Existence and Freedom

Existence and Freedom

Towards an Ontology of Human Finitude

Calvin O. Schrag

NORTHWESTERN

UNIVERSITY

PRESS

This volume has been published with the aid
of a grant from the Purdue Research Foundation.

Library of Congress Catalog Number 61–14317

Printed in the United States of America

Foreword

It was not so long ago that William James made his famous attacks on the abstractness and artificiality of the academic philosophy of his day and called for a "radical empiricism" which would do justice to "the world of concrete personal experiences" which, as he said, is "multitudinous beyond imagination, tangled, muddy, painful, and perplexed." In Europe there was an answer to this appeal in the form of what is now known as existential phenomenology. In America the answer has been perhaps delayed and certainly more devious. Nevertheless there is little question that James expressed a need deeply rooted in our tradition and still widely felt. Hence it is not surprising that there is now a growing interest here in European phenomenology. But we tend to think of it rather as a special school of philosophy than as an empirical discipline capable of yielding stable results that can be confirmed by investigators coming from radically different backgrounds and traditions.

Professor Schrag has accepted this widespread feeling as a challenge, and in working out his answer, he has drawn on many sources and has corrected many particular misunderstandings. The task of exploring the human *Lebenswelt*, as Husserl called it, by the non-reductive methods of phenomenology has only just begun. But there is already an extensive and significant body of literature in this field largely unknown to English and American readers. Professor Schrag's knowledge of this literature is far-ranging, penetrating, and exact. His comments on Heidegger and on the philosophical aspects of Kierkegaard's thought, though often original and sometimes controversial, are well founded and illuminating. Even though one may feel that he has not done full justice to some of the important differences in the authors he treats, he has shown many significant points of convergence and has gathered them together into a meaningful pattern. The world of our lived existence, with which James was concerned, is not a mere chaos of subjective impressions and constructions.

It is now clear that ordinary language, the language of the *Lebenswelt*, has patterns of its own, quite distinct from those of the technical languages derived from it. In the same way it has also become clear that the *Lebenswelt* itself has spatial, temporal, and existential orders of its own quite distinct from those that have been found in the objects of the special sciences or in the objective systems of traditional philosophy. This life-world is constituted by a different kind of fact and by a different kind of meaning. If it is to be explored and understood, it must be explored in a different way that will leave its distinctive structures intact. The phenomenologists of Western Europe, moved by the insights of Kierkegaard and James, have embarked on such an exploration which is now in progress. Professor Schrag has given us an accurate account of the general nature of this exploration and of some of its more significant results to date. This book is an important contribution to the growing literature of existential philosophy and phenomenology that is now appearing in this country.

JOHN WILD

Northwestern University

Acknowledgments

The specific task which I have projected in this study is not that of simply offering a summary of the dominant themes and concepts of existentialism. I trust that these dominant themes and concepts will be clarified throughout the book, but the guiding intention which underlies the whole work is that of elucidating how an existentialist ontology is possible. Throughout the book I argue that an existentialist ontology was already implicit in Kierkegaard's writings, later to reach its most systematic expression in the philosophy of Heidegger. The writings of Sartre and Jaspers, as well as Marcel and Berdyaev, are also examined for their ontological significance. The ontology which finally emerges in existentialist thought is what I have called an ontology of human finitude.

I wish to express my thanks and acknowledge my indebtedness to Professors John Wild and Paul Tillich, who have given me invaluable advice on many points. The central thesis which is elaborated in the present work was investigated during my graduate studies at Harvard, where my close associations with Professors Wild and Tillich provided both the inspiration and direction for a disciplined study of existentialism. Other scholars who have taught me and who have contributed both directly and indirectly to the realization of the following undertaking are Professor Julian Hartt of Yale University and Professor Karl Löwith of Heidelberg University. Not to be overlooked are the helpful suggestions and criticisms which I have received from my students, both at Purdue University and the University of Illinois. The *Revue Internationale de Philosophie* has kindly given me permission for the use of parts of my article, "Phenomenology, Ontology, and History in the Philosophy of Heidegger," published in 1958 (No. 44, fasc. 2); and *The Personalist* has permitted me to incorporate in chapter v part of my article, "Kierkegaard's Existential Reflections on Time," published in 1961 (Vol. XLII, No. 2). I am also most grateful to the Purdue Research Foundation for a generous grant which made it possible for me to engage in a summer of uninterrupted study and research, at which time the present study reached its final form, and for a further grant in aid of publication. Finally, I wish to express my appreciation to Mrs. Ruth Bessmer for her technical help with the preparation of the manuscript and to Miss Judith Kay Dyer for her competent assistance in correcting the proofs.

CALVIN O. SCHRAG

Purdue University, 1961

Contents

Introduction

The Athenian Socrates, for whom philosophy was a way of living as well as a way of thinking, advanced the maxim "Know thyself" as the guiding motif in his search for wisdom. The history of Western thought, in its manifold expressions, can be understood as both a revealing and a concealing of the knowledge demanded by this Socratic dictum. It is hoped that the following pages will make clear in what way this is indeed the case. The philosophy which has most sharply pointed out the ambiguities of the Western tradition as it seeks to deal with this most basic problem of man's knowledge of himself is the philosophy today known broadly by the name of existentialism. Devoted to a foundational and rigorous examination of the human condition, existentialism has emerged as an emphatic philosophy of human finitude in which the concepts of finite freedom, temporality, historicity, non-being, estrangement, anxiety, death, guilt, and resolve are central. Already in Kant's *Critique of Pure Reason,* with its classic demonstration of the finite character of a human reason which fractures itself when it seeks for a rational unification of the conditions of experience, we see the inauguration of a philosophy of finitude. It was not, however, until the advent of existentialism that this philosophy of finitude found its deliberate and disciplined expression. Existential thinking as a concrete way of life can certainly be found in ancient and patristic philosophy—Socrates and Augustine are cases in point. But existentialism as a distinctive philosophical movement first received its impetus through the reflections and formulations of the early anti-Hegelians—Kierkegaard, Marx, and Feuerbach—who lived and wrote during the first part of the nineteenth century. Protesting against the vicious abstraction of reason from existence in Hegel's rationalism and essentialism, Kierkegaard, Marx, and Feuerbach staged a timely return to the realities of lived experience. Hegel had proclaimed that the rational is the real and the real the rational. The counter-claim of Kierkegaard, Marx, and Feuerbach was that there is a qualitative disjunction between thought and reality, between essence and existence. For all that Hegel had to say about the logical and necessary mediation of opposites, the fact remained for these anti-Hegelians that thought and reality had not come together and that existence was still estranged from essence. Kierkegaard grasped this existential truth most clearly in his examination of man's concrete ethico-religious existence, in which he found a continuing estrangement of the self from itself and from God. Marx expressed the disjunction of thought and reality, and essence and existence, in another domain—man's concrete socio-economic existence. Marx argued that in Hegel's dialectical interpretation of history the reconciliation of particular existence and universal freedom was a reconciliation in thought only; and it was a reconciliation through which Hegel succeeded in placing himself outside of history itself. In history as Marx understood it, socio-economic classes warred against each other, capitalists depersonalized workers, and creative artists were transformed into paid laborers. And as Kierkegaard elucidated man's experience of finitude and estrangement in ethico-religious existence and Marx in the socio-economic sphere, so Feuerbach sought for an elucidation of man in concrete sensory-biological existence. It was Feuerbach who penned the words: "Do not wish to be a philosopher in contrast to being a man." Thought, insisted Feuerbach, can never be dissociated from the concrete thinker who apprehends himself in the movements of his immediate bodily existence.

The existential reflections of Kierkegaard, Marx, and Feuerbach, which grew out of their reaction against Hegel, were never formulated by these thinkers into an explicit and deliberate philosophy of existence. The philosophy-of-life (*Lebensphilosophie*) movement represented primarily by Nietzsche, Bergson, Dilthey, and Scheler, which followed closely on the heels of the early anti-Hegelians, contributed much to a further clarification of man's immediate lived experience. Contemporary existentialism, represented primarily by Heidegger, Jaspers, Sartre, and Marcel, succeeded the philosophy-of-life movement and is in some sense a continuation of it. It is in the philosophical reflection of these contemporary existentialists, especially Heidegger, that a structural analysis and ontology of human existence is formulated. This ontology, as we have suggested, is in its fundamental intention a philosophy of human finitude. Although this philosophy is expressed differently among the various existentialist thinkers, there is a basic similarity with regard to methodological procedures as well as formulation of structural concepts. The author is prepared to argue, in opposition to certain contemporary interpreters who characterize existentialism as a philosophy of perfervid individualism in which no common existentialist themes are disclosed, that a common perspective on the nature of existence underlies the apparent diversities of the respective thinkers. That there are differences must not and cannot be denied, but these differences arise for the most part on a level other than that of existentialist analysis. Kierkegaard was a Christian, and Sartre is an atheist. Martin Buber is Jewish, and Marcel is Catholic. Heidegger in his later works shows strong influences of a Boehme-like mysticism, and Jaspers remains strongly indebted to German romanticism. These are significant differences, to be sure, but they are as such adventitious to the elucidation of the fundamental question, "What does it mean to exist?" Kierkegaard sought an answer to the problems which existence poses, and he found it in the faith-relationship in which the solitary individual confronts his God. Sartre accepts neither faith nor God. Yet a similar statement on the finite and problematic character of existence is found in both Kierkegaard and Sartre. This would indicate that existentialism as a philosophy of human finitude can make no pronouncements either for or against the specific ethical and religious commitments through which man finds either immanent or transcendent meaning for his life. It may, and indeed does, show that the character of existence is such that man achieves his integrity through resolute choice or loses his integrity through a retreat from choice, but existentialism as a philosophy can in no way prescribe a religious or non-religious point of view. It is for this reason that the distinction between theistic and non-theistic, Christian and non-Christian existentialism is in the last analysis a spurious distinction. It is predicated on a misunderstanding of either the task of existential analysis or the nature of religious truth—or both. There is no Christian existentialism. However, there are Christians who are existentialists, and throughout the history of Western thought it has been Christian thinkers such as Augustine, Pascal, and Kierkegaard who have most sharply focused the problem of existence. Thus existentialism must never be identified with nor set in opposition to religion. Yet the question concerning the relation between existentialism and religion does arise and must be given studied attention and consideration. Paul Tillich in the United States and Rudolph Bultmann in Germany are the two prominent contemporary theologians who have dealt specifically with this question.

Just as the question of the relation between existentialist philosophy and religion constitutes a special area of enquiry, so also does the question of the relation of existentialism to psychotherapy and psychiatry. As Bultmann and Tillich have made use of Heidegger's structural analysis of human existence in their theologies, psychiatrists Ludwig Binswanger, Eugene Minkowski, Rollo May, Jordan Scher, Victor Frankl, and others have found the insights of Heidegger's understanding of man to be crucial for their psychiatric programs. The most systematic formulation of the relationship of existentialism to psychotherapy which has appeared to date is found in Binswanger's book, *Grundformen und Erkenntnis menschlichen Daseins*.[1] Binswanger argues that psychiatry and psychotherapy can function properly only when they are rooted in an adequate conceptual framework which provides clarification of the nature of man *as such*. He finds this adequate conceptual framework in Heidegger's basic existentialist concepts, which include care or concern (*Sorge*), anxiety (*Angst*), non-being (*Das Nichts*), being-unto-death (*Sein-zum-Tode*), temporality (*Zeitlichkeit*), guilt (*Schuld*), and resolution (*Entschlossenheit*). Victor Frankl has developed a school of psychotherapy known by the name of "logotheraphy" which is directly influenced by existentialist modes of thought. As the name indicates, logotherapy approaches the therapeutic process as one which concentrates on the search for *logos*, or a structure of meaning, through which an existence that is in a state of alienation or estrangement can be integrated. Correcting the Freudian reductivism which sees emotional frustrations as bound up with the curtailment of the "will-to-pleasure," logotherapy broadens the operational context of the causes of mental and emotional disturbances and focuses attention primarily on the threat to man's "will-to-meaning." Mental and emotional disorders, it is argued, in the last analysis arise from an inability to find meaning in a finite and problematic existence.

Existentialism has also found its way into the literature of the twentieth century. Many existentialists, particularly of the French wing, are both professional philosophers and literary artists. Jean-Paul Sartre is known to philosophers for his formidable essay on phenomenological ontology, *L'Être et le Néant*, but he is also of course the author of numerous plays and novels. Albert Camus was primarily a novelist, but he also wrote a philosophical essay on metaphysical rebellion, *L'Homme Revolte*, and a treatise on absurdity and suicide, *Le Mythe de Sisyphe*. Gabriel Marcel has complemented his *Journals* and philosophical writings with engaging plays which embody some of his philosophical elucidations. Existentialist themes, particularly the theme of anxiety in its various modifications, were certainly present in the poetry of the nineteenth-century French artists Baudelaire and Rimbaud, as well as in the poetry of Rilke. Baudelaire in his *Fleurs de Mal* poignantly expresses the anxieties of boredom and emptiness. Rilke in his *Duino Elegies* depicts the anxiety that man faces in the confrontation with his death. Franz Kafka, both in his novels and in his short stories, deals with some of man's most basic existential anxieties. The anxieties of meaninglessness and loneliness are powerfully expressed in *The Castle*, and the anxiety of guilt is elaborated in his novel *The Trial*. Dostoevsky in his emphasis on the tragic and demonic dimension of human freedom has dramatically depicted the finite existence of man in its primoridal nakedness. Chekov and Ibsen, Eliot and Auden, Faulkner and Tennessee Williams have all exemplified existential motifs in their literary works. Contemporary interpreters of existentialist thought—William Barret, for example, in his book *Irrational Man*—have devoted particular attention to the question of the relation between existentialism and literature. The existential attitude is also present in certain varieties of modern art. The Expressionist school, in its dissatisfaction with the Impressionist's preoccupation with "surface realities," seeks to return to "depth realities" and in so doing discloses the inner movements of the human spirit in both its turbulence and creativity. The paintings of the German Expressionists Ernest Kirchner and Erich Heckel, of the Dutch artist Van Gogh, and of the Norwegian Edvard Munch, are all powerful depictions of existential concern. The advent of cubism is another case in point. The fragmentations of lines, points, planes, and shadows which one notices in a cubist painting disclose the inner depth of a fractured and discontinuous existence.

We thus see that an existential understanding of man is expressed in contemporary movements of theology, psychiatry, literature, and art. The philosophical question which must now be posed and pursued is to what extent this understanding of man can be independently clarified and formulated into an existentialist ontology. The conviction of the author is that this is possible and that its possibility was already suggested in the reflections of Kierkegaard. However, an ontology of existence is only implicitly present in the writings of Kierkegaard, for he was primarily an ethico-religious thinker searching for an answer to his all-absorbing question: "How can one become a Christian in Christendom?" It was the philosophical task of Heidegger to explicate and systematize Kierkegaard's implicit ontology of existence into an existentialist and universal doctrine of man. The result of these efforts has been a movement toward a philosophy of human finitude. It is at this point that contemporary philosophical reflection on existence finds itself. Any pre-Kantian metaphysics which seeks for a rational unification of experience has become highly problematic because we are aware of the finite and fractured character of experience which seeks unification. But as Kant himself realized, an ontology of human finitude is possible. It is toward an examination of this ontology, as it emerges in the thought of the existentialist thinkers, that the following pages are devoted.

Existence and Freedom

I

Methodological Foundations

1. The Existential Thinker

"It is impossible to think about existence in existence without passion," writes Kierkegaard in his *Concluding Unscientific Postscript*.[1] Thought is inextricably bound up with human projects and decisions. Knowledge is always in some sense action. For the existentialist there can be no talk of the "passionless calm of purely speculative knowledge" which Hegel recommends in his *Science of Logic*.[2] It is on this point that Kierkegaard singles out Hegel as the chief offender. In the eyes of the existential thinker, Hegel's system is a fantastic distortion of truth and a most marvelous scheme of irrelevancy, a "facile deification of pure thought." [3] Writing in his *Journals*, Kierkegaard says that had Hegel stated in the preface to his *Logic* that the work was merely an experiment in thought, which had still begged the question in certain places, then we would certainly have to say that he was the greatest thinker who ever lived. But as it is, Hegel believed that he had explained existence through his logic, and with this belief he becomes a comic figure—he sees himself *sub specie aeterni* and forgets that he is an existing individual.[4] The Hegelian system makes the existential subject accidental and transforms him into something objective, indifferent, and impersonal. He becomes intellectually vaporized in the rarefied heights of pure thought. The comic predicament is precisely that the system embraces thought, only to lose the thinker. Thus it becomes a satire on the thinker himself. It is a fantastic feat of intellectual construction in which the artificer himself does not live. "A thinker erects an immense building, a system, a system which embraces the whole of existence and world history, etc.,—and if we contemplate his personal life, we discover to our astonishment this terrible and ludicrous fact, that he himself personally does not live in this immense high-vaulted palace, but in a barn alongside of it, or in a dog kennel, or at the most in the porter's lodge." [5] Hegel equated existence with pure thought and thus transformed existence into an abstract possibility which could find expression only within a logical unity of concepts. It was in this way that Hegel was driven to formulate a system. But this system, argues Kierkegaard, neglects the fundamental fact that it is impossible to think about existence except *in* existence and that it is impossible to think in existence without passion. Kierkegaard uses the terms passion, earnestness, inwardness, and subjectivity interchangeably and through the use of these terms indicates the inextricable unity of thought, action, and decision. Sartre's notion of *engagement* is clearly reminiscent of Kierkegaard's notions of passion and subjectivity. Jaspers expresses the same idea through his use of the German word *Handeln*, which denotes the interpenetration of knowledge and action. Heidegger develops a similar view in his discussion of the projective character of understanding (*Entwurf-character des Verstehen*). Understanding in Heidegger's analysis is never an objective and detached apprehension. It arises only in and with our existential projects which already involve us in decision and action. We know ourselves in our existence only through our decisions. Resolve and decisive action bring me to a knowledge of myself.

It is at this point that certain possible misinterpretations need to be avoided. The attitude expressed by the notions of passion, *engagement, Handeln,* and *entwerfendes Verstehen* should not be interpreted as voluntarism or irrationalism. The distinctions between voluntarism and intellectualism, rationalism and irrationalism, as Heidegger in particular points out, are questionable distinctions—at least insofar as they are used as a point of departure in philosophical enquiry. The very definition of philosophy in terms of the rational involves a questionable pre-judgment. In this pre-judgment, thought is already objectified, truth becomes an attribute of a statement, and *logos* (as structure of meaning) is reduced to logic, which has to do with the manipulation of valid and fallacious propositions. This reduction and falsification was already present in Greek thought through the formulation of Aristotelian logic. And Kant was right, Heidegger believes, when in the introduction to his *Critique of Pure Reason* he stated that logic had not advanced a single step since Aristotle. Its path of development was fixed. The only step which can be taken is to recover the immediate experience of reality which preceded the falsification of thought as *ratio*, expressed in terms of formal logical statements.[6] It was this intellectualism and rationalism which later brought about voluntarism and irrationalism as an inevitable reaction. When man discovered through his awareness of the tragic and destructive implications of his freedom that he was not simply, nor first and foremost, a rational animal, the rationalistic foundations of his tradition were shattered, and voluntarism emerged as a corrective. But the attitude and movement of voluntarism were still within the confines of intellectualism. It was shaped by what it protested against. This voluntarism reached its fulfillment in the thought of Nietzsche, who interpreted all life and existence as an expression of a primordial will-to-power. It is in this sense that Nietzsche stands at the end of a philosophical tradition.

Existentialism is thus neither intellectualistic nor voluntarisitic, neither rationalistic nor irrationalistic. It transcends the distinctions. The validity of thought is in nowise denied. What is denied is that thought can be reduced to a rational, objectifying, theoretical activity. Kierkegaard, often the whipping boy for those who interpret existentialism as a philosophy of irrationalism, speaks most positively of thought, as long as it is rooted in existence. It is precisely the task of the existential thinker to *think* his existence. He must penetrate his concrete particularity and existential involvement with thought which has universal validity. The existential thinker is a thinker and an existing individual at one and the same time. He lives his existence at the same time that he thinks it. "If thought," says Kierkegaard, "speaks deprecatingly of the imagination, imagination in its turn speaks deprecatingly about thought; and likewise with feeling. The task is not to exalt the one at the expense of the other, but to give them an equal status, to unify them in simultaneity; the medium in which they are unified is *existence*."[7] Kierkegaard's far-reaching reservations about Hegel arise, not because Hegel was a thinker, but because he identified thought with the rational and the logical. We must distinguish, cautions Kierkegaard, between "pure thought" and "abstract thought." Pure thought is the theoretical and detached thought of the "spectator of existence." Abstract thought is that which reflectively examines and describes existence by preserving a relationship with it.[8] The latter was persuasively exemplified by the Athenian Socrates. The thought of Socrates abstracted from existence but still retained an indissoluble link to that from which it abstracted. The philosophical reflection of Socrates was a reflection stimulated through passion and interest. Kierkegaard's high regard for Socrates becomes evident on every page of his writings. Socratic irony, Socratic dialectic, Socratic ignorance, and Socratic maieutic artistry permeate the whole of his work. Writing in his *Journals* he says: "What our age needs is another Socrates, someone who could existentially express ignorance with the same cunning dialectical simplicity."[9] It is in Socrates that Kierkegaard finds the existential thinker *par excellence*. Socrates "concentrates upon accentuating existence."[10] His peculiar merit was that of constantly reminding the knower that he was an existing individual. Heidegger shares Kierkegaard's high regard for Socrates and speaks of him as the "most able thinker of Western thought."[11]

As Hegel falsified the Socratic meaning of passionate thought by converting it into a reified pure thought, so also he falsified the Socratic existential dialectic by transforming it into a logical dialectic. Kierkegaard never tires of satirizing the intricate movements of Hegel's logical dialectic, but he has no intention of dispensing with dialectics properly understood. A denial of the dialectical, he argues, leads only to "superstition and narrowness of spirit."[12] Kierkegaard variously characterizes his dialectic as "existential"; "dialectic of inward appropriation"; "Greek"; or "qualitative" as distinguished from "quantitative." In an entry in his *Journals* he informs his reader that "everything depends upon making the difference between quantitative and qualitative dialectic absolute. The whole of logic is quantitative or modal dialectic, since everything is and everything is one and the same. Qualitative dialectic is concerned with existence."[13] Quantitative dialectic, or the dialectic of Hegel's logic, remains forever poverty-stricken in expressing the inward movements of the existential thinker as he apprehends himself in relation to a real becoming. In logic, movement and existential becoming are intruders. Logical entities are determinations of essence which are necessary and fixed. They are essentially, as Heidegger says, something "already-there" (*Vorfindliches*).[14] Here there can be no talk of a real becoming; and if there can be no talk of a real becoming, then there can be no talk of existence, for existence *is* becoming. For this reason, everything Hegel has to say about process and becoming in his *Science of Logic* is ultimately illusory. Qualitative dialectic, on the other hand, takes becoming seriously and seeks, through the employment of a Socratic maieutic artistry, to elicit an inward appropriation of the truth which discloses itself in man's concrete existential movements. It was this which accounted for the greatness of Socrates as a teacher. He was an occasion for the disclosure of existential truth.

The truth disclosed in Kierkegaard's qualitative dialectic is properly understood as *inward appropriation*. Truth is "an appropriation-process of the most passionate inwardness." [15] There can be no truth without inward appropriation. Speaking as an existential thinker Kierkegaard writes in his *Journals*: "The thing is to find a truth which is true for me, to find the idea for which I can live and die." [16] Truth is not something which I *possess* or *have* but rather is something which I *am* and *live*. Heidegger makes the same point when he says that man is not a being who possesses truth but is a being who is part of the truth (*Dasein ist in der Wahrheit*). The metaphor of ownership when applied to the relation of the individual to truth is grossly misleading. This is already to objectify truth, to think of it as an object which I would grasp in the same way that I would grasp a piece of chalk. But the truth of existence is not an objective truth in this sense. Existential truth is a mode of existence and a way of life. It is something which one *is* rather than *has*, something which one *lives* rather than *possesses*. This distinguishes the objective accent from the subjective accent. The objective accent falls on the WHAT; the subjective on the HOW. Existential truth is truth as subjectivity. Kierkegaard refers in a number of his works to the Old Testament story of David and Nathan as an illustration of his "doctrine" of subjective truth. Nathan comes to David with a story: There lived two men in a city. One man was a rich man with a huge flock of sheep. The other was a poor man with nothing save one ewe lamb, which as his sole possession was his pride and joy. Now it happens that a stranger passes through the city, takes nothing from the rich man but steals from the poor man his sole possession. Upon hearing the story, David, his anger kindled, boldly pronounces, "This man surely ought to be put to death." To which the prophet Nathan replies: "Thou art the man!" The story of the two men and the stranger was an objective story which David could analyze in terms of a theoretical detachment. But "Thou art the man" constituted another story; it effected the transition to the subjective.

We have used the term, "subjectivity" in describing Kierkegaard's concept of existential truth. Some of the later existentialists, especially Heidegger, have called our attention to the possible misinterpretations which can arise from the use of the term and have suggested the desirability of avoiding its usage entirely. Out of context it would seem to suggest an epistemological subjectivism, which has become the peculiar fate of much post-Cartesian philosophy, stemming primarily from Descartes' isolation of the epistemological subject as a thinking substance. But existentialism is as far from an epistemological subjectivism as it is from an epistemological objectivism. Indeed, it finds that the subject-object dichotomy as an epistemological distinction obscures the clarification of the immediate experience of existence as it is actually lived. The experience of existence in its immediacy precedes the split between subject and object as noetic designations. There is a level of experience in which the contrast between subject and object has not yet arisen. This does not mean that the distinction as such is invalid, but it does mean that it is a later and subordinate distinction which is itself grounded in a primordial experience of being. The existentialist concept of "being-in-the-world," arising from man's pre-theoretical encounter with his existential world of personal and practical concerns, as we shall see later, is the primary phenomenological concept through which it becomes possible to undercut the subject-object dichotomy. Hence, when Kierkegaard formulates his doctrine of truth as subjectivity, this must in no way be confused with a variety of epistemological subjectivism. John Wild, in his interpretation of Kierkegaard, has submitted the helpful distinction between "noetic subjectivism" and "existential subjectivism." [17] Noetic subjectivism gives priority to an isolated thinking subject which constructs around itself sense impressions beyond which it cannot proceed, which then involves it in an "ego-centric predicament." Noetic subjectivism gives priority to epistemology. Existential subjectivism, on the other hand, does not direct primary attention to the knowing mind in epistemological abstraction from existence. It seeks rather for an elucidation of the experience of the active *existing subject* in contrast to the isolated *thinking subject*. Existential subjectivism gives priority to ontology or being. Knowing is itself a mode of being. Misinterpretations of Kierkegaard's use of the term subjectivity can be avoided only when these two different meanings are borne in mind.

The existential thinker has the corresponding task of understanding himself in his existence, and he has the task of communicating this self-understanding to others. Insofar as the truth of existence is not an objective truth as are the "truths" of mathematics and empirical science, the method of its communication will have to be indirect rather than direct. Truth in mathematics can be directly communicated because the symbolic relationships are clearly and distinctly present to the abstracting intellect. Knowledge in natural science, although constituting a different order of abstract knowledge, is also directly communicable because the observations are open to sensory inspection and empirical verification. But these kinds of knowledge appear relatively late in man's awareness and already constitute a thematization of particular kinds of experience. The immediate understanding of our existence occurs on a level in which we *are* the truth which we seek to communicate. On this primordial level of experience truth is indelibly personal, and communication will have to employ the indirect method of Socratic elucidation. The existential thinker cannot express the truth of his existence in a manner or mode which is rationally compelling or scientifically verifiable, for this truth exists in advance of any objectifying, either rational or scientific. Thus existentialists often use the literary forms of journals, diaries, and personal letters. Kierkegaard's *Either/Or*, Volume II, takes the literary form and style of a letter written under the pseudonym Judge Wilhelm. These writings function as an occasion for the development of self-understanding on the part of the reader. The existential thinker elucidates through description his immediate experience and invites the reader to interrogate his own experience to see whether he finds a similar existential topography. These existential elucidations are indelibly personal, but they are at the same time occasions for the disclosure of the human condition. As such they have a special character and must be consistently distinguished from a biographical account of one's private and internal mental and emotional states. Kierkegaard is not offering us a description of the adventitious details of his private life. He uses indirect communication to show us what it means to exist.

2. *Phenomenology and Existentialism*

It may seem to the reader that to begin a discussion on existentialism with a consideration of methodological procedures is making a most unexpected circuit. For is not existentialism a continuing criticism of those philosophies which ascribe a priority to methodology and thus often conceal through their methodological preconceptions the data which are to be investigated? The existentialists have repeatedly pointed out the danger of losing one's self in methodological analysis at the expense of never arriving at the data themselves. A continual preoccupation with methodology leads to philosophical sterility. Heidegger calls our attention to a classic quotation appearing in the introduction in Lotze's *Metaphysics*: "The continual sharpening of the knife is tedious, if there is nothing to cut." [18] Also, a preconceived method may distort rather than disclose a given subject matter through an imposition of an arbitrary and unwarranted restriction on the breadth, range, and richness of human experience. Scientism affords a clear-cut instance of such an imperialism of methodology. Applied to human existence, the scientific method, which is an objectification of experience, discloses this human existence only by converting it into an object and thus distorting it. This does not mean that the scientific method has no validity when applied to its proper sphere of knowledge, which may include certain levels of human existence, but it does mean that when stretched beyond its elastic limits the scientific method conceals as readily as it reveals. Scientistic absolutism leads to methodolatry. A method becomes an idol—an idol which later is found to have feet of clay.

Existentialism has made a timely contribution in cautioning us against methodological strictures and distortions. Although it does not give priority to methodological formulation, it does approach the datum of existence in a certain manner, which for purposes of analysis can be examined with respect to intention and form. This approach to the investigation of existence is an approach which seeks to retain an organic unity between the data and the descriptions in such a way that the data is immediately disclosed in the descriptions. This approach, in its broadest perspective, can properly be called phenomenological.

It is primarily Heidegger and Sartre who have consciously made use of the phenomenological method, but the method is implicit in all the investigations of Kierkegaard and certainly is suggested in Jaspers' illuminating description of the "boundary situations" (*Grenzsituationen*). Phenomenology, in its broadest intention, is an attempt to return to the immediate content of experience, and to analyze and describe this content as it actually presents itself. "Zu den Sachen Selbst!" was the guiding principle of the phenomenological method as first formulated by Edmund Husserl. This principle was appropriated by Heidegger and applied in his existential analytics. Phenomenology as the method of existentialist philosophy thus seeks to disclose and elucidate the phenomena of human experience as they present themselves in their existential immediacy.

This method of phenomenological description was already part and parcel of Kierkegaard's existentialism, although it was never systematically elaborated. The existential thinker must penetrate his concrete, lived existence with thought and describe this existence in its immediate disclosure. Kierkegaard's profound descriptions of the various modifications of anxiety and his elucidation of the three "stages of existence" indicate an underlying awareness and use of the phenomenological method. It is through the use of the phenomenological method that one penetrates to the structures of human subjectivity. Only in this way can the existential thinker discover the universal possibilities of his lived concreteness. "The majority of men," writes Kierkegaard in his *Journals*, "are subjective towards themselves and objective towards all others, terribly objective sometimes—but the real task is in fact to be objective towards one's self and subjective towards all others." [19] It is through an existential phenomenology that one can become "objective towards one's self"—that one can reflect upon one's immediacy and describe the possibilities which constitute the becoming of the self. Description in existential phenomenology is made reflexive upon the self. The existential thinker has the task of describing his own existence as he experiences it in its manifold concreteness.

Heidegger, as the student of Husserl, sought to reconcile phenomenology and existentialism in preparation for the development of a universal phenomenological ontology based upon an analysis of the "Existence of *human* being" (*Dasein*).[20] It was thus that Heidegger made explicit the methodological principle suggested in Kierkegaard's descriptions of existence and clarified the significance of the principle for the formulation of an ontology of human finitude. The distinctive feature of Heidegger's phenomenological ontology is that it takes its point of departure from the existing *Dasein*. The gateway to the deeper levels of reality is found in man himself as he seeks orientation in his world of concrete, lived experience. Kierkegaard had already made us conscious of the comic predicament of the Hegelian, who in his preoccupation with the universal march of objective history and the mediation of logical categories forgets his personal existence. Similarly Heidegger cautions us against losing sight of the historical *Dasein* in our study of "strange cultures" and world history. Only by strict adherence to the phenomenological formula, argues Heidegger, are we able to preclude "all abstract constructions and formulations, accidental findings, acceptance of merely apparently demonstrated concepts, and adoption of pseudo-questions which often present themselves as real problems." [21] The task of the phenomenologist is to analyze, describe, and interpret the original data. Heidegger rejects without qualification any a priori epistemological and metaphysical constructions which would focus upon mental and cognitive processes to the neglect of the phenomena themselves. In a phenomenological and existentialist ontology the original datum is existence itself, and the goal is that of providing a conceptual clarification of this datum by delineating its constitutive structures. The phenomenological procedure demands emancipation from all epistemological pre-judgments and a priori limitations, which can only distort or conceal the original phenomenon in question. The datum or phenomenon of existence is always prior to any epistemological theories concerning it. That is why epistemology, or the question of knowledge, can never provide a point of departure. It constitutes a secondary and subordinate enquiry. Being precedes knowing. Knowledge is itself borne and supported by being. This is the "ontological proof," as Sartre puts it in his *L'Être et le Néant*, which is foundational for all phenomenological description. Nicolas Berdyaev, the Russian existentialist, expresses this priority of being over knowledge when he writes: "Thinkers who devote themselves to epistemology seldom arrive at ontology. The path they follow is not one which leads to reality. The most creative modern philosophers, such as Bergson, M. Scheler and Heidegger, are little concerned with epistemology. Man has lost the power of knowing real being, has lost access to reality and been reduced to studying knowledge. And so in his pursuit of knowledge he is faced throughout with knowledge and not with being. But one cannot arrive at being—one can only start with it." [22]

In his explication of the meaning of phenomenology Heidegger appeals to the Greek language—a language which is intrinsically philosophical. A proper understanding of the phenomenological method, he argues, can be achieved only when the constitutive elements which comprise the term "phenomenology" are examined and the meaning of their juxtaposition is clarified. The Greek etymological elements of the term are φαινόμενον (*phainomenon*) and λόγος (*logos*), on the basis of which phenomenology can be understood in its most general sense as simply the logos or science of the phenomena. The substantive, *phai-nomenon*, is itself derived from the Greek verb *phainesthai*, which means: that which shows itself. Accordingly, "phenomenon" means that which shows itself (*das Sichzeigende*) or that which reveals itself (*das Offenbare*). "Phenomenon" understood as that which shows itself or manifests itself must clearly be distinguished from the term "appearance" (*Erscheinung*). Phenomena are not simply appearances, but rather *that which* appears or *that which* shows itself. Appearances are always referential to some phenomenon. Appearances are appearances *of something*—of that which shows itself. The bifurcation of appearance and reality, already suggested by Plato and subsequently absolutized by the Western tradition, falsifies and distorts man's immediate encounter with the phenomena. The immediate presentment of being is not that of "shadow" realities or sense data (as in British empiricism) but rather that of a phenomenon which shows itself in the manner in which it is.

The concept of the *logos* was used by Plato and Aristotle in the fundamental sense of discourse (*Rede*), which has the root meaning of δηλοῦν (*deloun*)—making manifest that which the discourse is about or that on which the discourse turns. Aristotle, Heidegger reminds us, explained this function of discourse more precisely in his use of the term ἀποφαίνεσθαι (*apophainesthai*). The *logos* as discourse "opens to sight" or "lets something be seen" (*apo*). And that which discourse "opens to sight" is precisely the phenomena, or that which shows itself (*phaines-thai*). Phenomenology must thus properly be understood as *apophainesthai ta phainomena*—to disclose or "open to sight" that which shows itself in the manner in which it shows itself. The main objective of the phenomenological method is to return to the primary data as they show themselves. It is intent upon examining the phenomena as they are given. Thus its program can be summarized by its cardinal principle, *Zu den Sachen selbst!*

The phenomenological method, as expressly stated by Heidegger, has roots in the existential descriptions of Kierkegaard but is more directly a legacy of the transcendental phenomenology of Edmund Husserl, who was Heidegger's illustrious teacher. In *Sein und Zeit* Heidegger tells the reader that his investigations in existentialist analysis have been made possible largely through Husserl's investigations in his *Logische Untersuchungen*, and that if his own phenomenological enquiry makes a further contribution to the explication of the datum itself, his thanks must go first and foremost to Husserl.[23] Heidegger follows the basic phenomenological impulse of Husserl in striving to get back to the data of immediate experience by circumventing obscuring preconceptions. But in the elaboration of his specific program certain divergences from his master become apparent. Heidegger's modifications of the Husserlian transcendental phenomenology stem primarily from his explicit existentialist orientation, as well as from his historical thinking which he inherited chiefly from the *Lebensphilosophie* of Dilthey. Husserl, at least in his early and middle stages, can hardly be called an existentialist and carried on a running debate with the *Lebensphilosophie* tradition. In his *Ideen zu einer reinen Phänomenologie und phänomenologischen Philosophie*, Husserl's investigations are geared to a development of "a pure descriptive science of essential being" which focuses its attention upon timeless essences rather than the fact of existence. "Pure or transcendental phenomenology," he writes, "will be founded not as a science of facts, but as a science of essential being (as 'eidetic' science); a science which consistently avoids facts and seeks exclusively for the establishment of a 'science of essences' (*Wesenserkenntnisse*)." [24] In this preoccupation with a knowledge of essences there is no interest in the individual existent. "The positing and intuitive apprehension of the essence does not in any way imply the positing of an individual existent; pure essential truths contain no assertions whatsoever relative to facts." [25] This involves what Husserl calls the "suspension" of the world of facts—to "place in brackets" the data of the natural standpoint. But this bracketed world of existence is precisely the world which Heidegger wants to describe and subject to a fundamental ontological analysis. Husserl's phenomenology, at least in this stage, remains a science of essences (*Wesenswissenschaft*). Heidegger's phenomenology, from beginning to end, is propelled towards existentialist analysis (*Existenzialanalytic*).[26] Hence it could be said that Heidegger's philosophy, at least in one of its aspects, constitutes an attempt at a reconciliation of the historical thought of Dilthey, the existentialism of Kierkegaard, and the phenomenology of Husserl. Heidegger's phenomenology is the phenomenology of historical existence. In Husserl's *Ideen* the influence of German idealism and Cartesian rationalism still seems to predominate. In his later works, and especially in his unpublished manuscripts, the door is opened to a more existential and historical approach to the *"Sachen Selbst."* Gerd Brand, in his carfeul and revealing study of the later and unpublished manuscripts of Husserl, has shown how this existentialist theme emerges

a disciplined analysis and description of the structures of the historical itself, rather than through an appeal to cosmological categories, which could overcome relativism only at the expense of losing the historical by reducing it to an extension of nature (as is the case in the non-historical thinking of Greek rationalism). The descriptive concepts of the phenomenological existentialist are universals, but they do not have the character of the universals of classical rationalist and essentialist philosophies. The terminological distinction submitted by Heidegger is the distinction between "existentials" (*Existenzialien*) and "categories" (*Kategorien*). "All explications arising from the analysis of *Dasein* are derived with reference to the structure of existence. Since they are determined with reference to existence, we call these characterizations of *Dasein existentials.* They are to be sharply contrasted with the characterizations of non-*Dasein* which we call *categories.*" [36] The historical character of *Dasein* precludes an application of cosmological categories to human existence. The cosmological categories of substance, quality, quantity, relation, and the like are applicable only to the mode of non-human being (*nichtdaseinmässiges Seienden*). The historical existence of human being must be described by "existentials." These "existentials" have a special character. Like the classical cosmological categories of rationalism and essentialism they are universals, but they are universals which are peculiar determinants of human existence and arise only in the process of its historical actualization. They are structures of human historicity, not cosmologically derived modes of classification. The zoological definition of man as an *animal rationale* is a categorial definition in which man is cosmologically classified in a given order of nature. But in this zoological definition the historical existence of man has not yet been penetrated and can never be penetrated as long as our conceptual analysis is drawn from an interpretation of nature. This does not mean that the classification of man as a rational animal may not tell us something about some rather obvious empirical determinations of his being, but the inner movement of his historical actualization remains concealed. The conceptual clarification of historical existence can proceed only through a disciplined delineation of the "existentials" which structure it. These "existentials" are directly "read off" from man's concrete, lived experience. Thus any philosophy of human existence must take cognizance of two levels of existence—existence in its concrete determination (the *existenzielle*) and existence as a universal condition (the *existenzial*).

The German word *existenzielle* has the specific denotation of a *concrete act of existing,* and the word *existenzial* denotes the *universal structure present in the concrete act of existing.* Although any English rendering of these words is likely to be inadequate, the distinction can be kept clear through the consistent use of the terms "existential" for *existenzielle* and "existentialist" for *existenzial.* The former has to do with man's immediate apprehension of himself in concrete psychological, sociological, or religious situations. It defines man's ontic understanding of himself. The latter designates the universal structures in the concrete and thus constitutes the level of ontological analysis. In one respect the distinction between the existential and the existentialist defines the difference between the existentialism of Kierkegaard and Heidegger. Kierkegaard is primarily concerned with existence as it is experienced in man's concrete ethico-religious situation. Heidegger is interested in deriving an ontological analysis of man. But as Heidegger's ontological and existentialist descriptions can arise only from ontic and existential experience, so Kierkegaard's ontic and existential elucidations express an implicit ontology. The ontological, in a phenomenological ontology, does not refer to a separate realm of Being which somehow "exists" independently of the concrete. If this were the case, the Heideggerian ontologist would become as comical a figure as the Hegelian rationalist, for both would be constructing mansions in which they themselves do not live. Heidegger, however, makes it clear that Being can never be investigated as something which is "in-itself." The ontological is indissolubly linked with the ontic. An existentialist-ontological analysis can only proceed from an existential-ontic understanding of one's being-in-the-world. "The task of an existentialist analysis of *Dasein* with regard to its possibility and necessity," says Heidegger, "is already indicated in its ontic constitution. . . . The existentialist analysis is finally rooted in the existential, i.e., ontic." [37] The existentialist analysis of the universal structures of existence is undertaken by a *Dasein* who is himself involved in the process of existing and first becomes aware of himself in his lived concreteness. This is Kierkegaard's persistent theme in his doctrine of the existential thinker. The existential thinker is always an individual already involved in the process of existing. "Existentials" as universal descriptions are thus structural possibilities arising from and returning to concrete, lived experience. Walter Biemel clearly states the case when he writes that "l'ontologique est précisément ce qui rend possible le 'concret.' " [38] Now Heidegger speaks of these structural possibilities as being a priori and transcendental, thus indicating his dependence on the transcendental philosophy of Kant.[39] But Heidegger does not mean by a priori and transcendental something which *precedes* the concrete; rather, concepts circumscribe the ever-present structure of the concrete. In Heidegger's hermeneutic of *Dasein* they define the horizon of man's concrete, historical possibilities. An example from Heidegger's philosophy may help to give us a preliminary clarification of this all-important distinction between the existential and the existentialist. As an historical being who is always arriving from a past and facing a future in which he must make decisions, man exists either authentically or unauthentically. He can either shoulder his responsibility through resolute choice and commitment, or he can retreat from the future and its call for decision and disperse himself in the present. To exist, then, means to exist either authentically or unauthentically. This is an existentialist-ontological determinate of human being. It defines a horizon of universal possibilities along which man's concrete possibilities are chosen. My concrete choice of authenticity in terms of a commitment to the Christian faith, Zen Buddhism, or the Communist party occurs on the level of existential-ontic experience. Being human means to live either authentically or unauthentically, but being human does not mean being a Christian, a Zen Buddhist, or a Communist. The content of the concrete existential commitment is in no way determined by man's ontological and universal possibilities, but the concrete existential commitment has its conceptual clarification within the horizon of these universal possibilities. When Kierkegaard speaks of the reality of sin, he expresses an existential self-understanding of a man who apprehends himself as qualified by estrangement from God. But this existential experience presupposes a structure of existence in which sin can be understood as a concrete possibility; it presupposes unauthenticity as a possible mode of existence. Correspondingly, the same would hold true of the relationship of faith to authenticity. Faith is an indelibly personal and concrete encounter which for the believer provides the focal point of an integrated and committed life. But this faith, from the phenomenological point of view, finds expression only within the horizon of man's possibilities *as a man*, one of which is authentic existence. The specific clarification of this faith in terms of its revelatory components belongs to the domain of theology and not philosophy.

We have examined some of the implications of man's historicity for the formulation of a phenomenological ontology and the possible avoidance of historical relativism. Insofar as the data to be investigated and described show an indelible historical character, the descriptions of a phenomenological ontology cannot be the scientific descriptions of a cosmologically oriented philosophy with its traditional categorial mode of analysis. Such descriptions would only conceal the historical by surreptitiously transforming the historical into an extension of the natural. And man, as we shall see in our analysis, possesses a history rather than a nature; or to express it somewhat paradoxically, history *is* his nature. This does not mean, however, that one necessarily falls into point-of-view philosophizing and historical relativism. If historical existence does not permit structuring through an application of the cosmological categories of nature, this does not mean that it is simply an unknowable and discontinuous succession of lived experiences. It may have structures which are uniquely its own and which must be understood through the historical itself. Phenomenological ontology, which takes its point of departure from the hermeneutic of *Dasein*, constitutes this attempt to delineate man's universal historical possibilities (*Existenzialen*) through an existentialist-ontological analysis. The formulations of this existentialist ontology will be presented in the following chapters.

4. *Existential Intentionality*

We have already seen that the existential thinker moves on a level of experience which precedes the noetic split between subject and object. Prior to any theoretical thematization the existential thinker finds himself in a world of practical and personal concerns. The existential self never cognitively begins itself but always finds itself already existentially begun. It is given to itself as a going concern—thinking, planning, hoping, rejoicing, regretting, and despairing in an immediately encountered life-world. This pre-cognitive relatedness to a world of existential concerns we shall call *existential intentionality*. Kierkegaard had already suggested this existential intentionality, particularly in his three works *The Sickness Unto Death*, *The Concept of Anxiety*, and *Either/Or*; but it was primarily Heidegger, utilizing some of the seminal insights of Brentano and Husserl, who first formulated the notion of existential intentionality as philosophical motif. In the three works just mentioned, Kierkegaard develops a graphic description of the phenomenon of mood in some of its central modifications such as anxiety, boredom, melancholy, and despair. These moods, as understood by Kierkegaard, are not to be confused with isolated psychic states or emotions. They do indeed have a psychological expression, but they perform first and foremost a revealing function. They disclose aspects of the concrete life-world as it shows itself in its existential immediacy. Anxiety discloses my freedom by bringing me to an immediate awareness of my future in which reside my possibilities for self-actualization. Boredom and melancholy disclose various threats in my world-orientations, which find expression both in the estranged relationship which I experience in myself and in my estranged relations with others, by dint of which genuine communication reaches an impasse. In despair I always despair *over* or *about* something and thus already disclose a certain intentional relatedness of myself with the "objects" of despair. I despair over a loss of fortune or a loss of a friend and in this despair find facets of my life-world simultaneously disclosed. Mood in its various modifications must thus properly be understood as an *intentional disclosure*. The existential self is intentionally related to a world in which mood functions as a liaison. But mood must also be understood as a *situational determinant*. It has an intentional specification as a revealing factor, but it is also a determinant of the human situation itself. It is a qualification of the very being of the self and hence manifests itself as a universal possibility of human existence.

Heidegger, like Kierkegaard, analyzes mood (*Stimmung*) as an intentional or revealing phenomenon. The English word "mood" does not fully succeed in rendering the meaning of the German word *Stimmung*. *Stimmung* has connotations of attunement as well as familiarity which express more adequately the notion of an existential intentionality. In his pre-cognitive experience man finds himself attuned to a world with which he is familiar by virtue of his practical and personal concerns. Heidegger deems it significant that Aristotle treated the phenomenon of fear in his *Rhetoric* (B5 1382ᵃ 21) rather than in his *Psychology*. The idea is thus conveyed that fear is to be viewed principally as a revealing or disclosing factor. Fear discloses a mode of *Dasein's* relation to his natural and social environment in his existential world.

Sartre has shown in a most illuminating way in his *L'Être et le Néant* how shame, as a possible expression of consciousness, discloses a social modality of my being-in-the-world—my encounter with the Other. I experience shame only insofar as I became an object for the Other, who threatens my world with his look. I am ashamed of myself in the presence of the Other, who threatens my existential projects and at least momentarily determines who I am. In the experience of shame I recognize myself as a fixed and dependent being who exists for the Other. I experience myself as having "fallen" into a world in which my subjectivity is threatened through the Other's transformation of me into an ensemble of objective properties. This experience of shame discloses an implicit comprehension of my lived world in three dimensions: the "I" as consciousness, the "me-as-object," and the "Other" as mediator. "I am ashamed of *myself* before the *Other*." [40]

The foregoing descriptions and elucidations by Kierkegaard, Heidegger, and Sartre constitute an attempt to arrive at a pre-cognitive level of experience which undercuts the subject-object dichotomy and which is characterized by an existential intentionality. This endeavor is carried out by all existentialists and provides one basic characteristic of existentialism as a philosophical program. There are central themes that characterize existentialism as a distinct mode of philosophizing, and this is certainly one of them. Kierkegaard speaks of the priority of the ethically existing self over the thinking self. Jaspers in his program of *Existenzerhellung* describes existence as the "source" (*Ursprung*) which precedes all theoretical activity.[41] Marcel in his book *The Mystery of Being* discusses the "existential indubitable" as the centrally significant factor of immediate experience which is the prius of all reflection.[42] Heidegger develops the notion of a "preconceptual understanding of Being" (*vorbegriffliches Seinsverständnis*), and Sartre speaks of a *cogito préréflexif* which is itself the foundation for the reflective ego. To be sure, Sartre's views on consciousness and the ego differ significantly from those of Heidegger; yet he agrees with Heidegger, as well as the other existentialists, that the primacy of cognitive knowledge must be abandoned. And it is precisely this point which is at stake in his notion of the *cogito préréflexif*. Cognitive consciousness becomes secondary and subordinate. The being of the knower in his existential projects is initially revealed in his pre-reflective acts.[43]

The neglect in modern philosophy of this preconceptual understanding and existential intentionality, the existentialists are quick to point out, has its roots in the Cartesian bifurcation of the thinking and the existing self, in which the thinking self is given priority. It has become fashionable, says Kierkegaard in his *Journals*, for all modern philosophers to begin their philosophies, "Once upon a time there was a man, and his name was Descartes." Descartes' legacy to modern philosophy was his *cogito ergo sum*, but this, as Kierkegaard points out in his *Postscript*, resolves itself into a pure tautology. "If the 'I' which is the subject of *cogito* means an individual human being, the proposition proves nothing: 'I am thinking, ergo I am; but if I *am* thinking, what wonder that I am': the assertion has already been made, and the first proposition says even more than the second. But if the 'I' in *cogito* is interpreted as meaning a particular existing human being, philosophy cries: 'How silly; here there is no question of your self or my self, but solely of the pure ego.' But this pure ego cannot very well have any other than a purely conceptual existence; what then does the *ergo* mean? There is no conclusion here, for the proposition is a tautology." [44] The philosophical tradition which stems from Descartes errs precisely in this preoccupation with the thinking self to the neglect of the existing self. The real subject is not the cognitive subject—it is the existing subject. "That the knowing spirit is an existing individual spirit and that every human being is such an entity existing for himself," says Kierkegaard, "is a truth I cannot too often repeat; for the fantastic neglect of this is responsible for much confusion." [45]

Heidegger repeats Kierkegaard's criticism of Descartes. Descartes overlooked that consideration which is most important: the meaning of the *sum* which is presupposed by the *res cogitans*. "With the *cogito sum* Descartes claimed to provide philosophy with a new and certain foundation. However, what he leaves undetermined with this 'radical' departure is the kind of being characterizing the *res cogitans*, or more precisely stated, the ontological meaning of the *sum*." [46] The Cartesian *cogito* is not the primary datum. The primary datum is existence, and this in Heidegger's sense of already being-in-a-world. [47] In the philosophy of Descartes the self is reduced to a lonely, isolated epistemological subject, an Archimedean point, from which a theory of knowledge is to be formulated which can assure it of its own existence as well as the existence of the objective, external world. This form of *Fragestellung* was bequeathed to Kant, who affirmed it to be a scandal of philosophy and universal reason that a proof for the reality of the external world was still wanting. The real scandal of philosophy, counters Heidegger, is not that such proof has been late in arriving but that such proofs are always awaited and attempted. Heidegger's phenomenological approach with its doctrine of existential intentionality undercuts the subject-object dichotomy established by Descartes and, at least in part, inherited by Kant. [48] A Cartesian epistemological point of departure resolves itself ultimately into a pseudo-problem, for in his immediate preconceptual experience man already experiences himself intentionally related to a world in which he loves and hates, rejoices and despairs, lives and dies. The *cogito* is in no sense prior, entrusted with the task of mediating between itself as subject and its world as object. Cognition is itself a mode of *Dasein* grounded in the primitive experience of being-in-the-world. For Heidegger, "Knowing does not create a 'commercium' of the subject with a world, nor is it the result of an influence of the world upon the subject. Knowing is a mode of *Dasein* grounded in his being-in-the-world." [49]

Heidegger's existential intentionality, which underlies his *Dasein*-world correlation, was forcefully suggested in the implicit phenomenology of Kierkegaard. It also has its philosophical roots in the thought of Brentano and Husserl, and adumbrations of the doctrine can be found in late medieval philosophy, particularly in the philosophy of Duns Scotus. In his study on the doctrine of the categories in Duns Scotus, Heidegger points out that Husserl's notion of intentionality was already present in Scotus' doctrine of the *modi significandi activi.*[50] But it is with Brentano and Husserl that intentionality first becomes the fundamental presupposition of the phenomenological method. In his *Ideen* Husserl made the notion of intentionality the central theme of his philosophy. "To the essence of every actual *cogito* there always belongs a consciousness *of* something." [51] Intentionality is thus the basic structure of consciousness. The act of consciousness (*noesis*) is always directed toward its intentional object (*noema*). Heidegger follows Husserl in his accentuation of the theme of intentionality, but he regards as more inclusive the framework in which intentionality properly functions. For the early Husserl, the intentional relation of the fact of knowing and the thing-as-known is primarily a cognitive or theoretical operation, which he calls "pure consciousness." Here Husserl's point of departure is still the Cartesian *cogito.*[52] Heidegger, however (and Husserl in his later writings), sees the intentional structure as being present not only in the realm of consciousness, understood as cognitive experience, but in the whole of man's precognitive awareness, or what we have called existential intentionality.[53] Man intends his world not only in perceiving and judging but also in his use of tools or utensils in his daily practical concerns (*Besorgen*) and in his encounter with and response to other selves who share his world, which Heidegger calls "personal concern" (*Fürsorge*). Prior to any cognitive reflection there is a primitive existential awareness, by which man is already intentionally related to his world through his projective concerns and primordial *Stimmung*. Heidegger has not only broadened the classical doctrine of intentionality, but he has existentialized and historicized it. He has placed it squarely into the historically lived world of immediate experience, thus avoiding the objectification of reality which was the peculiar fate of the Cartesian *cogito*. It is this new conception of world which is here the crucial determinant. Man is not an isolated epistemological subject. He is a field of projects in which a world is already disclosed through an existential immediacy. He has his world with him, so to speak, in his preoccupations and concerns. Intentionally speaking, world is never there without man, and man is never there without world. Man's being is always a being-in-the-world. It is to this existentialist concept of the world that we must give our attention in the following chapter.

II

The Existentialist
Concept of World

1. Man as Being-in-the-World

THE FOUNDATIONAL PHENOMENON in an existentialist ontology is the primordial consciousness of being-in-the-world. Self and world are correlative concepts. "If no *Dasein* exists, there is no world," writes Heidegger.[1] "Without the world there is no selfhood; without selfhood, without the person, there is no world," is Sartre's formulation.[2] This experience of being-in-the-world constitutes the point of departure for a phenomenological description of existence. It is that "datum itself" (sought in the Husserlian attempt to recover the *Sachen selbst*) which provides the experiential prius from which all explications originate.

The immediate datum of being-in-the-world, although primitive, is not simple. It encompasses various special horizons into which existence is projected. World itself is experienced only through its various horizons or existential modalities which provide the contextual backgrounds for the structuring of my experience. I experience my world as a surrounding environment (*Umwelt*) in which tools and utensils are at hand (*zuhanden*) for the execution of my practical projects. My environmental world or *Umwelt* initially discloses itself as a world of accessible utensils (*zuhandenen Zeugwelt*), but it also discloses itself as a world of nature (*Umweltnatur*) in which there is night and day, rain and sunshine, heat and cold. This world of nature, first disclosed in its immediacy, later can be scientifically objectified and apprehended as being simply on hand (*vorhanden*) in contrast to being at hand (*zuhanden*). That is to say, nature when objectified is translated into the mode of thinghood (*Dinglichkeit*). But the horizon of my environment, both instrumental and natural, is not the only horizon of my being-in-the-world. There is also the modification of my world as *Mitwelt*. My world is a communal world, or a world that I always share with others. The third horizon of my being-in-the-world is world as uniquely my own, or world experienced in the mode of self-relatedness. Ludwig Binswanger has sought to describe this experience of self-relatedness as a mode of world-orientation in his concept of *Eigenwelt*.[3] It is the phenomenological description of the structure of self-relatedness that will yield an answer to the question, "Who am I?" These different horizons or modifications of world—environmental, communal, and self-relatedness—must be understood as interrelated and interdependent phases. They can and must be independently analyzed in a phenomenological description, but in man's immediate and pre-cognitive understanding they are given only in their structural interdependence.

The central point in this existentialist concept of the world is that it is understood in a pre-objective and pre-cosmological sense. As long as one insists upon viewing the world in terms of objective and cosmological categories, the immediate experience of the world, of which the existentialist speaks, will remain concealed. As soon as we ask, "*What* is the world?" then we have already preconditioned the answer through its objective formulation—as did Descartes. The existentialist meaning of the world is disclosed only when the question is subjectively formulated: "*How* do I exist in the world?" Here, as elsewhere, Kierkegaard's distinction between the objective accent which falls on the *what* and the subjective accent which falls on the *how* must be kept in mind. This in no way means that objective scientific analysis and experimentation, as a disciplined procedure of investigation, is denied or even called into question. The common charge that existentialism is anti-scientific (science understood in the sense of controlled observation and experimentation as it is carried out in the special sciences) is wholly groundless. The "scientific world" circumscribes a most legitimate area of human endeavor but is only part of a much broader world of experience in which man discovers himself as a human being before he decides to be a scientist. There can be no conflict between existential analysis and scientific experimentation. There is a conflict, however, between existential analysis and scientism as a philosophy, for scientism seeks to reduce the human life-world to quantitative determinants and mathematical abstractions in which the scientistic philosopher himself, for the most part, does not live.

The philosophical objectification, and hence falsification, of the world as disclosed in immediate experience stems primarily from the Cartesian subject-object dualism in which the *res cogitans* as a thinking substance is in some strange way related to a world defined as *res extensa*. The concept of world as understood by Descartes designates an extensive continuum, measured in terms of coordinates, which provides the "container" for individual substances and qualities. Both self and world in Descartes' thought are classified as substances, and the self is conceived to be in the world in the same way that any given substance coinheres in another substance. The relation between the self and world is a cosmological relation directly analagous to the relation which obtains, for example, when a lectern is *in* a lecture room. The Cartesian analysis, as Heidegger is quick to point out, distorts man's primitive and immediate experience of being-in-the-world by converting the self and the world into substances or objects (in the final analysis, the *res cogitans* is for Descartes an "object" as is all other intramundane reality) and conceiving the relation of "being in" (*In-sein*) as quantitatively determinable. In the existentialist view the world is not an objective spatial container into which man, improperly understood as a substance, is placed. Man and world are not things or objects which can be understood in terms of the categories of substance, quality, quantity, etc. These categories apply only to non-human reality, which presents itself in the horizon of on-handness (*Vorhandensein*) as a special modification of the *Umwelt*. The relation of "being-in" is not a cosmological relation. The "being-in" of *Dasein* is an "existential" (as distinct from a category) and points to a constitutive structure of human reality. The existentialist concept "being-in" never signifies an objectively spatialized coinherence. *Dasein* is in the world in the sense that he lives, dwells, and sojourns in the world.[4] The relationship here is not an objective, spatial relationship but is the more primitive relationship of involvement "in" and preoccupation "with" one's world. The immediately given world is the world of existential preoccupations and concerns. *Dasein* is in the world in the sense of "being preoccupied, producing, ordering, fostering, applying, sacrificing, undertaking, following through, inquiring, questioning, observing, talking over, or agreeing." [5] Walter Biemel has aptly characterized Heidegger's concept of being-in-the-world as an attitude of familiarity (*être familier avec . . . être-auprès*), which he then distinguishes from the purely spatial proximity of being-beside (*être-pres*).[6]

Descartes' error of ascribing primacy to the cosmological and substantive interpretation of both self and world isolates the thinking self as an epistemological point and can be avoided only when one permits the world to show itself as it actually is—i.e., in its manifold, lived concreteness. The epistemological problem as it was formulated by Descartes, then inherited by Hume and British empiricism more generally, is one which every schoolboy knows. How do we acquire knowledge of the external world? Descartes argued that we first have to prove the existence of an infinite and perfect God, who, by virtue of his perfection in goodness, could not possibly deceive the sensing and thinking self. Descartes' argument for the existence of God, however, came off rather badly when it fell under the critical axes of Hume and Kant. Hume's conclusion—inevitable if one ascribes validity to the Cartesian point of departure—was skepticism. There is simply no empirical verification for the reality of the external world. All that is given to experience is a changing flux of sense impressions, argues Hume. This led Hume to doubt not only the reality of the world as an object of this sense experience but led him to doubt the reality of an existing self which has these sense experiences. Fortunately, however, in his less "philosophical moments" Hume could return to the *Lebenswelt* and find the world immediately given in playing a game of billiards! It is the *Lebenswelt* which turns skeptics into actors; and in this unexpected transition, the skeptic is forced to acknowledge that a world of projects of existing selves is already disclosed. Kierkegaard expresses this with graphic irony when he writes in his *Journals:* "The real trap in which to catch the skeptic is ethics. Since Descartes they have all maintained that, during the period in which they doubted, they might not make any definite statement with regard to knowledge but that they might act, because in that respect one could be satisfied with probability. What a tremendous contradiction! As though it were not far more terrible to do something about which one was doubtful (for one thereby assumes a responsibility) than make a statement." [7] Both Kierkegaard and Heidegger have incisively pointed to the falsifications of immediate experience which arise when the Cartesian world, with its subject-object dichotomy, is given priority. An existentialist phenomenology seeks to cast aside this distorting veil by returning "to the data themselves" as they are given in man's lived experience. This does not mean that the subject-object distinction cannot have validity in its own right. But it does mean that the distinction is a relatively late emergent in our experience and has its ontological foundation in the primary phenomenon of being-in-the-world. In an existentialist analysis, the subject-object dichotomy is undercut but not annihilated.

We have suggested that the existentialist concept of world is properly approached with the Kierkegaardian question "How?" rather than the objective question "What?" Heidegger, in his essay *Vom Wesen des Grundes* argues that the pre-Socratics understood the world existentially rather than in terms of the objective totality of on-hand beings. "Already in the decisive beginning of ancient philosophy something important emerges. *Kosmos* does not mean this or that present being, nor the totality of all beings, but rather signifies situation [*Zustand*], i.e., the *how* in which this being is *in the whole* of that which he encounters." [8] In this early period of philosophy, which preceded the confining metaphysics of Aristotle and the epistemological constrictions of Descartes, thinkers could still experience Being as it disclosed itself. Equally significant, says Heidegger, is the fact that in Christianity the ontic and existential understanding of world refers to a concrete situation of man, a situation defined in light of his religious self-understanding. "It is no accident that in the new ontic understanding of existence which emerged in Christianity, the relation of *kosmos* and human *Dasein*, and therefore the concept of the world, is intensified and clarified. The relation is so fundamentally experienced that *kosmos* is used as a term denoting a manner of human existence itself. *Kosmos ontos* means for Paul (see I Cor. and Gal.) not primarily the conditions of the 'cosmological' but rather the condition and situation of *Man*, the manner of his relation *to* the cosmos, and his attitudes towards goods and possessions. *Kosmos* is the being of man in his godless disposition (*sophia toi kosmou*). *Kosmos ontos* denotes *Dasein* in a determinate 'historical' existence, in contradistinction to another mode already present." The Gospel of John, continues Heidegger, also expresses this central existential and ontic understanding of the world: "World designates the ground-structure of human *Dasein* in its disrelationship to God, *the character of human being* as such." [9] The New Testament presents a powerful expression of the existential understanding of world. This view, argues Heidegger, was also the view of Augustine and was later expressed in certain aspects of Kant's philosophy.

Kierkegaard's intention as a religious and ethical thinker was to give further clarification to this existential and ontic understanding of world expressed in the New Testament and in Augustine (we might also add Luther and Pascal). But Kierkegaard was also a philosophical genius, and in his fragmentary philosophical observations already suggested the existentialist and ontological concept of world as it was explicitly developed by Heidegger—probably more than Heidegger himself realizes.[10] This is particularly true in his descriptions of the structure of self-relatedness in *The Sickness Unto Death*, where most of the structural concepts of Heidegger are anticipated. Part I of this book, Kierkegaard tells us, does not deal with the God-relationship. It is a dialectical analysis which proceeds within the definition of the "human self." In Part II of *The Sickness Unto Death* the human self acquires a new qualification in that it is now understood in its relationship to God—it becomes a "theological self." [11] The genius of Kierkegaard was that of penetrating the relationship between the universally human and the religiously concrete. It was Heidegger who made it a cardinal principle of philosophy that existentialist-ontological formulations must never sever themselves from the existential-ontic, but it may be that Kierkegaard had already exemplified this principle with a greater consistency than that of his existentialist successor.

The theme of alienation or estrangement is central to an understanding of man's primordial experience of the world as a field of human concerns. Kierkegaard's descriptions of the experience of alienation in the *Eigenwelt, Mitwelt,* and *Umwelt* remain unsurpassed in the literature of the West. Man is alienated from himself, from other selves, and from nature. The "sickness unto death" is the sickness of despair, phenomenologically understood as estrangement of the self from itself. Despair is a fracture in the structure of self-relatedness. Moreover, man is estranged not only from himself but from others. There is a fracture in man's communal world. Kierkegaard's penetrating descriptions of the depersonalization of individuals in crowds are often overlooked by those who tend to see in Kierkegaard only an *Eigenwelt*. As Marx had pointed to the disruption of the communal world in the conflict between the landowner and the worker, in which the landowner depersonalizes the worker by transforming him into a commodity along with land, capital, and tools; so Kierkegaard formulated a graphic description of man's alienation in a society in which the crowd is ever threatening to transform him into a number or a cipher. Estrangement is also experienced in man's relationship with nature. Having erupted into history, man is no longer in perfect union with nature. He loses the security which characterizes his pre-historical identity with nature. This transition to historical existence then confronts man with a consciousness of his body, his sexuality, and his biological death, in which his breach with nature becomes apparent. This theme of man's alienation from nature is central to Kierkegaard's *The Concept of Anxiety*, where it is given a most profound statement. It is thus through man's experience of estrangement in his anxiety and despair that the various horizons of the existential world disclose themselves. As we have shown in chapter 1, there is an existential intentionality—an intentionality of mood—which precedes any cognitive determination of the character of one's world. Man's being-in-the-world, in its estranged and threatening character, is initially revealed through the various modifications of mood. This is why Heidegger insists that "we must, in fact, in a fundamental *ontological* manner entrust to 'mere mood' (*blossen Stimmung*) the primary uncovering of world. A pure perception, even though it penetrates the innermost veins of the being of on-handness, is never able to disclose that which threatens one." [12]

Before proceeding to a structural analysis of the different horizons disclosed in man's being-in-the-world, we might note a further point of clarification concerning the use of the term "world" as an "existential." We have spoken of the world as an "existentialist concept." This means that it is an ontological designation presupposed by ontic description. Heidegger expresses this most clearly in *Sein und Zeit* when he writes: "*Weltlichkeit* is an ontological concept and denotes the structure of a constitutive movement of being-in-the-world. This we understand as an existentialist determinant of *Dasein*. *Weltlichkeit* is, therefore, an 'existential.'" [13] We must not forget, however, that the existentialist and ontological are always rooted in the existential and ontic. The ontological is not a separate realm "off by itself"; rather, it designates the structure of the concrete and hence is that which, when it is disclosed, provides the concrete with its conceptual clarification. Heidegger ascribes to his concept of world an a priori and transcendental status. "World" as a concept is a transcendental or an indispensable condition for experience through which one's concrete encounters in their various horizons are understood. According to Biemel, world for Heidegger as an existential is *"ce qui rend possible tous les étants intramondains; it est partout pré-supposé."* [14] The concept of world as an a priori and transcendental factor indicates the universal possibilities of our encounter with intramundane beings. Heidegger makes it clear that a priori in no way means a construction of the mind. The Freiburg philosopher will have no truck with a subjective idealism in which an isolated ego constructs the objects of its world. "With *Dasein* as being-in-the-world, non-human ontic beings are already disclosed." [15] Nowhere does Heidegger deny the independent reality of trees, stones, and mountains. In this respect, he says, his philosophy would agree with the thesis of realism. But in its fundamental intention and movement an existentialist-ontological understanding of the world overcomes the realism-idealism problem itself. The realism-idealism problem is still posed in terms of the subject-object framework of interpretation. Heidegger seeks to disclose the ontological foundation which precedes any split between subject and object, and this foundation he finds in the phenomenon of world itself. World as a concept functions thus as the transcendental background for man's concrete intramundane orientations. Heidegger's use of the transcendental method points up the relation of his philosophy to that of Kant and to the whole tradition of *transcendentale Philosophie* which Kant inaugurated. In a sense Heidegger stands squarely in this tradition, as becomes apparent in his classic interpretation of Kant's *Critique of Pure Reason*. As Kant's transcendental unity of apperception constituted an attempt to establish the universal conditions under which empirical knowledge was possible, so Heidegger's transcendental concept of world indicates the universal horizon of intramundane orientations and projects. What is lacking in Kant is a full development of the field concept of world and its relation to the theoretical consciousness. Kant recognized that the "I" can never be separated from "thinking," but Kant failed to see that the "I think" always presupposes a fundamental, pre-cognitive, constitutive relation to the existential world. One might say that Heidegger has substituted for Kant's transcendental unity of apperception, grounded in theoretical consciousness, a more foundational transcendental *Weltlichkeit* grounded in the pre-cognitive experience of already being-in-the-world.

2. Structural Analysis of the Environmental World

The phenomenon of world is disclosed in one of its manifestations as a surrounding environment intentionally related to the practical projects of the existing *Dasein*. This surrounding environment (*Umwelt*) is uncovered in man's everyday existence through the instrumentality of tools or utensils (*Zeug*). The environment which is existentially proximate to *Dasein* is thus the environment in the modification of *Zeugwelt*. My environment is initially disclosed as a world of tools which I use to realize the plans and anticipations of my everyday concerns. These tools which I use to carry out my projects are at hand (*zuhanden*). They are the instruments that I use circumspectly (*umsichtige Besorgen*) to order the environment and make it malleable for my projects. The environmental world is therefore indissolubly linked with man's existential projects. As an instrumental complex this environment can disclose itself as beneficent, but it can also disclose what Sartre has called a "coefficient of adversity." My pen can run out of ink, my car can have a flat tire, my light bulb can burn out, the sun can be too hot, the wind can be too strong, etc. All of these coefficients of adversity frustrate my projects of practical concern, but at the same time they are what they are because of my projects. As Sartre points out, it is only in light of man's projects that the wind can appear as a head wind or a good wind.[16] My environment is thus initially disclosed as a field of practical concerns (*Besorgen*) in which my projects succeed or are shattered by virtue of the introduction of coefficients of adversity. Heidegger's favorite illustration of the disclosure of the *Umwelt* through the manipulation of tools is that of the hammer and the act of hammering. In the practical concerns of *Dasein* a hammer is first disclosed as a *Werkzeug*. It is a utensil or tool with which one hammers, thus fulfilling a given project. As utensil or tool, the hammer is present in the mode of at-handness (*Zuhandensein*). But the hammer can be present in another mode. If no longer in use or no longer referential to my practical concerns, the hammer is given as a *Korperding*, or physical object, instead of a *Werkzeug*. It is at hand no longer but simply on hand. As physical object the hammer can be scientifically analyzed and described in terms of its primary and secondary qualities.

But this scientific analysis is already at second remove from the reality of the *Umwelt* as it is immediately encountered. The heaviness of the hammer is not initially the heaviness of an object which has the quantitatively determined weight of 10 pounds; rather, it is the heaviness of a utensil which in reference to my practical concerns renders difficult the act of hammering. The mode of at-handness is thus the primitive mode of man's orientation in the *Umwelt*. The mode of on-handness comes later in man's understanding of his world. It is secondary and subsidiary in that it has its foundation in man's encounter with his world as a world of tools.

In this orientation through the use of utensils the spatiality of the environment is disclosed. At-handness has the character of existential proximity. Tools which are at hand are in a vicinity (*Gegen*) in which they have a place indicated by my practical concerns. The space of the surrounding world is thus understood in terms of existenital nearness and remoteness. Tools are either accessible, i.e., they are in their place, or they are absent from their place and thus remote from my projects. Place is where a utensil belongs. The place of a pen, for example, is its existential proximity for the writing of this book. Clearly space is here understood not in terms of a three-dimensional geometrical coordinate, which is somehow objectively given and then filled with on-hand things or objects. Indeed the primordial space of the world is not a dimension at all; it is a direction. It is a direction of human care in which distance is not that of metrical measurement but that of distance experienced as existential remoteness and nearness. The spatiality of being-in-the-world is first a *lived* space. The geometrically derived space with its dimensional loci and metric measurements is a later abstraction from a primordial lived space of immediate experience. When in my everyday existence I say that the way to my friend's house is a short way, shortness is understood not in terms of a quantitative stretch of geometric space but in terms of my initial project in which I have related myself to my friend in a special mode of concern. The space involved is not that of longitude and latitude but the space which Proust has so penetratingly elucidated in his descriptions of the distance between "Guermantes' way" and "Swann's way." Indeed, the way to my friend may be existentially nearer than the walk across the hall to my neighbor in the adjoining apartment, because my neighbor is only on the fringe of my concerns—he is existentially remote. So also the space enclosed by the walls of my apartment is not initially apprehended through metric measurements. It is first apprehended as being either too large or too small for the purpose which I have projected and seek to realize. It is either suitable or unsuitable for living in the manner which I have chosen.

Spatiality must thus first be comprehended as an "existential" which defines the environmental horizon of my projects. Spatiality as a category is a secondary and derivative designation which arises later in human experience. The modes of being-in-the-world through which these two approaches to spatiality are uncovered are the modes of at-handness and on-handness respectively. A categorial determinate of space can be derived only when the world is approached as being on hand and thus objectified. If the primoridal space is an existential and lived space, then one falsifies the initial disclosure of world-phenomenon when one describes the world as being *in* space. The world is neither in space (realism), nor is space in an epistemological subject which constructs its world (idealism). Properly speaking, space is in the world. Spatiality is a mode of world-orientation. The surrounding environment is not a spatial box which exists prior to the world-phenomenon. The environment is not arranged and spread out in a pure space that already exists. As a horizon of *Weltlichkeit* it is disclosed through a phenomenological investigation as a complex of places defined by the directions of practical concern.[17] Spatiality is an existential ingredient of the world in the mode of at-handness. To exist in the world is to spatialize it through the instrumentality of tools. These tools through which spatiality is disclosed have a referential (*Verweisung*) character and disclose the world in its bearing-complex (*Bewandtnis*). World-phenomenon is referential or vectorial. This constitutes the basis for Heidegger's doctrine of existential intentionality. The tools which I use refer to other tools, to the users of the tools, to the projects of the users, and to the whole complex of which these are a part. The environmental world is thus disclosed in its referential unity (*Verweisungzusammenhang*), which evinces an "instrumental" intentionality. A tool or utensil always has the character of being useful (*etwas, um zu*). Each utensil refers to another utensil. Pen, ink, paper, blotter, table, lamp, furniture, window, door, room—all suggest a referential structure of the world. The inner connectedness of this referential structure is what Heidegger calls the bearing-complex (*Bewandtnis*) of the environmental world. The *Umwelt* is disclosed as a Gestalt in which the phenomenon in its referential structure has its place relative to the projects of everyday concerns.

Now the question concerning the relationship of this existentialist description of the environmental world to any ontic scientific corpus of knowledge immediately arises. If indeed the existentialist analysis is to ring true, then it must provide the conceptual clarification for man's understanding of himself in his concrete orientation, whether this concrete orientation be biological, pyschological, sociological, or theological. Disciplines presuppose a concept of world, and before man becomes a biologist or a theologian, he is already existentially involved in the world. For this reason, a phenomenological description and ontological delineation of the structures of the primordial world-phenomenon must be undertaken. This is what Heidegger means by a fundamental ontology which seeks for a disclosure of Being (*Sein*). There also remains the task of relating the various areas of ontic investigation which deal with beings (*Seiendes*) in their special concrete situations. This task is that of metaphysics. Metaphysics seeks for a unifying perspective of the totality of that which concretely is. It seeks to discern the formal relationships among the various sciences and must further seek to explicate the connection of these formal relationships to the fundamental ontology in which metaphysics is itself rooted.[18] The metaphysician has the task of pursuing the question of how Gestalt psychology, for example, is clarified by the existentialist analysis of the referential structure and bearing-complex of being-in-the-world; of how the field theory of sub-atomic physics expresses an ontic level of the field conception of being-in-the-world; of how the social theory of the self in sociology is an ontic manifestation of a universal determinant of *Mitsein*; of how concern as an "existential" defining the universally human is a clarification of an ultimate theological concern about the holy. Heidegger's fundamental ontology, although not denying the possibility of metaphysics thus understood, does not take these issues into account. Heidegger distinguishes his philosophical-ontological concept from a special theological-ontic interpretation when he says that "world in the sense of 'being-in-the-world' in no way designates earthly being in contradistinction to the 'spiritual.' "[19] This is a special existential and ontic understanding of the world. Heidegger's interest resides in an explication of that ontological understanding of the world in terms of which any special ontic understanding has its conceptual clarification. This does not mean, as is often suggested by interpreters of Heidegger, that Heidegger has lost his existential moorings. This is only to say that an ontological analysis of man's being-in-the-world cannot draw its formulations from any one special area of ontic investigation—biology, psychology, theology, etc. To derive the structures of the universally human from a theological analysis of man in terms of sin and grace (as Karl Barth would seem to do) is to invite a theological imperialism which is just as vicious as a biological reductivism that interprets man solely through biological drives and needs. World is already presupposed in one's religious orientation as well as in one's biological orientation. The existentialist ontologist is concerned with a structural analysis of world-phenomenon as it shows itself in the whole manifold of existential and ontic experience.

Foundational studies in the field of psychiatric phenomenology and its relation to existentialist analysis have shown that the idea of lived or oriented space is basic to an understanding of neurotic and psychotic behavior.[20] The mentally and emotionally disturbed patient has lost his orientation in his lived space. Merleau-Ponty, the French phenomenologist, has given careful attention to the phenomenon of lived space and its psychiatric relevance. The emotionally healthy man, he observes, is guaranteed against delusion or hallucination because of the particular structure of his space.[21] Binswanger in his psychiatric studies describes what he calls "attuned space" (*gestimmter Raum*). This is an emotionally conditioned spatial experience in which the character of lived space has an indelible emotional coloring. Space is full or empty, expanded or constricted, depending upon one's mood. Love is "space-binding" in that the object of love is experienced in a nearness in which the geometric determinants of distance are transcended. Happiness expands the attuned space, sorrow constricts it, and despair makes it empty. Schizophrenic experience is characterized by a loss of spatial consistency, either gradually or suddenly. The space of the schizophrenic dissolves and loses its structure, and thus his whole emotional integrity is threatened.[22]

Studies and clinical investigations in psychiatric phenomenology are of utmost significance for an ontology of existence in that they help to delineate the peculiar relation between the existentialist and the existential, as the latter is subject to a specific ontic investigation. Any ontology of existence, if it is to remain true to immediate experience, must in its elucidation of the universally human provide guiding concepts for the ontic regions of being.

Our structural analysis of *Umwelt* has disclosed the basic existentialist concepts of at-handness and on-handness which circumscribe the two fundamental modes of our surrounding environment. These modes in their respective moments disclose the spatiality, referentiality, and bearing-complex that characterize the world as a field of practical concern. World-phenomenon thus presents itself in the horizon of environment. But here an important point must be underscored. The horizon of environment never surges up as an independent modality. The communal world and self-relatedness are always already there, and the three coexist, so to speak, in their primordial presentment. I experience my existential world as a *surrounding environment* which I share *with others*. The interpenetration of these horizons becomes evident in a consideration of the human body. My body is experienced as mine. It is a lived body through which I realize a project of being-in-the-world, or through which my project is limited or even shattered. But also my body is inextricably bound up with a biological environment of evolutionary development, of drives and instincts, of needs and physiological appetitions—all of which are items in my world of care. Also there is my body as it exists for others, which leads me to appraise myself as in some sense a body already looked at. This is to say that body is itself coextensive with world. My body is spread out over the different horizons of the world. It is omnipresent. To have a body and to experience world are one and the same thing.[23] The meanings which attach to my body as it concretely lives simply cannot be exhausted by an ontic analysis of objective factors such as physiological and biological determinants. Rollo May has pointed out that Freudian psychoanalysis as well as behavioristic psychology have restricted their interpretations of man to this special ontic area of the existential world and have developed a physiological and biological reductivism in which communality and self-relatedness are excluded. Heidegger makes the same point when he speaks of the "confusion of biologism," by which man is interpreted simply as a continuation of physiologically and biologically conditioned life processes. Man's body, in such a point of view, is no longer the lived body spread out over the horizons of the world but is an abstracted, objectified, and lifeless body which exists for biologists, physiologists, and physicians only. This does not discredit medicine and biology except to point out that their investigations circumscribe a particular ontic region of the *Umwelt* which has been abstracted from a primordial world-phenomenon. "That physiology and physiological chemistry can analyze man scientifically as an organism is no proof that in this 'organismic', i.e., scientifically understood body, the essence of man is to be found," says Heidegger.[24] The common charge that existentialism has neglected the phenomenon of body, particularly in its ontic environmental upsurge, may have some basis. Heidegger indeed has little to say about the body in his existentialist analysis. Sartre and Merleau-Ponty, however, from different perspectives, have given close attention to the phenomenon of the body as lived, and one must not forget Kierkegaard's penetrating discussion of the body in its bearing upon sex, which is developed in *The Concept of Anxiety*. The self as described in Kierkegaard's dialectical analysis is never "pure spirit." After man's historical disruption from nature, he must actualize himself as a sexual being. For Kierkegaard the erotic is always bound up with spirit, and the body with the soul. His essay "The Diary of the Seducer" in the first volume of *Either/Or* is a classic expression of the sensual side of man's world orientation. Although Kierkegaard's discussion on the lived body is fragmentary and never systematically formulated into an existentialist analysis, his grasp of the unity of the sensual and the spiritual is profound.

3. *Structural Analysis of the Communal World*

The world as immediately presented has an irreducible communal aspect which existentially qualifies all of man's concerns, theoretical as well as practical. Kierkegaard saw clearly the relevance of this communal character of existence, although at times it is given a subordinate consideration in his writings. Discussing the idea of friendship in Aristotle, Kierkegaard concludes that "his category is thus in a certain sense more perfect than the modern view which bases justice upon duty, the abstract categorical—he bases it upon the social sense." [25] Thus he finds in Aristotle's teaching on friendship in the *Nicomachean Ethics* a more adequate principle for ethics than in Kant's category of duty. Kierkegaard also provides a clear statement of the social character of being-in-the-world when he writes: "He who has ethically chosen and found himself has himself as he is determined in his whole concreteness. . . . But although he himself is his aim, this aim is nevertheless another, for the self which is the aim is not an abstract self, which fits everywhere and hence nowhere, but a concrete self which stands in reciprocal relations with these surroundings, these conditions of life, this natural order. This self which is the aim is not merely a personal self but a social, a civic self. . . .

The personal life as such was an isolation and hence imperfect; in the fact that through the civic life he comes back into his personality, the personal life manifests itself in a higher form." [26] To the above passages one could add numerous quotations from Kierkegaard's exegesis of the Biblical text "Thou shalt love thy neighbor," which he develops in his provocative book *Works of Love.* Christianity, he says in one place, "transforms every relation between men into a conscience relationship and thus also into a love relationship." [27] Similar suggestions of a social view of the self can be found in the *Journals.* "I should have been ashamed before God, and my soul would have been troubled, if I had become so self-important that I behaved as though 'other men' did not exist." [28] Thus to say that Kierkegaard did not take seriously the social character of existence and foundered on a radical and unqualified individualism would seem to be a most questionable generalization. An existential elucidation of man's being-with-others, particularly in its ethical and religious implications, is certainly present in the writings of the Danish thinker. However, it is first in the existentialist ontology of Heidegger that *Mitsein* is delineated as a structural element in the phenomenon of being-in-the-world. Heidegger has ontologized the ethico-religious notions of Kierkegaard in his attempt to develop a universal phenomenology of existence. *Mitsein* becomes an "existential" which indicates a most fundamental horizon of my being-in-the-world. As *Dasein* is never given without a surrounding environment, so *Dasein* is never given without the Other. "Insofar as *Dasein* exists at all," says Heidegger, "he has the modality of being-with-others." [29] Not only is the communal character of man revealed in his actual encounters with others; it is disclosed in his experience of being alone (*Alleinsein*). Man's experience of being alone presupposes a being-with-others. Man is alone only because the other is away or absent. In various ways man is separated from others and thrown back upon his aloneness, but this aloneness is itself a mode of being-with-others. Thus *Dasein* possesses an indelible communal character. In society and in solitude, *Dasein* is structurally a communal creature.

Karl Jaspers, although harboring certain reservations about the possibility of an existentialist ontology, expresses basically the same theme when he writes that self-being and being-in-communication are inseparable.[30] Sartre's existentialism, by virtue of his conscious attempt at a phenomenological ontology, is on this point more akin to Heidegger's than to Jaspers'. In *L'Être et le Néant* Sartre has formulated this ontology through a systematic delineation of three basic ontological distinctions: *en-soi* (in itself), *pour-soi* (for itself) and *Autrui* (Other). The *en-soi–pour-soi* distinction indicates the fundamental rupture in Being. The *en-soi* is being in its total plentitude, characterized by fullness, density, and completeness. It is perfectly coincident with itself, having neither potency nor movement. The *pour-soi*, on the other hand, constitutes the moment of separation or eruption from the plentitude of the *en-soi*, and the conditions for the separation are consciousness, the power of nihilation, and freedom. The *pour-soi* thus indicates the being of man as free consciousness. But there is a third ontological element disclosed in the world of the *pour-soi* as it projects itself in its freedom—*Autrui*. Consciousness finds itself in a state of coexistence with others. In my projects I find the Other already present as a threat to my freedom and self-affirmation. Through his "look" the Other shatters my world by sucking me into the orbit of his projects and shearing me of my unique possibilities. He transforms me into an object. The Other, in the philosophy of Sartre, surges into my world only as a factor of negativity. No positive or authentic communication is possible. The Other is always *"la mort cachée de mes possibilités."* I can affirm my freedom and unique possibilities only through dissociation from the Other, but this can never be realized, for the existence of the Other is an irreducible fact. I do not constitute the Other; I encounter him. And in this encounter he strives to affirm himself by rendering me into a possibility for him. I can affirm myself only by transforming the Other into an object, and the Other can affirm himself only by transforming me into an object. This constitutes the irreducible conflict of consciousness with the Other which makes Garcin declare in the conclusion of *Huis Clos*, "L'enfer, c'est les Autres." Marcel, Sartre's fellow countryman, has sought to correct Sartre's negativistic interpretation of *Mitsein* with a doctrine of "inter-subjectivity" which provides for a positive and creative communion of selves.

Man's being-with-others must thus be understood in relation to its two possible qualifications—being-with in a negative and mutually self-destructive manner, and being-with in a positive and mutually self-creative manner. Heidegger has given a conceptual clarification to this distinction in his use of "authenticity" and "unauthenticity." The ontological basis for the distinction between authenticity and unauthenticity is the qualitatively different relation which obtains in the projects of my *Umwelt* from those in my *Mitwelt*. The relation of man to the

Umwelt, in which he is preoccupied with tools which are at hand, is characterized as a relation of practical concern (*Besorgen*), but the relation which obtains in the encounter of *Daseins* is properly called personal concern (*Fürsorge*). "The characteristic of practical concern is not a feature of communality, even though in communality other intramundane beings are encountered, as is the case in practical concern. The being to which *Dasein* relates himself in his communality does not appear in the modality of at-hand utensils but is himself *Dasein*. This being is not the object of practical concern but rather stands in the relationship of personal concern." [31] The Other, understood in his proper perspective, is never a tool which performs a function for me, nor is he an on-hand object or thing which can be objectified through quantitatively determined knowledge. The categorial analysis which applies to the environmental world does not apply to the communal world. When the Other is reduced to an instance of at-hand or on-hand being, then his unique personal freedom evaporates; he is depersonalized and becomes an instrument and an object.

Existential philosophy has contributed more to a clarification of this depersonalization and dehumanization in man's unauthentic being-with-others than all the academic ethical systems propounded in Western thought. Marx was one of the first to call our attention to the destructive depersonalization which occurs when the entrepreneur transforms the worker into a tool and a commodity and thus puts a cash value on him. In modern technological society the machine and the instrument of production become the standards for defining human behavior, and man becomes identified with the wrenches which he uses to turn the bolts on the assembly line, or even with the bolts themselves. Man, in short, is sucked into his environment and there loses his identity. As Marcel has shown so profoundly, man becomes identified with the functions of his environment. "Surely everything both within him and outside him conspires to identify this man with his functions—meaning not only with his functions as worker, as trade union member or as voter, but with his vital functions as well. The rather horrible expression 'time table' perfectly describes his life. So many hours for each function. Sleep too is a function which must be discharged, so that the other functions may be exercised in their turn. The same with pleasure, with relaxation; it is logical that the weekly allowance of recreation should be determined by an expert on hygiene." [32]

This phenomenon of the depersonalization of the Other, particularly as it expresses itself in the guise of public conformity, is elucidated in Kierkegaard's book *The Present Age*. Although written primarily as a cultural critique of nineteenth-century Denmark, the book speaks to *our* present age with an unequivocal relevance. Kierkegaard saw clearly that for the most part being-with degenerates into an appalling public conformity. Authentic interpersonal relations are sacrificed on the altar of that "monstrous abstraction" called the public. Kierkegaard maintains that the "levelling process" has made the category of the individual virtually extinct. "It must be obvious to every one that the profound significance of the levelling process lies in the fact that it means the predominance of the category generation over the category individuality." [33] The decisions of the individual are made by the public or the crowd, and in making the decisions for the individual, the crowd becomes the criterion of truth. Then we have that most ludicrous view of life, says Kierkegaard, "which conceives that where the crowd is, there also is the truth, and that in truth itself there is need of having the crowd on its side." [34] In this public "existence" of the masses the self and the other self have only numerical significance. "By seeing the multitude of men about him, by getting engaged in all sorts of worldly affairs, by becoming wise about how things go in this world, such a man forgets himself, forgets what his name is (in the divine understanding of it), does not dare to believe in himself, finds it too venturesome a thing to be himself, far easier and safer to be like the others, to become an imitation, a number, a cipher in the crowd." [35]

The most effective instrument of the public in its process of depersonalization is the press. The press, writes Kierkegaard, is the place where "men are demoralized in the shortest possible time on the largest possible scale for the lowest possible price." [36] The press levels the exceptional to the average, makes the significant trivial and the trivial sensational. "One hardly knows whether to laugh or cry," writes Kierkegaard in his *Journals*. "The evening paper apologizes because the review of my *Works of Love* is immoderately long. And a few days later the same paper publishes in an article about the same length a police report of a theft." [37] The press is simply an instrument of the public. It is controlled and influenced anonymously and prints only what the public wants to see, think, choose, and believe. Any attempt at authentic communication is curtailed. Any ideas which might challenge the status quo or man's everyday preconceptions of what is required of him as a unique individual in his responsibility to other individuals are suppressed, and the voice of the public continues to be heard throughout the land.

This public levelling, depersonalizing in the crowd, and trivializing effected by the press produces indifference and superficiality in one's talk. Talk becomes, like the public itself, a mere abstraction. Thoughts are expressed, but it makes little difference who expresses them, for they are the thoughts and desires of the public and of no one in particular. "People's remarks are so objective, so all-inclusive," Kierkegaard notes, "that it is a matter of complete indifference who expresses them, and where human speech is concerned that is the same as acting 'on principles.' And so our talk becomes like the public, a pure abstraction. There is no longer any one who knows how to talk, and instead, objective thought produces an atmosphere, an abstract sound which makes human speech superfluous, just as machinery makes men superfluous." [38] Just as in the press so in our everyday talk authentic communion remains concealed. No genuine content is communicated, because the talk itself has become objectified and deprived of its personal quality. The speakers are themselves accidental to what is said. The talk could just as well be that of another, for what is expressed is simply the thought of *everyone*. This talk which is the talk of the public, continues Kierkegaard, produces an astounding superficiality in which conversation becomes a "meaningless repetition of names, of 'absolutely reliable' private information of what this and that person—mentioning all their names—had said, etc., etc. . . ." [39] The indifference and superficiality of this talk is vividly expressed in Kierkegaard's banquet scene in *Stages on Life's Way*, which might offer a striking parallel to the atmosphere of any twentieth-century cocktail party. "So then they dined. Soon conversation had woven its beautiful garland about the guests, so they sat there crowned with it. At one moment the conversation seemed to be in love with the food, then with the wine, then again with itself; at one moment it was as though it was on the point of signifying something, then again it meant nothing at all." [40] Whether T. S. Eliot drew some of his material for the writing of *The Cocktail Party* from Kierkegaard remains questionable. Actually, he did not need to. All that was necessary was a glance into the *Mitwelt* as it shows itself. The phenomenon is there ready to be analyzed and described.

Heidegger, the ontologist, has formulated Kierkegaard's fragmentary but illuminating descriptions of the unauthentic qualification of existence into a set of interrelated "existentials" which delineate the universal structures of the concrete experience of unauthenticity. The primary "existential" in this structural analysis of unauthenticity is the "anonymous one" (*Das Man*). The German term, *Das Man,* cannot

adequately be rendered into the English language because of the idiosyn-
crasies of the German grammar which are involved in its composition.
In the German the article, *das,* when it refers to the grammatical subject,
Man, transforms the subject from its masculine (and thus personal)
gender, namely "der" which is the proper German usage, into a neuter
(and thus impersonal) gender. This grammatical function of *das,* however, does not remain constant throughout the German, for it is grammatically correct to speak of *das madchen, das kind,* etc. But the German
construction of *Das Man* denotes specifically an impersonal, anonymous,
and neuter "who" (*Wer*). "The 'who' is neither this person nor that
person, neither man himself, nor a particular man, nor the summation of
all. The 'who' is the neuter, *das Man.*" [41] Probably the least inadequate
translation would be to translate the term either as the "anonymous one"
or the "impersonal one" or simply as the "one." The central connotation
is that of anonymity and depersonalization. To exist in the mode of the
"anonymous one" means to exist in the *Mitwelt* in such a way that both
the self and the other self are reduced to the status of on-hand being and
deprived of their existential freedom which alone makes communication
possible. "In this mode of being," says Heidegger, "the self of the unique
Dasein and the self of the other have not yet found themselves, i.e., they
are lost. Man exists in bondage and unauthenticity." [42]

The self of *Dasein* and the other self which he encounters in this
unauthentic mode of the "anonymous one" are selves which move in
the realm of the customs, habits, and conventions of everyday life. They
have succumbed to what Heidegger calls the "everydayness" of existence.
Man for the most part lives and orients himself in this mode of everyday
existence. He is introduced to the *Mitwelt* via this everyday existence.
When he apprehends himself as a going concern, he finds that he has
already taken on the mechanical habits, the established customs, and the
accepted conventions of everyday life. The "anonymous one" is further
characterized by a mediocrity (*Durchschnittlichkeit*) in which the average becomes the measure of his possibilities and the final standard of his
existence. He lives by a spurious "golden mean" in which social behavior
is calculated on the basis of socially binding "laws of averages." This leads
to a levelling process (*Einebnung*) in which the unique possibilities of
existence are flattened and all originality is trivialized. Publicity
(*Öffentlichkeit*) is another structural element of the "anonymous one"
in his mode of unauthentic communality. Man "opens" himself to the
public, conforms to its demands and opinions, accepts its criteria or

standards, and retreats from personal commitment and responsible decision. As Kierkegaard points out, the public becomes my decision-maker. I think what the public thinks, I feel what the public feels, and I do what the public does.[43]

These various modifications of the unauthentic "anonymous one" receive further clarification when they are understood in relation to the threefold structure of talk (*Gerede*), curiosity (*Neugier*), and ambiguity (*Zweideutigkeit*). Heidegger makes it clear that his structural analysis is not to be understood as a moral critique or as an aspiring philosophy of culture. It must be properly regarded as an explication of the ontological structures present in man's concrete experience of the communal world. His ontological analysis can only provide the philosophically clarified concept of a world-horizon in relation to which ethical questions can be reasonably raised. Every ethical interrogation presupposes a structure of human existence. An existentialist ontology has for its specific task the clarification of this structure.

Talk is an unauthentic modification of speech. Like speech it is a form of communication, but it is a form of communication which merely expresses the accepted, everyday, average, and shallow interpretations of the public. That which is talked about is not really understood. One merely listens to the talking itself. Thus nothing new is added. No decisive content emerges. Everything means the same, for everyday existence always speaks in the same clichés. In talk the primary relation to the essence of that which is discussed is lost. The real subject matter of the discussion remains concealed. Nothing is authentically understood. "Talk is the possibility of understanding everything without appropriating the content," Heidegger says.[44] This talking often assumes an authoritative character, and things become so simply because they are said to be so (*"Die Sache ist so, weil man es sagt"*). This unauthenticity of talk is not limited to vocal or audible conversation. It expresses itself in scribbling (*Geschreibe*), an unauthentic form of writing, as well as in reading. The reader, levelled to an average and everyday understanding of things, is not able to distinguish that which is originally creative from that which is merely repeated in talk. Instead of disclosing human existence in its true perspective, unauthentic talk, writing, and reading only contribute to its concealment. The talking itself is disclosed but never that which the talk ought to illuminate. The content remains hidden in the talk, writing, and reading of the "anonymous one."

The second structural element, curiosity, indicates the tendency

of the "anonymous one" to look for things simply for the sake of finding novelty. There is no earnest attempt to understand the truth and
falsity in what one investigates, only an insatiable desire to explore
everything in one's present environment. Thus in his curiosity the
"anonymous one" sacrifices himself to the present. He loses himself in
the present preoccupations which arouse his curiosity but which he never
seeks to understand.[45] Here we begin to see the relevance of time, which
later becomes the decisive "existential" in Heidegger's distinction between the authentic and the unauthentic. Curiosity is one way in which
Dasein sinks into the mode of an on-hand presence, thus separating himself from his remembered past and projected future, which are inseparable moments of his being-in-the-world. Never being satisfied, the
"anonymous one" is always "on the move" (Unverweilen), looking for
something new. This restlessness invites dispersion (Zerstreung) and
flightiness (Aufenhaltslosigkeit). The "anonymous one," curious about
everything, is everywhere and nowhere. He has no center. He loses his
integrity. It is now no longer a question of decisive thought and action.
Unity of purpose and commitment to truth are suppressed, and the
existence of both the self and the other self dwindles in a nameless and
frustrating cycle of sterile activities.

Ambiguity is the third element in the threefold structural constitution of the "anonymous one." In the everyday talk of the public, everyone makes pronouncements about everything. This places the "anonymous one" in a situation in which he is unable to discern what is
authentically understood and what is only talk. Everything seems as
though it might be genuinely comprehended and properly expressed.
Yet at its very source it is grossly misconceived. On the other hand, what
appears misunderstood may be genuinely comprehended. This existential ambiguity pervades all thought and action of the "anonymous one."

The foregoing "existentials" comprise Heidegger's attempt at
phenomenological description of the Mitwelt as it shows itself in the
unauthentic mode of the "anonymous one." For the most part man
exists in this unauthentic mode, and hence the phenomenon of being-
with-others first presents itself in this manner. Man first discovers himself
in the everyday, average, levelled, and public world of Das Man. But
unauthenticity is only one qualification of man's being-with-others.
Though Sartre does not, Kierkegaard, Heidegger, Jaspers, and Marcel
envision the possibility of an authentic communality (eigentliches
Miteinandersein). To what extent their doctrines of authentic com-

munality remain arrested or undeveloped is a relevant question and must be dealt with, but it is indisputable that these thinkers make much of authentic communal existence. Kierkegaard has described this authentic existence in his doctrine of the stages and in his *Works of Love*. The self exists authentically when it becomes free to shoulder its responsibility and open itself for a commitment, religiously defined as a commitment to God who commands a resolute love of one's neighbor. Heidegger's structural analysis of authenticity clarifies the universal possibilities in which Kierkegaard's existential ethico-religious commitment (as well as any other existential commitment) may become concrete. This structural analysis in Heidegger has as its guiding motifs the phenomena of resolve and conscience. Resolve brings the self to a personal concern for others. In this personal concern for others, the authentic self becomes the conscience for the other and frees each for his own unique possibilities. "Only the resolve taken on by himself brings *Dasein* to the possibility of freeing the other for his own possibilities. . . . The resolute *Dasein* can become the conscience of the other." [46] Having freed himself from the unauthentic dispersion of the "anonymous one," *Dasein* has the responsibility of aiding the other in the achievement of his integrity by becoming the "voice" of conscience for him. Similarly, Jaspers has heavily accented the theme of responsibility to and for others. "In communication I sense a responsibility not only for myself but also for the other self." [47] Like Kierkegaard, Jaspers sees love as the source of authentic communication. "Love is not yet communication but is the source through which communication is illumined." [48] Finally, Marcel has presented a profound statement on authentic communication in his discussion of creative inter-subjectivity, which we will consider in chapter vii.

4. Structural Analysis of Self-relatedness

The third horizon disclosed in man's primordial experience of being-in-the-world is the horizon of self-relatedness, or the world which I apprehend as being distinctively and uniquely my own. This field of phenomena is what interpreters of existentialism have referred to as the

Eigenwelt. The *Eigenwelt* is the region in which I become aware of my selfhood, experience the "I." We search this region for an answer to that puzzling question, "Who am I?" Again, we must keep in mind that the three horizons of world, *Umwelt*, *Mitwelt*, and *Eigenwelt*, are interdependent and disclose themselves in a simultaneous upsurge. Neither of the three horizons are prior to any of the other two. What *is* prior is a primordial experience of being-in-the-world in a vague, confused, pre-thematic sense. In the words of Marcel, "What is given to me beyond all possible doubt is the confused and global experience of the world inasmuch as it is existent." [49] But this global experience of world in its initial disclosure is not yet thematically differentiated into its various horizons. The world around me, the world of the other, and my world are given simultaneously. In my primordial experience I do not differentiate between what is mine and what is not mine. The global world existing as an immediate datum of experience is blurred, vague, and confused. Through a phenomenological investigation I then find that different horizons of this vague global experience of world show themselves. I uncover an environmental world through the use of tools in my practical concerns; I uncover a communal world through my personal concerns; and I uncover myself as that being who expresses concern about himself by asking the question, "Who am I?" There can thus be no question of finding an "I" given without the world—as in the philosophy of Descartes. The "I," the self, emerges within the world. It is for this reason that Heidegger's distinction between *Dasein* and *self* is most helpful. The "being-there" of *Dasein* is the primordial world experience of being spread out over the different horizons, projected into each of them. The experience of selfhood is a specific qualification of *Dasein* as *Eigenwelt*. It arises when *Dasein* manifests concern for his Being and relates himself to his Being.[50] This reflexive character of selfhood through which the self relates itself to itself is that which makes possible a knowledge of one's self, love and hate of one's self, and choice of one's self.

This concept of the reflexivity of the self, which is the basis for all self-knowledge and ethical action, was stated and elucidated with dialectical profundity in Kierkegaard's *Sickness Unto Death*. In the opening lines of the book we read: "Man is spirit. But what is spirit? Spirit is the self. But what is the self? The self is a relation which relates itself to its own self, or it is that in the relation (which accounts for it) that the relation relates itself to its own self; the self is not the relation but (consists in the fact) that the relation relates itself to his own self." [51] The same point is expressed in Kierkegaard's book *Training in Christianity*: "What is it, then, to be a self? It is a duplication." [52] The possibility of reflexivity or duplication is precisely that which constitutes selfhood. To be a self is to be able to look at one's self, love one's self, become estranged from one's self, be anxious about one's self, and evaluate one's self. The self can have knowledge of itself through becoming "objective" to itself. It can transcend itself and examine, describe, and appraise itself—as did Socrates when he was about to be condemned to death and spoke of his condemnation like a third person. [53] Selfhood involves the possibility of self-transcendence in knowledge. The self can experience itself in its immediacy through suffering, and then it can transcend itself and *see* itself as a particular suffering self. In all self-knowledge the reflexive and duplex character of existence is presupposed. Jaspers has given a careful formulation of this concept of *Selbstreflexion* in his *Philosophie*: "In the extraction from the 'ego' as consciousness in general; from the domain of the empirical 'I'; from the given characteristics of my essence; there emerges a *relation to myself* which is the avenue for a new conception of myself. In pure objectivity I examine who I am but find only a mass of particular facts; but I proceed beyond this objectivity to examine who I actually am and find that my identity rests *only on myself*. I am that being who is concerned about himself and in his relation to himself can decide who he is." [54]

Kierkegaard discusses the reflexivity of the self in connection with the phenomenon of despair, which in its fundamental character is estrangement within the self. The guiding thread for his discussion of selfhood thus arises from a concrete, existential experience of the negativities of existence. In despair, which is the "sickness unto death," man experiences an estrangement from himself. The self discovers itself in its despair as being in a wrong relation to itself. It experiences an internal fissure or fracture, turmoil, resentment, and negation. We will examine Kierkegaard's illuminating description of the different varieties of despair in a later chapter. Our interest here is only to clarify the meaning of reflexivity as it is revealed in the phenomena of despair, choice, and self-acceptance.

The pivotal datum in this relating activity of the self is the datum of consciousness. "Generally speaking, consciousness, i.e., consciousness of self, is the decisive criterion of the self. The more consciousness, the more self . . . ," says Kierkegaard. [55] Augustine, in some ways an existential predecessor, in Book IX of his *De Trinitate*, had developed a most incisive analysis of the relational and reflexive character of self-consciousness. He distinguished in the structure of self-consciousness the subject which is conscious (which we might call the "I") and the object of which the subject is conscious (which correspondingly could be called the "me"). There is myself as subject, as that which is conscious, and myself as object, as that of which I am conscious. Augustine specified still a third factor in the experience of self-consciousness. There is the knowledge or the thought which mediates the consciousness of the "I" with the "me" of which the "I" is conscious. I am conscious of myself as being conscious. Now the self must not be understood as simply a summation of the three terms. These three terms are modes of one and the same self, in each of which the self is fully present. This is not a tripartite doctrine of the self. The difference between the three terms is solely a difference of relation. We have, then, a unitary self possessing this relational and reflexive structure.[56]

The consciousness that Kierkegaard and Augustine specify as the decisive determinant of self must not be understood as a purely rational consciousness which intends an abstracted essence. "Self-consciousness is not contemplation; he who thinks that it is has not understood himself," says Kierkegaard, "for he sees that he himself is meanwhile in the process of becoming and so cannot be a finished product as the object of contemplation."[57] Consciousness is not a mere rational or intellective phenomenon. It is inextricably bound up with will and feeling. "The more consciousness, the more will, and the more will the more self. A man who has no will at all is no self; the more will he has, the more consciousness of self he has also."[58] Kierkegaard suggests, in a certain sense, a voluntaristic understanding of consciousness; but in a more fundamental sense he suggests a level of consciousness which precedes the distinctions of intellect, will, and emotion. Kierkegaard's view is not that of a traditional "faculty psychology" in which intellect, will, and emotion are abstracted as faculties or properties of a substantial ego. The self is not a "something" which *has* intellect, will, and emotion; the self is a becoming consciousness of which intellect, will, and emotion are emergent modalities. Intellect, will, and emotion, as he says in the *Postscript*, are unified in existence.[59] And consciousness is always allied with the term "existence" as Kierkegaard uses it—as it is also allied with the terms "infinite passion," "earnestness," and "interest." These terms are all correlative in Kierkegaard's understanding and use of them.

The reflexive structure of consciousness is thus an integral constituent of my *Eigenwelt*. Another integral constituent is the element of individuality. Aristotle, in his *Metaphysics*, established the argument that in the order of actual being it is the individual, and only the individual, that exists. Nietzsche, in whose philosophy Western metaphysics experienced both its fulfillment and demise, contended that the "error of Being" was precisely man's preoccupation with Being as the highest and most universal concept to the neglect of the passions of the "Solitary One." Max Stirner, a contemporary of Kierkegaard, in his book *Der Einzige und sein Eigentum* protested against what he considered meaningless abstractions—God, the state, society, humanity—and focused his attention upon the unique and irreplaceable individual. Existentialist philosophy returns with a renewed emphasis to this concern for the individual. The individual is for Kierkegaard not simply one determinant of self among other determinants but is the determinant *par excellence.* He often referred to individuality as "my category" and considered it so inextricably linked to his name that he hoped it would be inscribed on his grave (which it was).[60] The self is a concrete and unique individual existent. Selfhood and individuality are inseparable. The self as it experiences itself in its self-relatedness is never a "humanity in general" or a *specie differentia* within a genus. Nor is it a universal consciousness which has a purely conceptual "existence." It was on this point that Kierkegaard most bitterly opposed the idealism and rationalism of Hegel. Hegel could confer significance on the individual only as a moment in the self-actualization of the universal consciousness of the Absolute Spirit. Hegel recognized that nothing great in history happens without passion and interest expressed in individual actors, but in his system these individual actors become the "victims" of a universal consciousness which defines their significance and determines their destiny. The closer the Hegelian system approaches its completion, the less important the individual becomes, and in the end the Hegelian finds himself unable to define the relation of the system to the existing individual. The individual is swallowed up by the universal-historical. "But Ethics has been crowded out of the System, and as a substitute for it there has been included a something which confuses the historical with the individual, the bewildering and noisy demands of the age with the eternal demand that conscience makes upon the individual." [61]

Kierkegaard's continuing criticism of the Hegelian universal consciousness must not, however, be construed as a denial of the validity of universals, properly understood. In Kierkegaard's existentialism essence, as universal possibility, is conjoined with the reality of existence. "When the ethical question is raised in connection with my own reality, I ask about possibility; only that this possibility is not an aesthetically and intellectually disinterested possibility, but as being a conceived reality it is related as a possibility to my own reality, so that I may be able to realize it." [62] The universal in Kierkegaard's analysis is a possibility in the self's concrete ethical reality and must be understood concretely in relation to this ethical reality. Instead of understanding the individual in terms of the universally possible, the universally possible must be understood in terms of the concrete, existing individual. This is the kernel of Kierkegaard's "existential subjectivism." "While abstract thought seeks to understand the concrete abstractly, the subjective thinker has conversely to understand the abstract concretely. Abstract thought turns from concrete men to consider man in general; the subjective thinker seeks to understand the abstract determination of being human in terms of this particular existing human being." [63] The self is thus a synthesis of the universal and the individual, but only in the sense that the universal is posited in the individual. Expressed another way, one could say that the individual is for Kierkegaard the bearer or the foundation of the universal. The individual is existentially and ethically prior to the universal. The individual is the foundational datum, but this entails no abrogation of the universal as a possibility in the concrete. "For the universal man is not a phantom, but every man as such is the universal man, that is to say, to every man the way is assigned by which he becomes the universal man. . . . Only when the individual himself is the universal is it possible to realize the ethical." [64] The self, as understood by Kierkegaard, is not an abstract individual—which is no individual at all —but rather that which expresses itself concretely as universal humanity. Insofar as the universal is founded upon the ethically existing individual, the universal becomes contingent. It is not something given but is something that must be achieved. Each individual must realize the universal in a concrete particular embodiment. It is in this sense that the universal is posited as the individual. The religious doctrines of Adam and Christ as representatives of a universal humanity are ontic formulations of this existentialist insight that the individual is the bearer of the universal. Kierkegaard's discussion of original sin in *The Concept of Anxiety* constitutes a theological landmark in the elucidation of this historic doctrine.

To describe Adam's sin is to describe original sin, for an individual man is at the same time himself and the whole race. By the same token, Christ as son of man is an individual who without losing his individuality becomes the responsible representative for all men.

Our structural analysis of self-relatedness in the thought of Kierkegaard has thus far disclosed two integral constituents—the reflexive structure of consciousness and the individual character of existence. These constituents are also central to the concept of *Dasein* in the philosophy of Heidegger. Kierkegaard describes the self as related to itself in the consciousness of an infinite passion. Heidegger describes *Dasein* as that being who is concerned for his Being and who in this concern relates himself to his Being. As concern or care (*Sorge*) was the dominant factor in the relation of *Dasein* to his environmental world in the mode of practical concern, and in his relation to his communal world in the mode of personal concern, so also it is dominant in the world of self-relatedness in which *Dasein* relates himself to himself. Concern thus emerges as a basic structural determinant of being-in-the-world. *Dasein* is that being who is concerned for himself, and through this concern he already finds himself disclosed. In the reflexive concern in which *Dasein* relates himself to himself, he discloses or reveals himself in the horizon of *Eigenwelt*. Disclosure (*Erschlossenheit*) is thus integrally a part of his Being. This, says Heidegger, is the proper understanding of the doctrine of the *lumen naturale*. "*Dasein* is illumined *as* being-in-the-world, not through another being but so that *Dasein* himself is the illumination." [65] Clearly Augustine, with his doctrine of illumination or truth as indwelling, is in the background of Heidegger's existentialism on this point. A formulation similar to that of Heidegger is given by Paul Tillich, who on this issue also stands quite squarely in the Augustinian tradition. Tillich proposes that "whenever man has looked at his world, he has found himself in it as a part of it. But he also has realized that he is a stranger in the world of objects, unable to penetrate it beyond a certain level of scientific analysis. And then he has become aware of the fact that he himself is the door to the deeper levels of reality, that in his own existence he has the only possible approach to existence itself." [66]

The phenomenological description of *Dasein* as a being who is concerned for his Being and who in this concern relates himself to his Being indicates a twofold character of *Dasein*: first, the "essence" of

Dasein resides in his existence, and, second, this existence has an indelibly personal quality.[67] The Being disclosed in my reflexivity of concern is uniquely and peculiarly my own.

The essence of *Dasein* resides in his existence. This assertion is basic to the whole Heideggerian understanding of man and lies at the foundation of his new interpretation of existence as *Existenz*. Heidegger cautions us against a possible confusion of existence as understood in his existentialist analysis (*Existenz*) with existence in its traditional metaphysical meaning of *existentia*. A failure to distinguish between these two in the Western tradition has made any adequate and foundational description and interpretation of the nature of man impossible. "It is precisely the ontological task to show that when we choose the term existence (*Existenz*) for the Being of this being, the term does not and cannot have the ontological meaning of the traditional term *existentia*. *Existentia* means ontologically on-handness, a modality which does not pertain to that being which has the character of *Dasein*." [68] In his letter *On Humanism* Heidegger uses the hyphenated word, "Ek-sistence," which has the special meaning of "standing-out," "being ecstatic," or "being projected." "Ek-sistence, ecstatically conceived, is neither materially nor formally related to *existentia*. Ek-sistence means to stand out in the truth of Being. *Existentia*, on the other hand, means actuality, reality in contradistinction to pure possibility as Idea." [69] Paul Tillich in his study on existential philosophy has called our attention to the meaning of the Latin root *existere*, which indicates the notion of "emergence (*heraustreten*). To exist thus means "to emerge" or "to stand out." [70] Heidegger has utilized this root meaning of existence in his analysis of *Dasein* and has formulated the character of this existence with regard to its implicatory notions of nothingness, finitude, temporality, anxiety, guilt, death, and resolve. The point which needs to be underscored at this stage of our discussion is that *existentia* is a category applicable only to the realm of non-human being, including the world-region of utensils, or the mode of at-handness, and the world-region of objects and things, or the mode of on-handness. Existence is an "existential" characterizing an ecstatic *Dasein* who in his innermost Being remains opaque to a categorial analysis. Confusion can be avoided, suggests Heidegger, if we apply the category of *existentia* solely to the realm of non-human being and reserve the term *Existenz* for the Being of *Dasein*. *Existentia*, in its traditional meaning, signifies that which is actual or real as distinguished from the conceptually possible. The statement that the essence of man resides in his existence is not a statement about man's actuality as such but is rather a statement pertaining to the manner or mode in which this actuality expresses the fundamental tenor or bearing of man's Being. The existence of *Dasein*, as Sternberger has pointed out in his study, has to do with the "specific mode of the Being of man" (*Die spezifische Seinsweise des Menschen*).[71]

The traditional forms of humanism which have classified man as an *animale rationale* have foundered precisely because of their use of the metaphysical category of *existentia* in their interpretation of man. The concept of rational animality is a category derived from an examination of life as a general and natural phenomenon. Man, in these various forms of humanism, is thus understood as simply an instance of animal life in general. He is *existentia* but not *Existenz*. He is a living entity among other entities, separated from plants, animals, and God only by his degree of rationality. But here the distinctive essence of man—his ek-sistence or ecstatic character—has not yet been uncovered. And to neglect this, argues Heidegger, is to sap man of his essential "humanism" and to reduce him to an extension of the life process.[72]

The second characteristic disclosed in *Dasein's* self-understanding as a being who is concerned about his Being is "personalness" (*Jemeinigkeit*). The Being of *Dasein* is always his own. Heidegger does not use the concept of the individual in his existentialist analysis. This, again, is a category which describes on-hand being (for example, this individual book or this individual tree) but is not applicable to *Dasein*. The "existial" of "personalness" replaces the category of "the individual." Nevertheless, Heidegger's insistence on the "personalness" of *Dasein* arises from the same existential insight as Kierkegaard's insistence on the individuality of the self. Both the self in Kierkegaard's analysis and *Dasein* in Heidegger's analysis are disclosed in their personal uniqueness and thus are never simply instances of a genus or class concept. *Dasein* in the reflexivity of his concern apprehends himself as a particular, unique, personal existent. But, as already suggested in Kierkegaard's analysis of the self, man is at the same time the existential bearer of a universal humanity. Only in and through the personal and concrete *Dasein* do the universal structures of existence become transparent. To be sure, Heidegger does not always make it clear when he is speaking of a particular *Dasein* which is uniquely and concretely one's own and when he is speaking of *Dasein* as a universal mode of human existence. However, the central idea that the concrete and the personal is the bearer

of the universal appears throughout the whole of his existentialist ontology and can be understood to constitute a cardinal philosophical principle of existentialist philosophy as such.

Our structural analysis of self-relatedness, as discussed in Kierkegaard and Heidegger in particular, has thus far disclosed the phenomena
of the reflexivity of consciousness or concern, the ecstatic character of
existence, and individuality (Kierkegaard) or personalness (Heidegger).
A further structural determinant of the experience of selfhood is finite
or conditioned freedom. The emphasis on freedom as a *character
indelibilis* of human existence emerges throughout the whole of Kierkegaard's writings and is equally central to Heidegger's analysis of *Dasein*.
"But what, then, is this self of mine? If at the first instant I were to give
the first expression for this, my answer is: it is the most abstract of
all things, and yet at the same time it is the most concrete—it is freedom," writes Kierkegaard.[73] The self is freedom.

Now can this freedom in any way be phenomenologically elucidated and described? Kierkegaard and Heidegger suggest that it can.
Kierkegaard describes freedom as the dialectical synthesis of possibility
and necessity. "The self is freedom. But freedom is the dialectical element in the terms possibility and necessity." [74] To understand the self
as freedom with regard to the polar elements of possibility and necessity is first of all to understand the self in its dynamism as a self which
is in the process of becoming itself. "A self, every instant it exists, is in
process of becoming, for the self κατὰ δύναμιν . . . is only that which it
is to become." [75] The self is a dynamic process of self-becoming. This
interpretation of the self in terms of a dynamic, becoming, and striving
character is highly reminiscent of Plato's concept of *eros* as it is formulated in the *Symposium*. As in Plato *eros* is understood as a dynamic principle always in transition, in constant striving for fulfillment, reaching
out beyond what it is and what it has—so in Kierkegaard's analysis the
self κατὰ δύναμιν is a being constantly striving to become itself. The similarity between Kierkegaard and Plato on this point is noted by Kierkegaard himself when, in the *Postscript*, he makes an explicit reference to
the Greek concept of *eros* as a clarification of what is meant by existence.[76] The self is intrinsically dynamic. Any analysis of self in terms
of categories of substantial self-identity or monadic immutability conceals the inner dynamism and active striving which characterizes the self
in its lived becoming. The self strives, changes, seeks to become that

which it is not yet. At no time is the self completed and finished. It is always actualiz-ing, never actualiz-ed.

The self as freedom is in the process of becoming. But becoming can occur only within a polar structure of possibility and necessity. "For the purpose of becoming (and it is the task of the self freely to become itself) possibility and necessity are equally essential," says Kierkegaard.[77] Possibility indicates the open quality of the self, the "not yet" actualized possibilities, without which becoming could not occur. But neither can the self become itself without the structural pole of necessity. The self, without necessity, would have no actuality. Necessity, which is here existentially understood by Kierkegaard, is the structural element in the self which accounts for the fact that the self is *already there.* In every moment of self-consciousness the self finds that it is already given as a concrete totality of accumulated influences and past decisions. Necessity, says Kierkegaard, is that which characterizes the self as "a perfectly definite something." The self discovers itself as being already begun and oriented in a particular situation. The self has, in short, a destiny through which it has been shaped and given form. The awareness of this destiny of already being placed into a situation is graphically elucidated in a passage in Kierkegaard's book *Repetition:* "Where am I? How came I here? What is this thing called the world? What does this word mean? Who is it that has lured me into the thing, and now leaves me there? Who am I? How did I come into the world? Why was I not consulted, why not made acquainted with its manners and customs but was thrust into the ranks as though I had been bought of a 'soul-seller'? How did I obtain an interest in this big enterprise they call reality? Why should I have an interest in it? Is it not a voluntary concern? And if I am to be compelled to take part in it, where is the director? I should like to make a remark to him. Is there no director? Whither shall I turn with my complaint? Existence is surely a debate—may I beg that my view be taken into consideration?" [78] As we see from this passage, awareness of destiny is not a cognitive or theoretical awareness but an awareness determined by mood. I find myself thrust into a world which appears strange and uncanny. It is alien and threatening, and this strange threatening character of my situation can only be disclosed through mood. Pure contemplative thought always somehow bypasses it. I encounter my destiny or the necessity of myself not through abstract rational knowledge but through existential concern.

The self as finite freedom encounters necessity as a polar element in its being. Without necessity the self would be only potential freedom. It would be pure possibility, without a destiny and without concreteness. The self must be understood as a synthesis of possibility and necessity which means actual freedom. The freedom of the self is a freedom which is already actualized, though never completed. Necessity thus functions as a "check," a given condition, a factor of finitude in the self's becoming. Finite or actual freedom thus involves a synthesis of possibility and necessity. These are polar structures which in their dialectical unity constitute the self. "The self is just as possible as it is necessary; for though it is itself, it has to become itself. Inasmuch as it is itself, it is the necessary, and inasmuch as it has to become itself, it is a possibility." [79] In a summary paraphrase of this dialectical analysis of the self, one could say that the self is that which it has been (necessity) and becomes that which it is not yet (possibility). This, according to Kierkegaard, is the structure of finite freedom.

But this structural unity of possibility and necessity is subject to disruption. We have already seen that the self comes to an awareness of itself as a fractured and estranged self. This disrupted relationship is the "sickness unto death" or despair. We are now in position to clarify the meaning of this self-estrangement with the help of notions of possibility and necessity. Self-estrangement is the disruption of the polar unity of possibility and necessity. Significantly, Kierkegaard takes the concrete phenomenon of despair as his point of departure for the discussion of the polar structure of finite freedom. This keeps the polar structure rooted in the existential and the concrete. Possibility and necessity are not the rational constructions of a logical categorial deduction but are phenomenologically derived structures which clarify that which "shows itself" in man's lived experience.

The self is in the estrangement of despair when possibility outruns necessity. When the self no longer *has* itself as necessity, it loses itself as possibility. It runs wild in its freedom, constantly projecting possibilities but never choosing its actuality. Possibilities keep making their appearance until the self is lost in a sea of possibilities. Finally, "it is as if everything were possible—but this is precisely when the abyss has swallowed up the self." [80] In its radical freedom the self flounders about in possibilities but no longer maintains its relation to its past (which is still part of its being) by virtue of which freedom is already actualized.

As the self that flees from necessity is in despair, so also the self that retreats from possibility is in despair. A self which has succumbed wholly to necessity is still far from itself—it is only half itself. It has sacrificed itself to a fatalism or determinism. The freedom of the self is lost because its future as possibility is lost. It remains fixed in its past and its destiny, which is now transformed into fate. Kierkegaard speaks of this loss of possibility as the "suffocation" of the self. "The self of the determinist cannot breathe, for it is impossible to breathe necessity alone, which taken pure and simple suffocates the human self." [81] In the bondage of fatalism the self has no vision of the possibilities that transcend its destiny. It is bound to the destiny which it has by virtue of its past history, past decisions, and present environment. But the self is more than its past and present. Kierkegaard, and existentialists generally, will have no truck with deterministic psychology which would sacrifice the whole of the self to a causally determined past and present. The self has an incontestable claim on the future, which from birth to perishing remains structurally a part of its being.

Keeping Kierkegaard's structural polarity of possibility and necessity in mind, we shall now turn to an examination of Heidegger's structural analysis of *Dasein* and attempt to show that the two thinkers present a basically similar description of the phenomenon in question. The three structural moments of the Being of *Dasein* are existentiality (*Existenzialität*), "fallenness" (*Verfallenheit*), and facticity (*Faktizität*). Existentiality, the future mode of human being, is prior to the other two, which are grounded respectively in the present and the past. However, for reasons which are not wholly clear (or perhaps for no reason), Heidegger begins his analysis with facticity and then takes up the discussion of existentiality and fallenness.

The facticity of *Dasein* characterizes his naked "thereness." This naked "thereness" is disclosed through the phenomenon of mood, which as we have seen in our discussion on existential intentionality, performs a revealing function. Mood puts me "in tune" with my facticity and thus unveils it. Mood is a most familiar and everyday ontic phenomenon. The ontological element present in this ontic experience is situationality (*Befindlichkeit*). Situationality is the determinant which expresses the perpetual finding of one's self as "already there." This perpetual finding of myself "there" is clarified by Heidegger through the delineation of three structures of situationality: abandonment; simultaneous disclosure of world-phenomenon (i.e., tools, environment, and others); and the threatening character of this disclosed world. *Dasein* finds himself abandoned in his naked "thereness." He is simply there, without explanation or rational support. His whence and his whither remain wrapped in obscurity; only the "brute that he is" shows itself.[82] *Dasein* does not bring himself into the world; he finds himself already abandoned there. He discovers himself as a going concern, thrown into a situation which he has not created, and remains in a situation as long as he is. The second structure of situationality "is an existentialist modality of simultaneous disclosure of world, being-with-others, and existence." [83] *Dasein* finds himself in a world in which an instrumental and natural environment, other *Daseins*, and his own unique existence are simultaneously disclosed. To have an environment is part of human facticity. I must use the tools which are at hand. I find myself in a situation in which the tools for the fulfillment of my projects are already given. To be sure, I can modify my environment through my free projects, but an irreducible conditioning and limiting of my freedom is always present. Sartre has described this element of facticity in a revealing passage: "Freedom implies therefore the existence of an environment to be changed: obstacles to be surmounted, tools to be used. Certainly it is freedom which reveals them as obstacles, but free choice can only interpret the meaning of their being. It is necessary that they be simply there, wholly brute, so that there may be freedom." [84] Likewise I find myself in a situation in which other selves have already conferred meanings on my world. I find selves which I have not created and meanings which I have not derived. Social customs, language, and stereotypes are revealed as already being there when I define my projects. Man finds himself in the presence of meanings and actions which have not come into the world through him. As Sartre expresses it, man "arises in a world which is given to him as already looked at." [85] This leads us to the third structure of situationality—the threatening character of the disclosed world. At every moment *Dasein* is threatened by the world to which he has been abandoned. His projects are threatened by utensils and things, by other *Daseins*, and by self-estrangement. The hammer which I use to build my bookcase can be broken; the muddy road or the sweltering heat can prevent my journey; the other self can dissolve my perspective of the world through his look, thus transforming me into an object, a being which is on hand; and in numerous ways I can experience estrangement in my *Eigenwelt*. Here the threatening character of my being-in-the-world is disclosed. Facticity must thus properly be understood in relation to these three structures of situationality—abandonment, disclosure of world through its various horizons, and world in its threatening character. This facticity of *Dasein*, Heidegger cautions us, must not be confused with the factuality of an at-hand or on-hand being. Facticity is a structural moment in the Being of *Dasein* himself. As such it is indissolubly linked with responsibility. Having found himself in a situation, *Dasein* is confronted with the responsibility of determining what significance this situation will have in his future decisions—what role it will play in his project of becoming that being which he is not yet. But this implies that *Dasein* is in a real sense beyond his situation. He can transcend it in freedom. *Dasein* in his freedom thus becomes responsible for his situation, but at the same time his freedom remains forever a freedom-in-a-situation. The freedom of *Dasein* is limited and finite.

The clarification of *Dasein* as that being who is beyond his situation through his freedom can be achieved only after we have examined the second structural moment in *Dasein's* self-relatedness: existentiality. The revealing or disclosing agent of this constitutive factor is understanding. As mood discloses *Dasein's* facticity, so understanding discloses *Dasein's* existentiality. Yet, one must never dissociate mood from understanding nor understanding from mood. Each interpenetrates the other. When man becomes aware of his facticity, he already has an implicit understanding of himself, but this understanding does not become explicit until he has "projected" himself out of his situation into his future possibilities. In this way understanding transcends facticity and discloses the existentiality of *Dasein* as protention (*Entwurf*) and possibility (*Möglichkeit*). "The modification of *Dasein* as possibility has its existentialist foundation in understanding. *Dasein* is not a being on hand which possesses in addition a possibility; rather, *Dasein* is primarily possibility of being. *Dasein* is what he can be, and how he can be is his possibility." [86] In his understanding *Dasein* is disclosed to himself as basically and principally possibility. Possibility, says Heidegger, is the most fundamental and positive ontological determinant of *Dasein*.[87] Possibility in the Heideggerian analysis, as previously in Kierkegaard's works, is not the empty logical possibility which describes the contingency of on-hand being; rather, it is properly acknowledged as *existential* possibility. Logical possibility as a category, which is the way it has been primarily used in the Western philosophical tradition, simply denotes that which is not yet real or that which is not necessitated in the region of on-hand beings. This possibility is lower than reality. It is empty and anemic—it has no existential life-

blood. Existential possibility, on the other hand, is a positive determinant of existential reality itself. *Dasein* himself *is* his possibilities.[88]

Dasein as possibility lives into the future. This constitutes the
protentional character of human existence. This protention of *Dasein*
is in a certain sense the counter-phenomenon of abandonment and
facticity in general. In his facticity *Dasein* finds himself abandoned in a
situation; in the protention of his existentiality he understands himself
as moving into a future. This protentional character of *Dasein* is implied
in Heidegger's analysis of "ek-sistence" as the essence of human being.
It is the essence of man to "stand out" towards his possibilities. To say
that *Dasein* has this protentional character does not mean that he enter-
tains some preconceived and predetermined plan of action. Possibilities
are not "things" which may or may not be added to the charter of his
Being; they are directions of his existence which are disclosed as an integral part of his being-in-the-world. *Dasein* is disclosed as already "protended" into a future, and as long as he exists, this protentional quality
attaches to his being. Thus Heidegger can say, as Kierkegaard did, that
man is what he becomes. Man is never a given factuality. He is what
he makes himself to be. As ek-sistence, or as an ecstatic being, he has an
uncontestable claim upon the future.

The third structural moment in the ontological constitution of
Dasein is fallenness. As mood is the agency of the disclosure of facticity,
and understanding of existentiality, so speech, particularly in the unauthentic mode of talk, discloses the fallenness of *Dasein*. Speech, properly
understood, is the articulation of man's present orientation in the world.
This articulation takes various forms. Audible speech is, of course, the
most common form, but man can also articulate his being-in-the-world
through listening and remaining silent. Silence often "speaks" more
decisively and more forcefully than the audible word. In these various
forms and counter-forms of speech there is a simultaneous revelation of
the communal world. Speech expresses the personal concerns that relate
me to others. But in this communion with others, *Dasein* exists for the
most part in the mode of the "anonymous one." Talk or gossip trivializes
authentic speech, curiosity binds man to the present, and ambiguity pervades his thought and action. Speech thus discloses that *Dasein's* authentic possibilities have been sacrificed through an everyday preoccupation with present concerns. Fallenness characterizes man as he is sacrificed to the present in his flight from his future and his past. "Fallenness

has its existentialist meaning in the *present*." [89] Facticity characterizes *Dasein* as already-in-the-world, having arrived from a past; existentiality characterizes *Dasein* as protentional or ahead of himself in his future possibilities; fallenness characterizes him as present with the world in everyday concerns. These three structural moments thus reveal the phenomenon which is to provide the final ontological meaning of human existence—time.

The similarity between the structural approach of Kierkegaard and that of Heidegger has already become apparent. The self as finite freedom is described by Kierkegaard as a synthesis of possibility and necessity, or future and past. But this structure of self is initially disclosed in a condition of disruption or fracture, existentially understood as despair. *Dasein* in Heidegger's analysis is a complex of existentiality and facticity, rooted respectively in the temporal modes of future and past. *Dasein* "exists factically" or is "abandoned possibility." [90] But for the most part *Dasein* is rendered present in the mode of fallenness, which entails a disruption of the temporal directions of past and future. Heidegger does not speak of this disruption in terms of despair as does Kierkegaard. Despair for Kierkegaard (which is later theologically defined as sin) is an existential and ontic datum and hence is one concrete expression of the mode of fallenness. Fallenness in Heidegger's analysis is an existentialist and ontological determinant which defines the universal horizon of all the concrete possibilities of estrangement. Thus, again, we see how Heidegger has ontologized Kierkegaard's ethical view of existence. More precisely, we see how Heidegger has rendered explicit Kierkegaard's implicit ontology of man.

Kierkegaard saw that passion and interest are foundational for an understanding of existence. These ethical notions of passion and interest are given an ontological illumination in Heidegger's concept of concern. Concern is the foundational "existential" which characterizes man's being-in-the-world. We have seen that man is related to his environmental world in the mode of practical concern, to his communal world in the mode of personal concern, and to himself as that being who is concerned for his Being. Thus concern shows itself as the most basic ontological element of *Dasein*. Concern permeates every horizon and region of man's being-in-the-world. Both in his authentic and unauthentic existence, concern pervades man's movements in the world. A pre-ontological understanding of human being in connection with concern is expressed in a Latin fable attributed to Hyginus, the compiler of Greek mythology. Heidegger sees in this fable a powerful expression of man's existential self-understanding.

> As Concern was going across a river, she saw some clay. Thoughtfully, she took a piece of it and began to form it. As she was contemplating that which she had made, Jupiter appeared. Concern begged Jupiter to bestow spirit upon her work. This wish Jupiter happily granted her. But when Concern wished to give her name to what she had made, Jupiter protested and demanded that his name be used. While Concern and Jupiter were disputing over the name, Earth arose and demanded that her name be used because it was she who had offered a piece of her body. The disputing parties sought out Saturn as judge, and he submitted the following decision: "You, Jupiter, as you have given the spirit, shall take the spirit at death. You, Earth, as you have given the body, you shall then again receive the body. But Concern, since she first formed this creature, may possess it as long as it lives. And since there is dispute concerning the name, let it be called 'homo,' for it has been made out of earth (humus)." [91]

The fable explicitly shows that it is Saturn (time) who submits the final verdict on this creature which has been formed. Time provides the final ontological meaning of concern. The unity of concern is a unity of the temporal ecstasies of future, past, and present. Concern is in advance of itself in its possibilities (existentiality); already abandoned in the world (facticity); and sacrificed to the present in its everyday preoccupations (fallenness). If concern is thus the unifying ground of being-in-the-world, it must have its final ontological meaning in time.

I I I

Anxiety and Finitude

1. Anxiety and Fear

THE SIGNIFICANCE OF the phenomenon of anxiety in existential thinking can hardly be overemphasized. Phenomenological description of anxiety in its various modifications is certainly one of the salient features of existentialism and may even be said to constitute its distinctive viewpoint.

It was primarily through Kierkegaard that the concept of anxiety came to be central to existentialist analysis. Kierkegaard's *Journals* are filled with recurring references to anxiety as it is experienced in various existential situations. For example, he speaks of the anxiety he felt in his relationship with his father; of the anxiety that drove him to excess in his relationship with Regina; and of "the anxiety of being alone in the world, forgotten by God, overlooked among the tremendous household of millions upon millions." [1] These are existential elucidations of special expressions of anxiety which he experienced in his personal life, but implied in them is the anxiety which characterizes the human situation.

The phenomenon of anxiety as a universal determinant of human existence is subject to a foundational examination by Kierkegaard in his book *The Concept of Anxiety*.[2] All later existentialists have drawn heavily from the seminal insights which Kierkegaard develops in this classic work. Heidegger acknowledges that it was Kierkegaard who, in connection with his psychological exposition of the problem of original sin, analyzed the phenomenon of anxiety more penetratingly than any of his predecessors. However, where Kierkegaard's analysis is directed primarily to the existential encounter and ontic description of original sin, Heidegger is interested in developing an existentialist and ontological analysis of anxiety as a structural determinant in universal human experience.

We have already discussed the cardinal significance of mood in our examination of existential intentionality. Mood is an intentional disclosure through which the human situation becomes transparent. Mood reveals the way I exist in the world. But mood is also a situational determinant. It defines my situationality and thus is a positive determinant of my being-in-the-world. Anxiety in its various modifications of boredom, melancholy, guilt, and despair are qualifications of the very being of man. These two sides of the phenomenon of mood—as an intentional disclosure and as a situational determinant—are inseparable moments of self-awareness. The self *is* as it discloses itself in its moods. Heidegger expresses the existential unity of this dual character of mood when he speaks of "the existentialist sameness of the disclosing with that which is disclosed."[3] It is precisely this which makes a phenomenological description of anxiety possible. The phenomenon of anxiety "shows itself" as it is immediately experienced and is thus susceptible to the phenomenological tools. There is no distinction here between a "mere phenomenon" and a "thing-in-itself" that underlies it, for such a distinction would lead the existentialist straight into phenomenalism. Anxiety *is* the thing-in-itself as it is initially disclosed in a pre-cognitive existential immediacy and then subjected to phenomenological analysis.

As a propaedeutic to the examination of the phenomenon of anxiety both Kierkegaard and Heidegger carefully distinguish between fear and anxiety. Both phenomena are modifications of mood disclosed in man's situationality and thus have a common ontological basis, but they are distinct in that each has a structure of actualization peculiar to itself. Fear is a phenomenon in which consciousness confronts a definite object, person, or event that can be specified as an intentional *terminus ad quem* and properly interpreted as the source for the experience of fear. Kierkegaard clearly expresses this when he says that fear and similar concepts always refer to something definite.[4] Heidegger makes the same point: "Anxiety is basically different from fear. In fear we are always in the presence of this or that determinate being which threatens us in this or that determinate manner."[5] Man fears an impending catastrophe, a loss of fortune, a possible punishment, or a criminal attack. In all these cases that which threatens as the source of fear is something definite or something which is localized in an object or a region of objects. As such it can be specified, lifted from obscuring adventitious details, and dealt with productively through the adoption of appropriate measures. Now in the phenomenon of anxiety no such definite object or specific referent is disclosed. We find no intentional *terminus ad quem.* Anxiety means precisely the negation of every such object. "If then we ask further what is the object of anxiety," says Kierkegaard, "the answer as usual must be that it is nothing. Anxiety and nothing regularly correspond to one another."[6] Thus anxiety discloses man's utter helplessness, or abandonment as Heidegger would say, in a world in which there are no protective supports. That which threatens cannot be overcome, because of its elusive character. It resists any objective specification which would make possible its endurance or eradication. In anxiety man experiences a dramatic encounter with nothingness which threatens his very being-in-the-world. When asked what it is that has made one anxious, one is prone to reply, says Heidegger, that "it was actually nothing."[7] Whereas in fear man is confronted with a definite object which constitutes the threat, in anxiety man encounters and discloses nothingness.

Fear and anxiety are thus two special forms of mood. Kierkegaard makes the distinction and then moves on to the discussion of anxiety without further elucidation on the peculiar character of fear. Heidegger, however, also presents a phenomenological description of fear and thus seeks to clarify its structural elements. His analysis of fear proceeds within the framework of a threefold classification: the source of fear (*Wovor der Furcht*), the act of fearing itself (*das Fürchten*), and the "why" or the purpose of fearing (*Worum der Furcht*). The source of fear —what *Dasein* fears the presence of—is always some definite utensil, object, or person. It arises either from the environmental world where it makes its appearance in the mode of at-handness or on-handness, or it arises from the communal world as the fear of the other self. Fear always threatens from one of these regions of the world, and the distinctive quality of the threat is that it can be localized and specified. I know which utensil it is that thwarts me or hinders me; I know what object has to be removed to enable me to achieve security in my world; and I know the particular person who threatens my own self-actualization. In all these instances the source of fear is definite and determinate, and in each case the source is disclosed as being prejudicial. It is a something which is always hovering and approaching, threatening to shatter and take away my security and my supports. Although the source can be determined, one cannot tell whether and when it will strike. It is always nearby. It may strike, and it may not. It may hit, or it may pass. The act of fearing constitutes the second structural element in the phenomenon of fear. The act of fearing is that which uncovers what is threatening and focuses upon it as the intentional object of fear. In the act of fearing, *Dasein* lifts the threatening factor out of its obscurity and brings it into the conceptual horizon. Fearing as an instance of existential intentionality performs the revealing or disclosing function. It is that in the intentional complex of *Dasein* and object which points to and reveals the object of fear. The purposive element of fearing, which constitutes the third structure, is reflexive upon *Dasein* himself. The purpose of fear is to reveal to *Dasein* his own endangered state and render explicit the abandonment that is part of his situationality. "The fearing discloses this being [*Dasein*] in his endangered state, in the condition of his responsibility," says Heidegger. "Fear always reveals, if only in intermittent explicitness, *Dasein* in his abandonment." [8] The purpose of fearing is to bring *Dasein* face to face with a threat or a complex of threats which surround him in his being-in-the-world. The fear experienced by *Dasein* exists for his own sake. *Dasein* has been defined as that being who is concerned for his Being, and fear expresses one dimension of this reflexive concern of *Dasein*. It must therefore be said that *Dasein* fears because of himself or for the sake of himself. The three elements—the source of fear, the act of fearing, and the purpose of fearing—thus comprise the structure of the phenomenon of fear. They are disclosed by the phenomenon as it shows itself in man's intramundane experience. Now the task of phenomenology, as we have seen, is precisely that of elucidating and describing the phenomenon as it shows itself in its existential immediacy. Heidegger's structural analysis and description of fear provides a clear-cut example of the application of the phenomenological method to the datum of existence.

The phenomenon of fear, in its various modifications of fright, hor-

hor, terror, and the like, constitutes the fearing character (*Furcktsam-keit*) of *Dasein's* being-in-the-world. We are again reminded not to conceive this characterization ontically. This is not a psychological description of fear in terms of psycho-physiological conditions, i.e., glandular, neural, and digestive functioning in response to given stimuli. Psychological analysis constitutes a scientifically legitimate enterprise, but it occurs on a level other than that of phenomenological description. Phenomenological description discloses fear as "an existentialist possibility of the essential situationality of *Dasein*." [9] Fear is a structural concept which definies a universal possibility of man's orientations and concerns as they are projected into the various regions of his being-in-the-world.

2. *Anxiety, Non-being, and Freedom*

In the preceding section we have seen that anxiety, as distinct from fear, must properly be understood as a confrontation with nothingness or non-being. This idea is part and parcel of the existentialism of Kierkegaard and Heidegger. Anxiety reveals or discloses nothingness. Kierkegaard writes: "And anxiety . . . is greatest of all before nothing. In that way the tempter and temptation insinuate that the one who succumbs to temptation has himself discovered the temptation; for, say the tempter and temptation: I really said nothing at all, what you are anxious about is nothing." [10] Anxiety and nothingness are thus correlative concepts. Paul Tillich, who has formulated a concept of anxiety similar to that of Kierkegaard and Heidegger in his book *The Courage to Be,* speaks of anxiety as "the state in which a being is aware of its possible non-being." [11] But not only is anxiety inseparable from non-being; it is also inseparable from the freedom which it presupposes. Any adequate phenomenological description of anxiety, therefore, needs above all to clarify the existentialist meaning of non-being and freedom and their interrelationship.

In his essay on metaphysics and in his book on Kant, Heidegger deals explicitly with the problem of nothingness and clarifies its significance for his ontology of human finitude. First he points out a common error in the approach to the problem. A problem or question if wrongly formulated will only further conceal the datum under investigation instead of disclosing it. Putting the question properly is a *sine qua non* for philosophical elucidation. This is particularly true in an examination of the significance of nothingness. Commonly the question is posed: "What is nothingness?" With the question so framed, the content is already misinterpreted in that nothingness is objectified and presupposed as *something*—as a "being" of some kind or another. But it is precisely from beings that nothingness is to be differentiated. Hence the question must be formulated differently so as not to prejudice an answer. The question must be existentially formulated: "Of what concern is this nothingness?" Now the common everyday talk of *Dasein* expresses this nothingness as a simple negation of intramundane beings. When *Dasein* first encounters anxiety, he concludes that what he is anxious about is actually nothing. Nothingness is here understood as "no-thing" in the realm of intramundane beings, i.e., it refers to no-utensil, no-object, and no-person. Ontically, this statement describes the state of affairs, but it tells us little of the ontological condition of nothingness. And it is the inquiry into this ontological condition which must precede any question of the not-being of intramundane beings as well as the question of logical negation. "We maintain: nothingness is more fundamental than not-being and negation," writes Heidegger.[12] Negative judgments are predicable only on the basis of a prior ontological condition. Now where is this prior ontological condition to be sought? Clearly not in theoretical thinking, since this thinking is always directed to an object, and nothingness is never an object. Nothingness cannot be "conceived" through a pure theoretical operation. It can be apprehended only in the experience of anxiety, which we have seen, functions as an existential intentional disclosure. According to Heidegger, "With the fundamental mood of anxiety we have reached the situationality of *Dasein* in which nothingness is revealed." [13] Nothingness is thus revealed as a constitutive factor of *Dasein's* being-in-the-world. This means that nothingness as an original and ontological condition is found in the Being of *Dasein* himself, disclosed in the structural moment of facticity as situationality but also, and more vividly, disclosed in the structural moment of existentiality as possibility. "This self-projection into nothingness is, not an occasional attempt at 'thinking' nothingness, but a happening which is the basis of all self-disclosure among beings and which must be elucidated through a fundamental ontological analytics of *Dasein* in connection with his possibility-of-being." [14] We have seen that in Heidegger's analysis of the structural moments in concern the primary determinant is existentiality as possibility. *Dasein* is always protended into his not-yet actualized possibilities. "To *Dasein* belongs, as long as he is, a not-yet." [15] This not-yet can be only partly actualized because of the inevitable exclusion of possibilities in the act of decision (*Ent-scheidung*), literally meaning "to separate" or "cut off." These excluded possibilities, nevertheless, are integral to the very Being of *Dasein*—they permeate his facticity insofar as he has already excluded or sacrificed possibilities in the past, and they permeate his existentiality insofar as actualization of future possibilities implies limitation and exclusion. These excluded existential possibilities, which structurally are a part of human being, comprise the nothingness which is here at stake for the existing *Dasein*. This is the meaning of Heidegger's statements in his essay on metaphysics and in his book on Kant when he describes *Dasein* as a "confinement in nothingness" (*Dasein heisst: Hineingehaltenheit in das Nichts*).[16] *Dasein* has nothingness within himself as an ingredient of his Being. His Being is a Being permeated with nothingness. Hence, says Heidegger, the familiar phrase of Hegel's *Logic*, "Pure Being and pure Nothingness are the same," does express a fundamental truth, provided that the relation is understood, not in terms of a conceptual immediacy as it was by Hegel, but in terms of an *existential* nothingness which is constitutive of finite being as such.[17] Nothingness thus becomes the basic determinant of human finitude. Finitude means limitation through self-actualization, a limitation which we have seen is disclosed in the inevitable exclusion of certain possibilities of *Dasein*—the "not yet" actualized and the "no longer" already sacrificed. This is the nothingness which threatens man's Being as long as he is and constitutes him as a finite creature. To be finite means to be a being who is limited by non-being. Quite clearly the notion of nothingness or non-being as an "existential" must not be confused with the concept of *nihil absolutum*. Heidegger in his study of Kant and Tillich in his *Systematic Theology* have sought to clarify the distinction between the relative and absolute, the dialectical and non-dialectical meanings of non-being. Tillich finds the distinction already present in Greek thought with its consistent differentiation between *me on* and *ouk on*. *Me on* is a dialectical notion which points to a relative negation of being; *ouk on* is a non-dialectical notion which points to an absolute negation of being—what Heidegger calls the *nihil absolutum*.[18] Non-being as the principle of finitude is non-being understood in its relative and dialectical character through which it becomes a constitutive factor of human being or *Dasein* himself. Anxiety in its disclosure of nothingness thus brings man to an awareness of his radical finitude, and whatever else is to be said of existentialist philosophy, it must be said that existentialism is an emphatic philosophy of human finitude. The principle of finitude is central to all the existentialist thinkers, and it emerges with particular emphasis in the philosophy of Heidegger. Heidegger interprets this philosophy of human finitude to be, at least in part, a legacy of Kant's critical philosophy. With his emphasis on the finite character of human reason and his insight into the negativities of moral striving, Kant paved the way for the development of fundamental ontology formulated in terms of finite structures.[19]

The non-being encountered in anxiety becomes at the same time the condition for finite freedom. Heidegger expresses this when he links nothingness with existentiality and possibility-of-being. And in asserting this theme he can immediately be identified as the philosophical successor of Kierkegaard, who in *The Concept of Anxiety* examined with an unparalleled profundity the interrelation of anxiety, non-being, and freedom. In Kierkegaard's analysis non-being is understood as an intrinsic quality of the self as possibility. The non-being of anxiety is the "alarming possibility of *being able*." [20] Non-being is thus indissolubly linked with the being of the self as finite freedom, where it is disclosed in the self's confrontation with its possibilities. Non-being resides in anxiety as "the reflex of freedom within itself at the thought of its possibility." [21] Insofar as the self's possibilities already constitute its being, the self is both being and non-being. Non-being is a constitutive dialectical factor in the self as finite freedom. This finite freedom calls the self to decision and confronts it with the responsibility of existence. It is precisely in this confrontation with the self's responsibility that anxiety is posited—an anxiety which can now be properly understood as the "dizziness of freedom." Anxiety thus discloses non-being and freedom which make possible man's finite self-actualization. Freedom is the presupposition for actualization, and *as the presupposition* it is disclosed in the first moment of consciousness as a freedom not yet actualized. It is the possibility of *being able* which precedes the actualization or concretization of any specific possibility. It is what Kierkegaard appropriately calls the "reality of freedom as possibility anterior to possibility." [22] Anxiety confronts the self with its essential, unactualized freedom which in the initial moment of consciousness holds an indefinite number of possibilities insofar as no possibilities have yet become concrete. In this unactualized freedom the self is both fascinated and repulsed by its possibilities for actualization; it is attracted to them, but at the same time shrinks from them.

Anxiety then becomes a "sympathetic antipathy and an antipathetic sympathy." [23] The self is fascinated with its possibilities because prior to choice everything is in its power. Kierkegaard refers to this as the "egoistic infinity of possibility." "Anxiety is at the same time the most egoistic thing, and no concrete expression of freedom is so egoistic as is the possibility of every concretion." [24] Thus the self is attracted to its actualization. We are aroused to freedom and fascinated by it. But at the same time we are in a state of antipathy toward freedom because this freedom brings with it the responsibility of choice. Thus man is placed in the ambiguous position where "he cannot flee from anxiety, for he loves it; really he does not love it, for he flees from it." [25]

Kierkegaard's analysis of the theme of anxiety is developed with the religious doctrine of original sin in the background. Anxiety as a structural determinant of the universally human is examined in connection with a specific ontic phenomenon—original sin as the primordial disrelationship with God. Anxiety, in its theological context, is understood as the presupposition and consequence of original sin. Already in the description of anxiety as the "reflex of freedom within itself at the thought of its possibility," the ontological context for the phenomenon of sin is set forth, insofar as sin is posited as a qualitative leap in the moment that freedom is actualized. Kierkegaard finds in the Biblical story of the Fall a most powerful and profound depiction of sin as a qualitative leap posited in the actualization of freedom. When we describe the sin of Adam, we describe ourselves, for Adam is at one time himself and the race. That which explains Adam also explains us.[26] In his original state Adam was in a state of innocence, which is to say that he was unactualized freedom. He was not yet determined as spirit, which means that he was not yet a self. In this original state selfhood was present potentially. This is the moment of dawning consciousness in which the unactualized self confronts the "reality of freedom as possibility anterior to possibility." Kierkegaard expresses this in his notion of dreaming spirit. "In his innocence man is not determined as spirit but is soulishly determined in immediate unity with his natural condition. Spirit is dreaming in man. . . ." Elsewhere he repeats, "In his innocence man was, in so far as he was spirit, a dreaming spirit." [27] In this state of innocence as a dreaming spirit or unactualized freedom, Adam encountered anxiety through the prohibition of God which confronted him with the "alarming possibility of being able." There was yet no specification of *what* he was able to do, but only the awareness of the possibility of *being able*. That is to say, anxiety disclosed to Adam his essential finite freedom—his freedom to choose. A knowledge of the *what* would have required the knowledge of the distinction between concrete choices of good and evil, which was consequent only upon the eating of the fruit. Hence Adam could not possibly have understood the words of prohibition—"Only of the tree of the knowledge of good and evil thou shalt not eat"—nor the words of judgment—"Thou shalt surely die." He was still in his state of innocence and had no conception of what it meant to choose between good and evil or what it meant to die. Yet the words of prohibition aroused his freedom and awakened in him a desire to actualize this freedom in concrete choices; and the words of judgment produced a "deterring conception"—an antipathy rather than a sympathy.[28] Thus anxiety is confronted in its ambiguous guise. It puts man before his possibilities that attract and repel, fascinate and terrify. Adam as dreaming spirit becomes subject to the ambiguity of anxiety. "The terrible becomes in this instance merely anxiety; for Adam has not understood what was said, and here again we have only the ambiguity of anxiety. The infinite possibility of being able draws closer for the fact that this possibility indicates a possibility as its consequence."[29] Here innocence arrives at its breaking point. Brought to an awareness of its possibilities through the ambiguity of anxiety, dreaming spirit is about to actualize itself and pass over into the full consciousness of existence. In the moment of this actualization there occurs the leap into existence, and with this leap, sin is posited as a concomitant.

In distinguishing between the two moments of consciousness—the awakening consciousness of dreaming spirit prior to the Fall and the full consciousness of actualized existence after the Fall—Kierkegaard is seeking to maintain a distinction between finitude and existential estrangement, between ontological anxiety as the awareness of finitude and existential anxiety as an awareness of finitude under the conditions of estrangement. He makes it clear that the anxiety of the dreaming spirit in its state of innocence is not yet guilt. "As Adam lost innocence by guilt, so does every man lose it. If it was not by guilt he lost it, neither was it innocence he lost; and if he was not innocent before he became guilty, he never became guilty."[30] In his discussion on the relation of existence to time Kierkegaard also suggests that temporality as an implication of finitude is not, as such, fallen or estranged. "We do not say that the temporal is sinfulness, but rather contend that because of the fact that sin is posited the temporal signifies sinfulness."[31] Man is not guilty or sinful because he is finite and temporal. In his essential finitude as unactualized freedom the determinant of guilt is not yet present. However, when guilt enters through the Fall in the moment of temporal actualization, then it becomes a determinant of existence itself, and one can properly say that the "temporal signifies sinfulness." The line which Kierkegaard seeks to maintain between finitude and estrangement is indeed thin, and it may be questioned whether he succeeds in consistently upholding the distinction. Yet it is evident that he intends to do so. And in this his thought is basically Augustinian: *Esse qua esse bonum est.* Man as a finite creature is not guilty by necessity. Guilt and sin are not ontological necessities. With Heidegger, on the other hand, the distinction between finitude and estrangement is dissolved. We have seen in chapter ii that *Dasein's* being-in-the-world is always already fallen. Fallenness is a structural determinant of man's *Eigenwelt*. In chapter vi we shall see that "*Dasein* as such is guilty." Existential estrangement is for Heidegger a necessary implication of human finitude.

The anxiety of innocence in which man initially faces his freedom is thus for Kierkegaard the presupposition of guilt and sin. This is the anxiety over his finitude. In this anxiety the determinant of sin is not yet present, but it is posited the moment the self actualizes its freedom. Hence sin must properly be understood as coming into the world through a "qualitative leap." Sin is posited as a general discontinuity of human experience which cannot be inferred from anything prior. It is simply there as an indelible characteristic in the actualized freedom of the existing self. "Sin presupposes itself, just as freedom does, and cannot be explained, any more than freedom can, by any antecedent." [32]

After sin has been posited, anxiety acquires two analagous expressions. On the one hand, it has its expression in the objective anxiety of nature; on the other hand, it becomes manifest in the subjective anxiety of the individual. By objective anxiety Kierkegaard means the effect of the original sin on the non-human sphere in the created order. "By the fact that sin came into the world, it acquired significance for the whole creation. This effect of sin in the non-human sphere of being I have called objective anxiety." [33] It is this effect of sin in the non-human world, argues Kierkegaard, that Paul had in mind when he spoke in his letter to the Romans of the "anxious longing of creation." With the positing of sin, creation itself enters a state of imperfection, and anxiety acquires a cosmic significance. [34] Because of this objective anxiety in nature, anxiety can be observed in animals as well as man. Subjective anxiety is that anxiety which is expressed in the sinful condition of the individual rather than the world of nature at large. Subjective anxiety is anxiety which has become united with freedom and as such is the peculiar determinant of human existence (non-human nature is devoid of freedom, except in an analagous sense). Now one might think, says Kierkegaard, that as soon as sin is posited, anxiety would be canceled, inasmuch as anxiety has been understood as the appearance of freedom before itself as possibility. It would seem that insofar as the qualitative leap is reality, possibility, and therefore anxiety, would be annulled. But this, argues Kierkegaard, involves a misunderstanding of the relation of possibility and reality. Human reality, as we have seen in the preceding chapter, is not a single factor. It is a structural polarity of necessity and possibility. Possibility remains as an intrinsic determinant of human existence. However, possibility insofar as it has undergone a qualification through the Fall makes anxiety reappear in a new guise. This new guise is anxiety in the context of an actualization which discloses a future that demands a choice of concrete alternatives. "So anxiety comes back again in relation to what was posited and in relation to the future." [35] Anxiety is not canceled when the self opts for actualization. It is now disclosed as the anxiety of the possible as future. "The possible corresponds precisely to the future. For freedom the possible is the future, and for time the future is the possible. Corresponding to both of these in the individual life is anxiety. A precise and correct linguistic usage associates therefore anxiety and the future." [36] In a passage in his *Christian Discourses* Kierkegaard vividly and dramatically expresses man's concrete, existential apprehensiveness of a future which fills him with anxiety: "Tomorrow I shall perhaps hunger, even if I did not today; tomorrow a thief will perhaps steal my riches, or a slanderer my honour, corruption my beauty, the envy of fate my good fortune—tomorrow, tomorrow! Today I stand on the pinnacle of fortune—oh, recount to me while it is still today a misfortune—quickly, quickly!—else tomorrow everything will be lost irrevocably. What is anxiety? It is the next day." [37] The anxiety of existence is the anxiety of the next day. The self becomes anxious about its future and dreads the possibilities of the morrow. Anxiety thus has a protentional direction—the self is anxious about that which it can become. But anxiety also has a retentional direction—the self is anxious about that which it has been. In its existential actualization the self is a polarity of possibility (future) and necessity (past). Both future and past are constitutive, structural moments of self. In the anxiety over the past, the past itself becomes present as a possibility. The past which can become a source of anxiety is a past which must stand in relation to possibility. If the past were a simple objectified past, severed from all possibility, then I could never experience anxiety over a past decision or a past misfortune. I become anxious about my past only insofar as it discloses itself as being susceptible to repetition, i.e., capable of being translated into a future possibility. "The past of which I am supposed to be anxious must stand in a relation of possibility to me. If I am in anxiety about a past misfortune, this is not in so far as it is past, but in so far as it may be repeated, i.e., become future." [38]

In this analysis of anxiety we have suggested further central concepts in Kierkegaard's thought—the reality of the past, the priority of the future, and the project of repetition—all of which need careful and detailed examination, which we must postpone for a later chapter. Our interest in the present discussion is to clarify the relationship between Kierkegaard and Heidegger in their intrepretations of anxiety, to see how Heidegger has rendered explicit the ontology of anxiety that was already suggested by Kierkegaard. Kierkegaard, as we have seen, formulates the concept of anxiety in relation to the ethico-religious notion of sin. Heidegger intends to develop a pure phenomenology of human finitude and estrangement which is presupposed by any special ontic analysis, whether it be theological, psychological, or sociological.

The two basic structural elements in Heidegger's ontology of anxiety are source and purpose. This basic structure corresponds with the structure of fear. Moreover, the two phenomenon are similar in that they both are at the same time intentional disclosures and situational determinants. Anxiety discloses *Dasein* in his anxious situations. This is what Heidegger calls the "existentialist sameness of the disclosing with that which is disclosed." Yet anxiety is distinguished from fear in that it is a "superlative disclosure" (*ausgezeichnete Erschlossenheit*) and a "preeminent situationality" (*Grundbefindlichkeit*). The fundamental distinction between anxiety and fear emerges more clearly when we examine the sources of the two phenomena and find that fear has its source in some region of intramundane being (a utensil, an object, or another person), whereas the source of anxiety lacks any intramundane determination—the source of anxiety is nothingness. "The source of anxiety is no intramundane being. Therefore it has no bearing-relation. The threat does not have the character of a determinate deprivation which meets the threatened in a specific factual possibility. The source of anxiety is completely indeterminate. This indeterminateness not only precludes the specification of a particular being which threatens, but indicates the irrelevancy of intramundane being as such." [39] Unlike the source of fear, the source of anxiety is never a definite and specific factor in the *Umwelt* or the *Mitwelt*. Anxiety, Heidegger writes in his essay on metaphysics, "is always anxiety in the presence of . . . but not in the presence of this or that." [40] When we then inquire what produces anxiety, we find that it is nothingness. We have already examined the inner relation between anxiety and non-being as they figure centrally in the thought of both Kierkegaard and Heidegger. The source of anxiety is nothingness understood in relation to man as possibility. Anxiety discloses the nothingness which belongs to *Dasein* himself—the nothingness of his not yet chosen possibilities and his already excluded and sacrificed possibilities. This nothingness is an intrinsic determinant of *Dasein's* Being as finite. Thus anxiety becomes the anxiety of human finitude. In classical thought an ontology of human finitude was suggested by Augustine when he took the reality of evil seriously and sought an explanation for it in man's tendency toward non-being. Nicolas Berdyaev, the Russian existentialist, has formulated the same theme in his concept of "meontic" freedom. Augustine and Berdyaev, Kierkegaard and Heidegger have described most profoundly man's encounter with nothingness and finitude as these are disclosed in the phenomenon of anxiety.

Purpose is the second constitutive element in Heidegger's ontology of anxiety. We must inquire to what end the anxiety of *Dasein* is directed. The answer is *Dasein* himself. *Dasein*, as that being who is concerned for his Being, encounters nothingness and becomes anxious about himself. The purpose of anixety is to bring *Dasein* to an awareness of his Being as it overflows the various horizons of his being-in-the-world. As anxiety achieves this purpose, it reveals three interrelated aspects of *Dasein's* being-in-the-world: (1) the strange and uncanny (*unheimlich*) character of his world; (2) his isolation and aloneness; and (3) his freedom for his authentic possibilities. Anxiety reveals the strangeness of *Dasein's* being-in-the-world by showing him that the world as encountered in his everyday, fallen existence is alien to his authentic Being. He thus becomes a stranger to the world. His being-in is disclosed as a "not-being-at-home" (*Un-zuhausesein*). The trusted everyday world of practical and personal concerns breaks down. What was before a refuge for security and contentment now becomes strange and puzzling. The world has nothing more to offer. Its former significance is shattered as everyday meanings evaporate. All protections and supports vanish. Nothing remains.

As his trusted universe of everyday concerns is dissolved, *Dasein* is thrown back upon himself in his solitary existence. "Anxiety isolates and reveals *Dasein* as a *'solus ipse.'* " [41] Solitude is disclosed as the path to authenticity. *Dasein* becomes aware that in his everyday preoccupations and concerns in his world he has lost himself in the publicity of the "anonymous one" and has suppressed his authentic possibilities.[42] He has turned away from himself and has taken refuge in the complacency, conformity, and contentment of the public. He moves in the realm of common everyday talk, curiosity, and ambiguity. He has made himself "at home" in the world. Hence he must now be isolated from his unauthentic practical and personal concerns and find himself in solitude. As Whitehead defined religion as that which one does in solitude, so Heidegger finds in solitude the way to authentic wholeness.

The third purposive aspect of anxiety is its disclosure of man's freedom for authentic choice. Anxiety discloses the unique possibilities which belong to *Dasein* and which he must choose to affirm his authenticity. "Anxiety," says Heidegger, "reveals to *Dasein being-toward* his unique possibilities, i.e., the being-free-for the choice of himself. Anxiety makes *Dasein* aware of his being-free-for . . . authenticity, aware of his Being as possibility, aware that he is always already thus free." [43] This was a persistent theme in Kierkegaard. Anxiety brings man to an awareness of his freedom. It discloses his future and makes him aware of what he can become. Anxiety breaks up the contentment and complacent trust of everyday existence, isolates man and brings him to his solitude, and makes him free for the choice of his authentic possibilities. For both Heidegger and Kierkegaard, anxiety is the gateway to authentic existence.

3. *Boredom and Melancholy*

The allied moods of boredom and melancholy, like those of fear and anxiety, play a significant role in existentialist philosophy. An exemplification and description of these closely related forms of existential disquietude can be found in both the literary and philosophic expressions of existentialism. Baudelaire's *Fleurs de Mal* contains numerous references to man's experience of *ennui* as he moves within the emptiness, and even sordidness, of a colorless existence. The writings of Sartre, Chekov, and Ibsen are equally rich in their poignant depictions of the mood of boredom as an inescapable phenomenon of human life. These exemplifications of the mood of boredom in literary existentialism are matched by an explicit philosophical formulation in the phenomenological descriptions of Kierkegaard, Jaspers, and Heidegger. Kierkegaard was the first of the existentialist philosophers to analyze boredom as a distinctive trait of the human condition. In his analysis and descriptions of this basic and pervading mood in human experience he first points out the similarity between boredom and anxiety. Boredom, like anxiety (in a sense, one could think of boredom as a specific modification or type of anxiety), reveals the nothingness which we have described as an indelible constituent of man's existence, and it produces a dizziness when man musters the courage to gaze into this nothingness which is part of him. We have already seen how anxiety can be described as the "dizziness of freedom." This is equally true of boredom or tedium. They confront man with his nothingness, his freedom, and his decision-demanding possibilities. But man has not yet found himself in this field of possibilities. He is driven from one undertaking to another and fails to find meaning in anything which he pursues. Finally, he is overcome with a nameless and gnawing emptiness as this nothingness continues to threaten his authentic self-actualization. "How terrible tedium is—terribly tedious. . . . The only thing I see is emptiness, the only thing I move about in is emptiness." [44] Boredom and tedium lead to an emptiness in which all meaningful contents of life are threatened. This mood of boredom is a universal characteristic which has plagued men from the very beginning. In the beginning of the race, and in the beginning of each individual (for the individual is always himself and the race), boredom is already there as a concrete possibility of human existence. "The gods were bored, and so they created man. Adam was bored because he was alone, and so Eve was created. Thus boredom entered the world, and increased in proportion to the increase of population. Adam was bored alone; then Adam and Eve were bored together; then Adam and Eve and Cain and Abel were bored *en famille*; then the population of the world increased and the peoples were bored *en masse*." [45]

In his description of boredom Kierkegaard distinguishes two forms or two different manifestations. In one form the self is bored with a particular object, event, or person. Like fear, this form of boredom is directed toward something specific and definite—something which can be determined as the specific cause for one's plunge into boredom. Although this form of boredom does disclose significant aspects of man's situation, it does not yet reach the heart of the matter. The nothingness and the genuine threat to one's being is disclosed only in the second form of boredom, in which there is no particular object or person with which one is bored, but simply one's self and one's being in the world. Heidegger, who follows Kierkegaard on this point, distinguishes the two forms of boredom with reference to the authentic and the unauthentic. Unauthentic boredom is always directed to particular utensils, objects, and persons in one's *Umwelt* and *Mitwelt*. In this experience of boredom *Dasein* is still lost in his preoccupations and concerns with intramundane beings and has not yet arrived at the awareness that it is he himself in his self-relatedness who is threatened. Authentic boredom brings man to a reckoning with this latter reality. In authentic boredom I am just bored—not with anything in particular. "Authentic boredom is still far removed when we are bored with a specific book, a movie, an undertaking, or our idleness. It appears when 'one is bored.'" [46] Only authentic boredom discloses my true situation. In unauthentic boredom I am still under the illusion that my boredom is simply dependent on an unfortunate turn of circumstances. If only the book were more engaging, the movie more intriguing, and my particular project more challenging, then I would be rid of my boredom! But this is to seek the cause and the cure for boredom in the realm of intramundane beings, where it can never be found. Indeed our involvement with books, movies, and various and sundry activities only provides us with a momentary escape from the authentic boredom which threatens us at the core of our Being. Authentic boredom discloses "the basic phenomenon of our being-there." [47] Boredom is revealed as a determinant of existence itself. Sartre elucidates the same point in his novel *Nausea*. Roquentin, the central character, expresses the basic phenomenon when he says: "I am bored, that's all. From time to time I yawn so widely that tears roll down my cheek. It is a profound boredom, profound, the profound heart of existence, the very matter I am made of." [48] As Kierkegaard had already shown, in this authentic boredom man is overcome with a feeling of emptiness. Man's activities and personal relations lose their meaning and their significance. Heidegger speaks of an "appalling indifference" (*merkwürdige Gleichgültigkeit*) which ac-

companies the onslaught of boredom. "This profound boredom, vacil-
lating like a mute fog in the abyss of *Dasein*, draws all things, people,
and one's self together into an appalling indifference." [49] All man's
practical and personal concerns become a matter of indifference. They
no longer hold any importance for the individual. No undertaking is
deemed worthy of his efforts. All human relations are trivialized. Man is
driven from one undertaking to another but is left empty and lost. For
a time he may forget himself in the publicity of the "anonymous one"
by seeking diversion and distraction in the average, everyday activities
of men, soliciting the contentment and quieting influence of the crowd.
But soon the contentment and the satisfaction derived from these
diversions vanish, and man is again left with an astounding indifference
and profound emptiness. Kierkegaard has graphically characterized
man's continuing search for diversion and distraction in his concept of
the "rotation method." The rotation method is the method which the
self uses to keep itself diverted. By this method it can keep on the move,
travel from place to place, experiment with new activities, search out
the amusing and the entertaining, and thus forget about itself. "One
tires of living in the country, and moves to the city; one tires of one's
native land, and travels abroad; one is *europamüde*, and goes to
America, and so on; finally one indulges in a sentimental hope of endless
journeyings from star to star." [50]

Philosophical anticipations of the phenomenology of boredom
as formulated by Kierkegaard and Heidegger can be found in the
writings of both Pascal and Schopenhauer. Pascal had already impres-
sively described man's abortive search for external distractions and
amusements through which he might divert himself and escape from
his *ennui*. Man seeks to suppress his existential disquietude by losing
himself in *divertissement*. Pascal singled out the chase, a popular sport
in his day, as a lucid example of the diverting function of recreation.
The object of the chase is not to acquire possession of the hare. If the
hare were given to the participants prior to the chase, it would certainly not be accepted. The function of the chase is that of diversion. It
keeps man from thinking about the human condition. Man cannot
face the painful task of reflecting upon himself; so he seeks constant
diversion in amusements, noise, and commotion. [51] So also Schopenhauer
had many illuminating things to say about man's experience of boredom. As soon as man has the opportunity to rest from his daily tasks
and concerns, *ennui* is already at the door, and means of diversion are

immediately sought. "The striving after existence is what occupies all living things and maintains them in motion. But when existence is assured, then they know not what to do with it; thus the second thing that sets them in motion is the effort to get free from the burden of existence, to make it cease to be felt, 'to kill time,' i.e., to escape from ennui." [52] This everlasting search for diversion through which he can "kill time" brings man to the point where he cannot stand to be alone. Solitude becomes unbearable. It is something to be avoided at all costs, for in solitude man is thrown back upon himself and is forced to gaze into the depths of his emptiness. This is the reason, says Schopenhauer, why penitentiary systems have been able to use solitary confinement as a means of punishment. Solitary confinement cuts off all avenues for diversion and distraction. It dissolves all routines of activity in which the self might lose itself. This loss of everyday routine also accounts, says Schopenhauer, for the common "Sunday boredom" which is peculiarly characteristic of the middle class. After the weekday schedule ceases, the individual has only himself on his hands. "In middle-class life ennui is repeated by the Sunday, and want by the six week-days." [53]

In all these instances of boredom we see a common denominator —a disclosure, however faint, of the self's nothingness and freedom, from which for the most part it seeks to escape through diversion. The self cannot face its finitude and its freedom and thus engages in endless routines which momentarily provide satisfaction. It seeks to escape its authentic boredom rather than accept it and face it courageously. It looks for supports in the realm of intramundane beings but finds only quicksand. The world of everyday concerns cannot liberate man from the disquietude of emptiness. Only by turning resolutely to himself, facing his freedom through the shouldering of responsibility and commitment, can the self wrestle successfully with its boredom.

The phenomenon of melancholy is a mood closely allied to that of boredom and has been given studied attention by certain thinkers of the existentialist persuasion. Kierkegaard, in certain circles, has acquired the epithet the "Melancholy Dane," although usually this epithet carries a derogatory connotation. Melancholy, like boredom, is characterized in the phenomenological descriptions of Kierkegaard by an enigmatic and nameless emptiness. "If a melancholy man is asked what ground he has for it, what it is that weighs upon him, he will reply, 'I know not, I cannot explain it.'" [54] Melancholy points to an indefinable discontinuity within human experience. Throughout his life Kierkegaard struggled with this undefinable, yet enveloping, discontinuity. His *Journals* and his book *Stages on Life's Way* present a running commentary on the various expressions of this melancholic qualification of spirit. His melancholy, he tells us, "descended in inheritance" from a father who was "prodigiously melancholy." Hence his "life began without immediateness, with a terrible melancholy." He was "brought up in melancholy," finding in it his most "intimate confidential friend." In his relation with Regina melancholy gripped him with its terror. And he was unable to understand Christ as savior who helps one out of misery "because of the unhappy melancholy which has, on one point, been a sort of practical madness." [55] Throughout the whole of his life melancholy with its threat of emptiness and meaninglessness was an immediately experienced reality. Kierkegaard's descriptions make it clear that this melancholy is not a mere psychological disturbance which can be relieved by a physician. He speaks of it as a "spiritual ailment" or a "hysteria of the spirit," which means that it is a condition of existence itself and not simply the result of socio-psychological conflicts. Kierkegaard, however, does not proceed to offer any clear differentiation between so called "neurotic melancholy" and "existential melancholy," and most existentialist literature is deficient on this point. One of the clearest statements on the distinction between the existential and pathological character of mood that has appeared in existentialist thought is that submitted by Paul Tillich in his *The Courage To Be*. Tillich defines existential anxiety in its various types as a structural condition of human existence itself, a condition that can never be removed, because it is part of what it means to exist. Pathological anxiety is the result of socio-psychological contingencies which produce unresolved conflicts in the personality of the individual (the specific definition of these conflicts varies with the different schools in psychopathology) and which can be removed through psychotherapeutic treatment. Pathological anxiety, according to Tillich, is "a state of existential anxiety under special conditions." [56] It is a state in which the individual cannot courageously face and accept his existential anxiety. The neurotic individual cannot accept the nothingness or non-being which is disclosed through anxiety, and by refusing to accept his non-being he remains unable to affirm the unique potentialities of his freedom. "He who does not succeed in taking his anxiety courageously upon himself can succeed in avoiding the extreme situation of despair by escaping into neurosis. He still affirms himself but on a limited scale. *Neurosis is the way of avoiding non-*

being by avoiding being." [57] Kierkegaard had already expressed this theme of courageous acceptance of man's existential anxieties when he wrote: "The one and only thing which is able to disarm the sophistry of remorse is faith, courage to believe that the state of sin is itself a new sin, courage to renounce anxiety without any anxiety, which only faith is capable of—not that it annihilates anxiety, but remaining ever young, it is continually developing itself out of the death throe of anxiety." [58] Kierkegaard and Tillich agree that existential anxiety cannot be annihilated. It is a universal determinant of the *condition humaine*. One does not overcome it by removing it. One overcomes it only by going through it, by courageously accepting it as part and parcel of one's being-in-the-world.

But for the most part the melancholy man seeks to escape his feeling of emptiness through an incessant, self-destructive, despiritualizing diversion. It is in Nero, says Kierkegaard, that we find the example *par excellence* of the melancholy nature which constantly seeks for diversion and distraction so as to flee from itself. Nero sought to overcome his melancholic spirit through an immersion into countless varieties of pleasure. He even appointed "ministers of pleasure" who were entrusted with the task of finding new ways to satisfy his desires. "Then he grasps after pleasure; all the world's cleverness must devise for him new pleasures, for only in the instant of pleasure does he find repose, and when that is past he gasps with faintness." [59] The same theme is developed by Kierkegaard in his essay "Diary of a Seducer." In this essay he portrays a young lover, a prototype of Mozart's Don Giovanni. The young lover has a poetic and melancholic nature but seeks to escape from it through a program of diverting seductions. He loses himself in pleasure, but after one pleasure has been gratified, another appears and with a greater intensity, until like Nero he has put himself into the bondage of a never satisfying search for gratification. Both Nero and the seducer are unable to accept the emptiness which qualifies them as existing selves. In his flight from melancholy Nero is ready to have a child dismembered before the eyes of its mother so as to provide him with another means of diversion. When this fails to chase away the emptiness, so the story goes, he burns Rome and sits and fiddles, but after the embers die, his melancholy returns as a phantom which will not be dispelled. This description of Nero's nature, Kierkegaard reminds us, has not been undertaken to busy our imagination or to occasion us to thank God along with the Pharisees that we are different from

Nero. Nero, he emphasizes, is "flesh of our flesh and bone of our bone," which is to say that in Nero a possible mode of human existence becomes transparent.[60] Boredom and melancholy, as related forms of existential disquietude, are structural conditions of man's existence. They define an aspect of the situation in which the self as actualized finite freedom concretely lives. They are irreducible qualifications of man's being-in-the-world.

4. Phenomenology of Despair

The phenomenon of mood has its most intensive expression in the experience of despair. In the language of Karl Jaspers, despair approximates the final limits of man's "boundary-situation" (*Grenzsituation*). The self in despair experiences a total loss of hope as the threat of nothingness, disclosed in anxiety, boredom, and melancholy, becomes overwhelming. In despair the self loses its very being as it is engulfed by non-being. The structures of self break down, and consciousness is dispersed. The unity and integrity of the self are dissolved. Kierkegaard's classic discussion of despair in *The Sickness Unto Death* still remains unsurpassed in existentialist phenomenology. In a previous chapter we have seen how Kierkegaard derived the elements of possibility and necessity as polar structures of selfhood through an examination of the phenomenon of despair. Then we noted that despair is most precisely defined as a disruption of this essential polarity of possibility and necessity. So also in his *Works of Love* Kierkegaard speaks of man's despair as a "disproportion in his inmost being." [61] Despair is a disruption, disrelationship, or disproportion of the elements which structure the interior of the self. The two basic elements are necessity, or the determinant of self as having been, and possibility, or the determinant of self as being not yet. Closely allied in Kierkegaard's analysis with the polarity of necessity and possibility is the polarity of finitude and infinitude which is equally important for an understanding of his phenomenology of despair. As the self is a synthesis of possibility and necessity, so also it is a synthesis of infinitude and finitude. "The self is the conscious synthesis of infinitude and finitude which relates itself to itself, whose task is to become itself." [62] The polar elements of infinitude and finitude, like those of possibility and necessity, characterize respectively the dynamic and formal factors of selfhood, by dint of which the self is actual freedom and concrete becoming. The finite, like the necessary, limits the self; infinity, like possibility, constitutes the open character of the self. "For the self is a synthesis in which the finite is the limiting factor and the infinite is the expanding factor." [63] The polarities of infinitude-finitude and possibility-necessity provide the structural elements in terms of which the concrete experiences of the self can be understood. The phenomenon in question is still the phenomenon of despair, which can now be conceptually clarified as the disruption of the structures of self-hood and described in relation to different types of despair.

In his delineation of a typology of modes of despair Kierkegaard subsumes all manifestations of despair under two primary forms: the despair of not willing to be one's self (the despair of weakness), and the despair of desperately willing to be one's self (defiant despair). These two primary forms have a variety of expressions, such as the despair of immediacy, despair about the eternal, and the despair of resignation. However, even the two primary forms in these various expressions can ultimately be reduced to a common denominator. All despair is finally grounded in the self's desire to get rid of itself. Even the self which desperately wills to be itself, as we shall see, wills to be a self which it can be only by negating itself as a self. Such a self strives for infinity and possibility at the expense of its finiteness and necessity. But just as the self as possibility needs itself as necessity, so the self which strives to make itself infinite destroys itself as finite self.

Prior to the two fundamental forms of despair, which are reducible to the despair of striving to get rid of one's self, there is what might be called a preliminary form of despair. This is the "despair which is unconscious that it is despair, or the despairing unconsciousness of having a self." [64] This form of despair, says Kierkegaard, is despair only in a very restricted sense. He characterizes it as an "ordinary view" or "vulgar view" which is bound to mere appearances, surface realities, and superficial perspectives. In this superficial form of despair the self has not yet arrived at a consciousness of itself as spirit, i.e., of itself as a self, and hence is unable to recognize its own despair. Jaspers, whose descriptions of despair parallel those of Kierkegaard, has formulated a clear statement of this superficial form of despair in which the reflexiveness of consciousness has not yet penetrated to the innermost being of the self. On this level of self-reflexion we are dealing, says Jaspers, with a self-consciousness which has come about purely by chance (*zufälliges*

Sichbewusstwerden), in which there is no active and dynamic relation of the self with itself. It is only an apparent and a momentary self-awareness in which there is no self-relation in passion and concern. Hence the self forgets itself immediately following the occurrence of self-awareness. There is no retention of the self in memory, and therefore any active relation of the self to its situation or facticity is precluded.[65] This superficial and unauthentic consciousness of despair, which has not yet penetrated to its true situation, regards despair as some rare phenomenon that results when one is momentarily dejected or discouraged over some set of circumstances. Thus despair is confused with transitory psychological states. This despair which is regarded as a rare phenomenon is further seen as occurring only in other persons but never in one's self. Just as the sick man tells himself that he is well, so the self constantly reminds itself that it is not in despair.[66] And to keep from falling into despair, it intensifies the rotation method of avoiding boredom and melancholy, with the hope of losing itself in distractions and diversions which will drive away the phantoms of despair. The self has not yet become fully conscious that it is *in* despair—that despair is a condition of its very humanity. This type of despair can be considered only as a preliminary form. Genuine despair breaks forth only when the self becomes conscious of itself as being in despair, and despairs either at not willing to be itself, or despairs in a desperate and defiant attempt to be itself.

The despair of not willing to be one's self is the despair of weakness. This despair involves a disproportion of the polar elements of the structures of the self in such a way that infinitude and possibility are sacrificed to finitude and necessity. Thus the self loses its integrity. The concrete expression of this disruption of the structures of the self is a despair over factors in the external environment, such as loss of fortune and loss of health. The self succumbs to necessity and sees itself determined by the externals which impinge upon it. If the externals are in his favor—if he has a respectable job, a substantial income, and a happy family—then man lives on the pinnacle, overjoyed with his good fortune. But when these externals are taken away, the self is thrown into despair. In this view the self sacrifices itself to external circumstances in terms of which it defines itself. It is circumstances which qualify the existence of the self as either hopeful or despairing; but a self which permits itself to be buffeted by circumstances has not yet found itself. "For the immediate man does not recognize his self, he recognizes (and here

again appears the infinitely comic trait) that he has a self only by externals. There is no more ludicrous confusion, for a self is just infinitely
different from externals." [67] Sucked into the orbit of his environmental
world, man continues to exist outside himself. He is riveted to his facticity
or necessity, and when the external factors in his environment frustrate
his projects, he plunges into despair because he has lost himself as possibility. He has lost his inner subjective freedom. He is bound to his environment. The sickness of such an individual, says Kierkegaard, results
from his loss of the "inward direction which is the path he ought to
have followed in order to become truly a self." [68] He strives to find himself outside himself and loses himself as an integrated self with a unique
existential freedom. He loses himself as possibility through which he can
transcend himself horizontally to the future, and he loses his infinity
through which he can transcend himself vertically to the divine.

This disruption of the structure of selfhood in the despair of
weakness has another aspect. Not only does the self which is sacrificed
to necessity and finitude abdicate freedom by seeking to find itself in
the external circumstances of its environment, but it also relinquishes
this freedom through a despairing plunge into the public "existence" of
society. It seeks to find itself in the external and objectifying talk, multitudinous activities, and soothing influences present in the *Mitwelt*.
"As the little child must be put to sleep by a lullaby, so these men
need the tranquilizing hum of society before they are able to eat, drink,
sleep, pray, fall in love, etc." [69] But these social sedatives have only a
momentary efficacy. When their quieting influence wears off, man is
brought back to consider himself, and he despairs because the supports
of his existence are disclosed as spurious. This despair may reach the
point at which all hope, as an implication of possibility, vanishes, and
life chained to necessity becomes unbearable. This may lead to suicide,
in which the despair of not willing to be one's self reaches its most intensive expression. The self cannot bear the disproportion of its existence
and thus strives to do away with itself. This may be a piecemeal self-
destruction through which the self invites the very external factors of its
environment over which it despairs to annihilate it. Or it may be a
conscious act of self-destruction through which the self seeks to destroy
itself by its own hands.

The second basic form of despair is defiant despair, or the despair in
which the self seeks desperately to affirm itself. In this form of despair
the disproportion is one in which possibility absorbs necessity and

finitude is lost in a fantastic striving after infinity. Again, the structures of existence are disrupted, and the very being of the self is threatened. Defiant despair is a despair in which the self refuses to recognize its necessity or facticity. It seeks to affirm itself as possibility alone—as a radical unconditioned freedom. It cannot accept itself as a self which is already begun in existence, defined by the concretions which characterize it as limited and finite. "The man's concrete self, or his concretion, has in fact necessity and limitations; it is this perfectly definite thing, with these faculties, dispositions, etc. But by the aid of the infinite form, the negative self, he wills first to undertake to refashion the whole thing, in order to get out of it in this way a self such as he wants to have, produced by the aid of the infinite form of the negative self—and it is thus he wills to be himself. That is to say, he is not willing to begin with the beginning but 'in the beginning.'" [70] In this form of despair the self suppresses the factors of its facticity and strives for a qualitative infinitude. It loses itself in its possibility and infinity. Such a self becomes, says Kierkegaard, a "hypothetical self." It has no actuality or concretion. It becomes a mirage which floats in a sea of possibilities. "So the despairing self is constantly building nothing but castles in the air, it fights only in the air." [71]

In despairing self-affirmation, this self seeks to constitute itself as an "experimental god." [72] It refuses to acknowledge any power over it and affirms for itself an infinite self-sufficiency. This despair is the despair of the Promethean self which strives to be a god. It despairs over its finitude and strives for infinity. But the self which makes itself infinite destroys itself as a self. Finitude and infinitude are polar structures of selfhood. The radical affirmation of one to the exclusion of the other leads to a negation of self as such. "No derived self can by regarding itself give itself more than it is." [73] Like Prometheus, the self which negates itself by striving for infinity (i.e. negates itself as finite) finds that it cannot escape the limits of its existence. This then is its occasion to take offense against its existence as qualified by necessity and finitude. "So he is offended by it, or rather from it he takes occasion to be offended at the whole of existence, in spite of it he would be himself, not despitefully be himself without it (for that is to abstract from it, and that he cannot do, or that would be a movement in the direction of resignation); no, in spite of or in defiance of the whole of existence he wills to be himself with it, to take it along, almost defying his torment." [74] Through the despair of self-affirmation man becomes defiant in the presence of limiting factors and protests against the condition of existence itself. Albert Camus has incomparably expressed this movement of defiant despair in his concept of metaphysical rebellion which he develops in his essay *The Rebel*. "Metaphysical rebellion," writes Camus, "is the movement by which man protests against his condition and the whole of creation. It is metaphysical because it contests the ends of man and creation. The slave protests against the condition in which he finds himself within the state of slavery; the metaphysical rebel protests against the condition in which he finds himself as a man." [75] Desperate self-affirmation leads to a self-elevation of one's self as infinite, which in turn leads to a defiant rebellion against the conditions of finitude.

Religiously understood, this despair of defiance is a rebellion against God. In bearing witness against the condition of its existence, the self takes offense against the Power through which the self has its being. "It wills to obtrude upon this Power in spite, to hold on to it out of malice," says Kierkegaard. "And that is natural, a malignant objection must above all take care to hold on to that against which it is an objection. Revolting against the whole of existence, it thinks it has hold of a proof against it, against its goodness." [76] In the second part of *The Sickness Unto Death* despair is defined theologically as sin, properly understood as rebellion against God. In the story of the Fall Adam affirms for himself a self-sufficiency which is equal to that of God. Man refuses to accept the fact that he is a creature, and he thus rebels against the source of his creation. In its rebellion the self clearly cannot consider any help from God. This would destroy the radical self-affirmation in its protest against existence. Kierkegaard suggests that we picture an author making a clerical error through a slip of the pen. Suppose that the error becomes conscious of itself as an error, rebels against the author, and in hatred refuses to be corrected, affirming itself in the protest: "No, I will not be erased, I will stand as a witness against thee, that thou art a very poor writer." [77] Such is the defiant protest of the self which refuses to accept its finitude and estrangement.

The boundary-limit of this despair of radical self-affirmation is suicide. This we have seen is also true of the despair of weakness. Thus we see that both of these fundamental forms of despair culminate in a common movement—an attempt on part of the self to get rid of itself. Suicide as an implication of defiant despair, however, has a different quality from that which ensues from the despair of weakness. The suicide of defiant despair is the final stage of a radical self-affirmation, in which freedom insisted upon as infinite, seeks its last desperate expression. Made aware that it cannot escape its facticity of being thrown into existence without being consulted, it strives in a last and desperate attempt to affirm its freedom by choosing its exit. Jaspers, discussing suicide in his *Philosophie* has shown how *Selbstmord* is always in some sense a movement within freedom.[78] The suicide of defiant despair is an expression of a spurious unlimited freedom; the suicide of the despair of weakness is an expression of a freedom trammeled by necessity. In *Either/Or* Kierkegaard defines the suicide of defiant despair as the "negative expression for infinite freedom." [79] The suicide negates his finite freedom by seeking to give it an infinite expression. But in doing so he loses both himself and infinity.

The various forms of despair described by Kierkegaard and some of the other existentialist thinkers are presented to the reader as universal possibilities of human existence. Despair is a phenomenon of existence which must be accepted before it can be overcome. In *Either/ Or* Kierkegaard speaks of "choosing despair," for only then does one genuinely become aware of the estranged character of human existence. A flight from despair constitutes a flight from existence itself. Despair cannot be removed as a condition of existence, but it can be faced courageously. Despair is "overcome" only by going through it, not by avoiding it. As Sartre has Orestes proclaim in *The Flies*, "Human life begins on the other side of despair." It is questionable, however, whether Sartre ever gets to the "other side." Kierkegaard does. The difference between Sartre and Kierkegaard resides in their respective theologies. And Sartre unquestionably has a theology—an atheistic theology, but a theology nonetheless. Sartre heroically accepts the non-existence of God and reconciles himself to the fact that man is a useless passion. Kierkegaard encounters and resolutely affirms a Power which constitutes the self and provides the condition for the courage to be one's self in which despair is taken up. But independent of their respective theologies, both Sartre and Kierkegaard endorse a philosophy of human finitude.

I V

Death and

Transitoriness

1. Existence and Mortality

"WITHOUT DEATH men would scarcely philosophize." These words, penned by Schopenhauer, express the paramount importance of death as a philosophical theme. Schopenhauer was not the first to apprehend the philosophical significance of death. Socrates had made it part of his mission in ancient Greece to teach men how to die. And the Stoics, both Greek and Roman, were profoundly concerned with death and sought to find its hidden meaning. Existentialism, in its movement toward a philosophy of human finitude, has given the theme of death a renewed and disciplined expression. The theme has been pursued with engaging insight in the philosophies of Jaspers and Heidegger in particular. In Jaspers' philosophy death is discussed as one of the "boundary situations" (*Grenzsituationen*) which define the human condition. (Other boundary situations are chance, suffering, conflict, and guilt.) Heidegger develops an ontology of death in which death is *"interiorized"* as a mode of existence itself (*Sein-zum-Tode*). But prior to these disciplined descriptions we already find an existential approach to death in the reflections of Kierkegaard, and similar themes emerge in the writings of all his spiritual descendants. Nicolas Berdyaev, whose existentialism bears an indelible Kierkegaardian stamp, says, "Strictly speaking, a system of ethics which does not make death its central problem has no value and is lacking in depth and earnestness." [1] In the literary camp of existentialism, the poetry of Rilke, particularly his *Duineser Elegien*, stands as an incomparable elucidation of man's confrontation with his having to die. André Malraux has made much use of the theme of death in his novels. And Albert Camus deals in a most provocative manner with death in connection with absurdity and suicide in his *Le Mythe de Sisyphe*.

Existentialist thinkers agree that death can be elucidated and described as a constitutive structure in man's situationality. It is disclosed in one's projects of concern as a boundary which limits the very concerns which are projected. It is a factor of destiny which makes its appearance as an irreducible limit to my possibilities. Death, existentially interpreted, is a phenomenon intrinsically related to human care or concern, disclosed in the protentional movement of this concern as it confronts its possibilities and their unsurpassable limit. Death thus understood is not simply a biological factuality which terminates a life process. It is an existential facticity which is part and parcel of man's being-in-the-world. The new determinant is an engaged consciousness or concern. Hence existential dying might be defined as a biological factuality interpenetrated with consciousness. This distinguishes death from the simple biological termination which characterizes non-human being. Kierkegaard, Jaspers, and Heidegger make it clear that, properly speaking, an animal cannot be said to die. Only when spirit or consciousness is posited, says Kierkegaard, can one properly speak of dying. [2] Jaspers observes that for an animal death is not a possible boundary situation, because the animal cannot "know" death. [3] Heidegger has sought for a more precise formulation of the phenomenon of death in his three distinctions of *Verenden*, *Ableben*, and *Sterben*. *Verenden*, meaning quite literally "coming to an end," properly characterizes plant and animal life. *Ableben* refers to the biological termination of human life, or man's ontic annihilation. And *Sterben*, or dying, is an existential modality in which this ontic annihilation is permeated with consciousness and is taken up in the movements of existential concern. "*Dying* is the genuine term for the *mode of being* in which *Dasein* is in relation to his death." [4] The death under consideration here is quite clearly not a simple cessation of life, nor the death of the "death-bed" viewed as a final and external biological occurrence. Death is an already present possibility of existence. It is a "being-unto-the-end" (*Sein-zum-Ende*) rather than a simple "being-at-the-end" (*Zu-Ende-sein*). Heidegger makes it clear that "death is a mode of being which *Dasein* takes over as soon as he is." [5] The issue here does not turn on the question of death as a biological universal, inductively derived through an observation of the empirical disintegration of human and non-human contingent bodies. This may be a legitimate categorial characterization of man's empirical being, but death as a determinate of human consciousness and concern is an "existential" rather than a category. Death as a simple biological universal expresses an unchanging factuality of intramundane beings, but death in connection with existence, and the penetration of this existence with consciousness and concern, is never such an unchanging and immutable fact insofar as the way I relate myself to death constantly undergoes modification. As Jaspers puts it, death varies with *Existenz*. [6] Death is a mode of human concern, indissolubly linked with the various projects of man's world-orientations, in which the transitoriness of existence is disclosed. This is what is meant when death is existentially defined as a constitutive structure of being-in-a-situation.

Death as a factor of human situationality is a phenomenon which embraces the whole of life. As Heidegger says, it is something which one takes over as soon as one is. Death and life existentially interpenetrate one another even though they are logical opposites. Berdyaev speaks of death as a manifestation of life and of life as a perpetual dying. The death experienced in life is occasioned by the transitoriness of existence which renders it impossible for man to fulfill his being in his temporal and spatial orientation. [7] This transitoriness is disclosed in the *Umwelt*, *Mitwelt*, and *Eigenwelt*. Leaving a familiar and beloved surrounding always produces a pulsation of anxiety because one becomes aware of the passing or transitory character of one's relation to his world of tools and world of nature. Every parting or farewell has a quality of finality. Death makes us aware that the friend or the loved one might never again be encountered. Berdyaev describes the anxiety which he experienced as a boy at every parting as an instance of this experience of death within life. The awareness of never again seeing the face of the stranger he had met, the town through which he had passed, the room in which he had resided for a few days, the tree or the dog which he happened to see—all this filled him with a mortal anguish which testified to the mortality of existence itself.[8] But death is most sharply experienced in the *Eigenwelt* when the self relates itself to itself and becomes conscious of its indelibly personal mortality. All existentialists, with the exception of Sartre, interpret death as a principle of individuation. It brings me back to the transitoriness of my personal being-in-the-world. Death is a phenomenon which I discover in my self and toward which I must assume some kind of attitude. I may seek to escape from it, but in fleeing I only suppress it. It cannot be overcome. It is a *character indelibilis* of my personal existence.

Death as a phenomenon of existence itself most radically places the meaning of life into question. Sartre finds in death the most extreme expression of the meaninglessness of life. Death renders life absurd. Death can never give life meaning. It is that which on principle removes all meaning from life. The absurdity of death necessarily ensues in Sartre's philosophy because the phenomenon remains for him simply a factual and external limit to man's subjectivity. Death for Sartre never appears as an existential possibility. It is a chance event which one encounters as a nihilation of one's possibilities. "This perpetual appearance of chance at the very source of my projects cannot be known as *my* possibility, but, on the contrary, as the nihilation of all my possibilities, a nihilation which *itself is no longer a part of my possibilities.* Hence death is, not *my* possibility of no longer actualizing presence in the world, but a *continuing possible nihilation of my possibles, which is outside my possibilities.*"[9] If death is wholly outside the realm of my possibilities, then any meaning is *ipso facto* excluded, because meaning is conferred only in relation to possibility. But by placing death outside possibility, Sartre places death outside existence itself, which ironically involves this most ardent spokesman for existentialism in a most unexistentialist interpretation. In the final analysis, Sartre has recourse to an Epicurean materialism in his understanding of death. As long as man lives, death is not; when man dies, he is not. In neither case does death emerge as a matter of existential concern. For Kierkegaard, Jaspers, Heidegger, and Berdyaev on the other hand, death is an interior possibility of the human self as concern or passion. Death for these thinkers threatens the meaning of human subjectivity but can also give meaning to this subjectivity. It is a possibility of human existence which can be authentically fulfilled or unauthentically suppressed. For Sartre death can never become an interior possibility—it can be a possibility only for the Other. "To die is to exist only through the Other." [10] In his death man becomes a prey for the Other who judges his life and praises or condemns it. Insofar as meaning is forthcoming, this is a meaning conferred by the Other. My death is a possibility for the Other but never for me. In Sartre's analysis death is wholly absorbed into the *Mitwelt* —a phenomenon disclosed only through my relations with the Other —and is deprived of any significance for the *Eigenwelt*.

Sartre's theme of the absurdity of death is consistently rejected by the other existentialists. The question which must be raised, says Kierkegaard, is that "of the possibility of finding an ethical expression for the significance of death." [11] The subjective thinker wishes to know how death will affect and transform his entire life. Death is thus viewed as "something to be related to the entire life of the subject." [12] Death for Kierkegaard is not an absurdity which renders all my existential projects ultimately meaningless, as for Sartre; death is itself a task or a possibility which calls the existing subject to decision by making him aware of the urgency of choice in the moment. Death thus takes on ethical significance for the whole of man's life. Death discloses the transitoriness of my existence and the finite character of my possibilities and confers upon each choice an earnestness and passion which would hardly come into question were man immortal. Thus Jaspers speaks of a possible fulfillment (*Vollendung*) in existential death.[13] Death can be appropriated in one's subjectivity and given an ethical significance. Heidegger has ontologized this ethical view of death expressed by Kierkegaard and Jaspers in his concept of death as a mode of existence, which can be either authentically or unauthentically modified. As soon as man is and as long as man is, he has before him the task of assuming some kind of attitude toward his death, and he must seek to relate his death to the whole of his existence.

The existentialist concept of death as a mode of existence must be clearly contrasted with the Freudian concept of the "death drive" (*Todestrieb*), although the two may be significantly related. Freud argued that psychical energy was drawn from a libidinal reservoir in which love and hate, the drive for life and the drive for death, were ambiguously intertwined. In every intensive affirmation of life Freud saw a correlative fascination with death. Indeed, every individual, he argued, unconsciously desires his own ontic annihilation. This is expressed in the "suicidal tendencies" of the various forms of masochism, in which the death drive becomes an instrument for the atonement of psychological guilt. In becoming accident prone, for example, the individual does away with himself piecemeal, not having the courage to entertain suicide as a conscious and deliberate action. Again, the death drive may be directed outward rather than inward, and we have the sadistic personality. However, in both expressions of the death drive as formulated by Freud we are dealing with pathological or neurotic instances of the experience of death as an ontic phenomenon. Death is pre-enacted, and sometimes actualized, as an empirical factuality, because of the inability of the individual to cope with the realities of life. Death when understood as a mode of existence remains intentionally neutral to any pathological modification that one's being-in-the-world may have. The existential attitude acknowledges death as a universal qualification of existence itself; the pathological attitude is a particular expression of destructive socio-psychological factors. The relationship between Heidegger's concept of *Sein-zum-Tode* and Freud's *Todestrieb*, is therefore a relationship similar to that which obtains between existential and pathological anxiety in general.

2. *The External View of Death*

Man has always found it necessary to devise some view of death. Sometimes death is viewed as a source of terror; other times it is seen as a welcome release from the anxiety of life. Death may be approached through a heroic resignation, or it may be the occasion for a cowardly retreat. It can be transformed into a martyrdom which gives expression to an ideal or a dedicated life, and it can be romanticized for its melancholy attractiveness. Death can be courageously accepted and affirmed, or it can become a matter of profound indifference. Whatever particular view man may hold, he cannot avoid assuming some kind of attitude and action toward his death. Now in all of his particular views on death we can distinguish between what Kierkegaard calls the external and the subjective view of death, or what Heidegger later refers to in his distinction between an unauthentic and authentic being-unto-death. Although everyone must assume some kind of attitude toward death, for the most part, says Kierkegaard, this attitude is one in which death is viewed as an external and objective phenomenon in such a way that the personal and unique death of the existing subject is comically ex-cluded. There are two such external views of death which Kierkegaard singles out for examination. One of these views is that represented in the naïvité of the pagan consciousness; the other is represented in the so-phistication of Hegelian intellectualism. The pagan view of death, says Kierkegaard, has elements which make it attractive and heroic, but it still remains at a distance from a true understanding of what it means to die. Kierkegaard alludes to Lessing's essay, *Wie die Alten den Tod gebildet*, in connection with this pagan view. In this essay he finds one of the finest representations of death in classical art. In reading this essay, he says, "one cannot deny that one is put in a mood of pleasur-able sadness by this picture of the sleeping genius, or by observing the beautiful solemnity with which the genius of death bows his head and extinguishes the torch. There is, if one will, something indescribably per-suasive and alluring in the thought of trusting oneself to such a guide, who is as tranquilizing as a recollection in which nothing is recol-lected." [14] Such a view of death is attractive, heroic, and alluring. It arouses no terror and instills no anxiety. It teaches a melancholy resigna-tion in which death is accepted without an appropriation of it as a sig-nificant factor in one's entire life. As such it lacks what Kierkegaard calls the "highest element," namely, subjectivity. The pagan view of death is still an external view; it views death from the outside. This external view of death, says Kierkegaard in his discourse on "The Decisiveness of Death," was clearly formulated in the materialism of Epicurus. "A pa-gan has said that death is nothing to be feared, for 'when it is, I am not, and when I am, it is not.' This is the jest through which the subtle ob-server places himself outside." [15] This external view makes no place for death as a determinant of subjectivity. Indeed, it has no relevance for the life of the existing subject. It simply remains an external limit to this subjectivity.

The awakening of a subjective understanding of death can come about only when the pagan view is pruned of its poetic sedatives and heroic resignation and death is disclosed as a genuine threat to existence. "When death appears in its true form as the lean and joyless reaper, one does not behold it without terror; but when, to mock men who imagine they can mock it, it comes upon the scene disguised, when only the spectator sees that this is death, this unknown figure which captivates all by his courtesy and causes all to exult in the wild abandon-ment of pleasure—then a profound horror seizes him." [16] A subjective apprehension of death requires the intentional disclosure of terror and horror as modifications of mood. We have already seen how mood functions as a basic element in the disclosure of one's being-in-the-world. Part and parcel of this disclosure is the indelible transitoriness of existence revealed through the terror and horror of having to die. But these modifications of mood must bring the self to an awareness of its own individual death. If they simply depict the horror and terror of death in general, the death of humanity, then the attitude toward death remains an external view. "Even if the conception used pictures of horror to delineate death and terrified a sick imagination, it is still only a jest if the individual merely thinks about death, and not about himself in death, if he thinks about it only as the fate of the human race, but not as his own fate." [17]

Classical paganism thus never arrives at a genuine understanding of the existential reality of death. The pagan view constitutes a flight or a retreat from death rather than a subjective penetration of it. Hegel's objective idealism falls under the same criticism. Kierkegaard sees in the Hegelian preoccupation with objective knowledge of universal history a fantastic neglect of a genuine understanding of death. "Before I pass over to universal history it seems to me I had better think about this, lest existence mock me, because I had become so learned and high-falutin that I had forgotten to understand what will some time happen to me as to every human being—sometime, nay, what am I saying: suppose death were so treacherous as to come tomorrow!" [18] In the System where the dispassionate spectator understands everything in terms of the universal and the general, death itself becomes "something in general." [19] With the suppression of the individual character of death in such a view there is a concomitant concealing of death's uncertainty. In general terms one can speak movingly and with great emotion about the uncertainty of death—and then end by submitting resolutions for the long life that lies ahead.[20] But this is precisely to forget the uncertainty of death, the fact that death might be "so treacherous as to come tomorrow."

Both the poetic view of classical paganism and the objectified view of Hegelianism bypass the capital importance of death for the existing individual. But also in our common, everyday, levelled understanding, what is existentially involved in dying fails to become transparent. Commonly we think of death as that which results when one takes a dose of sulphuric acid, or drowns himself, or goes to sleep in an atmosphere of coal gas. These are all objective and external observations about death in general which disclose little about our own individual death which we alone must die. Or we can acquire a most extraordinary knowledge of death in learning what the Stoics had to say about suicide, how Shakespeare's Juliet poisoned herself, how the poets interpret death, how the tragic hero dies in the last act, and what the clergy are accustomed to say on the subject in their funeral sermons. But for all this extraordinary knowledge of death, we must conclude, says Kierkegaard, that death is by no means properly understood. Death is still viewed as some kind of external fact instead of an imminent reality ever present in my personal existence.[21]

This external view of death elucidated by Kierkegaard is given a conceptually clarified formulation in Heidegger's ontological analysis of the unauthentic being-unto-death. Heidegger's analysis pursues the problem of death in connection with the structural determinants of "fallenness" and the "anonymous one." Our view of death is conditioned by our flattened existence and our loss of self as we are absorbed into the anonymity of *Das Man*. "*Dasein* dies factically, as long as he exists, but for the most part in the mode of fallenness." [22] In his average existence *Dasein* has lost himself in his everyday concerns and articulates his fallen being-in-the-world through the contentment and quieting influence of talk. It is this talk of the "anonymous one" which most forcefully expresses *Dasein's* unauthentic being-unto-death. Talk acknowledges death only as an external natural happening which is objectively apparent. Every day and every hour an unknown number of people die. In this talk, which is essentially a flight or retreat from death, the "anonymous one" grants that someday even he will have to die—but not for the time being. "Man in his evasive talk says: eventually man will have to die, but for the most part he remains secure." [23] Talk evades the existential problem of death because it speaks only for the "anonymous one," not for the unique and personal *Dasein* who must face death as an individual concern. People talk about death anonymously. They say that "one" must die sooner or later; eventually "one" will die; "everyone" someday will have to reckon with death. But this anonymous "one" is precisely "nobody"—i.e., nobody in particular. The "anonymous one" misconstrues death as something in general. Generally speaking, death is a scientifically and objectively indubitable fact. There is certainly strong evidence that everyone, at some time or another, will have to die. But in this talk the intrinsically individual and indelibly personal character of death remains concealed.

The unauthentic being-unto-death of the "anonymous one" constitutes a retreat from death as an existential reality. "The everyday being-unto-death as fallenness is a constant *flight from death*. This mode of being-unto-the-end is one of unauthentic understanding, concealment, and *retreat from death*." [24] Heidegger refers to Tolstoi's story "The Death of Ivan Ilyitch" as a literary depiction of this unauthentic retreat from death. After Ilyitch discovers that no cure for his illness is available, he is confronted with the terrifying possibility that he may die. But instead of courageously facing this possibility he seeks to escape from it by losing himself in the quieting influences of everyday expressions such as "not yet," "not yet for sometime," and "later probably"— all of which move in the realm of unauthentic speech or talk. In this flight or retreat from death there is a suppression of the authentic anxiety through which *Dasein* is brought to himself in awareness of his final possibility. Anxiety is suppressed, and death is transformed into an object of fear. It is viewed as an external biological factuality which happens to all men at the end of their life. Death thus becomes objectified. Man seeks to find the reality of death in the biological functioning of the organism which is open to the investigations and measurements of medical science. Death is equated with cessation of the heartbeat and curtailment of breathing. But as Kierkegaard suggested, in this objectified view of death the individual comically places himself on the outside. And as Ivan Ilyitch finally came to realize, there was something comic about viewing his death in connection with a floating kidney, a chronic catarrh, or an appendicitis. The reality of death for him did not reside in these physiological disturbances. It had its locus elsewhere, namely in the existential concern and anxiety which disclosed the indelible transitoriness of his existence. Fear can only disclose the empirical contingency of human life. Death as an existential phenomenon is revealed only through anxiety, but it is precisely this anxiety which is suppressed in the everyday movements of the "anonymous one," and hence man's being-unto-death remains unauthentic.

When the "anonymous one" has succeeded in suppressing the anxiety of his existential death, then the certainty of death is likewise concealed. To be sure, the "anonymous one" says that death will certainly come, but this everyday certainty is based on an empirical observation of the death of others, and thus remains immune to any subjective appropriation. As an empirical observation the phenomenon can have only hypothetical certainty. Hence it is necessary to qualify the statement that "all men die" with the qualification "so far as one knows." Death becomes highly probable but not existentially certain. It has an empirical rather than an apodictic certainty.[25] This empirical certainty may make *Dasein* aware of the factuality of death, but it cannot reveal the significance of death as an existential facticity. Remaining within the realm of empirical certainty, *Dasein* is unable to become certain of death as a reality for him. And in suppressing the certainty of death the "anonymous one" disguises its indefiniteness. *Dasein* retreats from the possibility that death may strike any moment. As Kierkegaard showed, the self seeks to conceal the possibility that death may come tomorrow. The "anonymous one" turns from this ever-present and imminent possibility to the pressing problems of his immediate practical concerns. Contenting himself with the talk of the public, he can proclaim that all concern with death is mere idle and morbid preoccupation. Thus he postpones thinking of death—at least, for the present, he says. The "anonymous one," in his average and levelled everyday existence, which he expresses through the talk of the public, lives and moves in an unauthentic being-unto-death.

3. Death and Subjectivity

The subjective thinker seeks to understand himself in his existence. He strives to penetrate and elucidate the concrete particularity of his lived experience. This, we have seen in an earlier chapter, is what Kierkegaard understands by truth as subjectivity. Truth is disclosed in the movements of human subjectivity, and the subjective thinker must seek to describe the geography of this subjectivity in which the truth of existence shows itself. It is hardly an accident that Kierkegaard's most suggestive comments on the phenomenon of death appear in his *Postscript* under the chapter entitled "The Task of Becoming Subjective." If man is to grasp the full existential significance of his death he must turn from the objective and the general to the subjective and the particular. Only in subjectivity does the existing individual confront the irremediable transitoriness of his existence. Subjectivity discloses death as an

indelibly personal phenomenon. Death, subjectively apprehended, becomes *my* death. It is a particular rather than a general death. It is a
death which I alone will have to die. "If the task of life is to become
subjective then the thought of death is not, for the individual subject,
something in general." [26] Death is disclosed in the concrete particularity
of human subjectivity as uniquely and irreplaceably my own. It is a
possibility of my existence which bears in a superlative manner the stamp
of my individuality. It is in this sense that death takes on significance
as a principle of individuation. In the subjective apprehension of my
death I am called back to myself—to the self which was lost in the external view of death where death applies to the "anonymous one" but to
nobody in particular. The principle of individuation for human existence is not an abstract signate matter but a unique existential possibility which confers upon my being a particular determinant of facticity.
Death marks the self off from universal mankind and from other individuals, each of whom must ultimately die their own death, and discloses the individual and irreplaceable character of the existing self.
Hannah Arendt, in her collection of essays on existential philosophy,
has argued that Kierkegaard was one of the first to understand death
as a principle of individuation.[27] John Wild makes the same point in his
study on existentialism when he writes, "The thought of death indi-
viduates me, and brings me back to the self that is my very own.
Kierkegaard intuitively recognized this when he said that each man
must die his own death." [28]

Coupled with the awareness of death as *my* death is the awareness of the indefiniteness of death. Death subjectively understood is not
a distant event which one thinks about when one attends a funeral or
passes a graveyard. Death is apprehended as being imminent every moment. My death is a death which may come tomorrow. Death is thus
understood as being at the same time the most certain and the most
uncertain event of my being-in-the-world. "In this way death is indeterminate: the one thing certain, and the only thing about which
nothing is certain," says Kierkegaard. "And no teacher can so effectively
compel attention to the subject of instruction as the uncertainty of death
when it points to the certainty of death; and no teacher can so keep
the thoughts of the pupil concentrated upon the one subject of instruction as the thought of the uncertainty of death when it trains the thought
to the certainty of death." [29]

In this subjective apprehension of death as an individual and imminent possibility, its relevance for the whole of existence is made manifest. Death is seen to permeate the whole of life and qualifies it at every instant. It is no longer viewed as a simple external and natural phenomenon which seems to happen to all people at some point in time and which has no reality until it arrives. Death when it becomes relevant for the whole of life is apprehended as a reality *already present.* The basic question which must be formulated, says Kierkegaard, is "whether death can be apprehended and experienced in an anticipatory conception, or whether its only being is its actual being." [30] Is death only when the individual is not, or can death be experienced in existential anticipation? Is it an external limit to my subjectivity, or does it interpenetrate it? Sartre, following the Epicurean view of death, places death outside the individual's experience of his inner subjectivity and defines it as simply a termination of this subjectivity. The only being of death is its actual being, and it can become real only when the individual is no longer. Sartre thus eliminates any existential significance that death may have for the individual subject. Insofar as death has any meaning at all in Sartre's view, it is a meaning which is relevant only for the Other. My death may achieve existential relevance and meaning for the Other, who must define the significance of my death in light of his own projects. But my death according to Sartre never enters my personal subjectivity. It is an irreducible absurdity for the one who has to die. For Kierkegaard, on the other hand, death is principally a factor of human subjectivity in which the anticipatory conception of death plays a determining role. Death has reality as a phenomenon which is present in the life of the individual himself. From the objective viewpoint this of course presents an insoluble problem. If death is viewed as an objective and external happening which comes only at the end of man's life, then death could never be understood prior to its occurrence. As Kierkegaard puts it, if death were to be understood scientifically through a process of experimentation, the individual would be involved in a comic sacrifice of himself upon the altar of his own experiment. If his existence goes out with his own experiment, he obviously cannot understand the results of his experiment, because he is no longer there. [31] But this application of a scientific and objective procedure to the phenomenon of existential dying leads only to a falsification of the problem. Clearly the individual can never understand his own death in this scientific and objective sense. But the individual can experience his death existentially. He can anticipate his final end and in this way relate death to his entire life. Thus the subjective task of the existing individual is to find the ethical significance which death has for his personal decisions and his shouldering of responsibility. Death as an imminent reality infuses every decision with existential urgency and importance. Death makes a difference for life. One decides differently when one's concerns have been interpenetrated with the reality of death. The reality of death gains a new expression, says Kierkegaard, when we ask what death is for the living individual. "We wish to know how the conception of death will transform a man's entire life." [32] Death belongs to life and must be appropriated in life. In this view death is not simply a contingent happening; it becomes a task or an existential project. Joachim Wach, in his illuminating book *Das Problem des Todes in der Philosophie unserer Zeit*, argues that the understanding of death as a task is a distinctive feature and contribution of the philosophies of Schopenhauer, Feuerbach, Simmel, and Heidegger. Death is described by these thinkers, he writes, "no longer as a point of termination which man seeks to suppress, no longer as an evil from which man flees, nor as a transition to a new, modified but still continuing existence, but rather death becomes a *task*." [33]

Death for the subjective thinker is a present reality. It is a constitutive element of life itself and figures significantly in all man's concrete existential projects. Thus death can receive a social definition in the context of the relation of selves with other selves, or it may be given a theological expression in the context of the relation of the self with God. Jaspers and Berdyaev have devoted some close attention to the reality of death in connection with the disruption of community, and Kierkegaard, using the phrase the "sickness unto death," has formulated a penetrating analysis of death religiously understood in terms of an estrangement from God.

Death has implications for the intersubjective communication of selves. Jaspers, in his discussion of the death of those nearby with whom I stand in communication, has shown how death discloses the transitoriness of our communal relations. In the death of a friend the severing of communication reaches its most intensive expression. For all time and all existence communication is cut off. I alone remain and am no longer able to address the deceased. In the presence of death there is only solitude. Everyone must die alone. But this solitude strikes both the one who is dying and the one who remains. If the communication between the two was genuine, then death as an existential constituent of life is experienced by both, although only the deceased is subject to death as an empirical factuality.[34] Berdyaev expresses the same theme when he speaks of every parting as an experience of death. Death expresses itself in life as severance from community. "We die not only in our own death," says Berdyaev, "but in the death of those we love." [35] If being-with-others is an intrinsic determinant of human being, as Heidegger maintains, then the death of others can be appropriated as a death within ourselves. The transitoriness of existence with its finite space and finite time reveals the boundary limits of the communication which is an integral aspect of our personal existence.

But death also has theological implications. Kierkegaard has sought to delineate these theological implications in connection with the concepts of despair and sin. The "sickness unto death" is despair, and despair religiously understood is sin. This understanding of death as a "sickness" must in no way be confused with a biological malady. Kierkegaard is here delineating a special existential-ontic expression of death as a mode of existence. The "sickness unto death" is the despair which is a constituent element in life itself. "Dying the death means to live to experience death. . . . The dying of despair transforms itself constantly into a living." [36] The "sickness unto death" as despair, and ultimately as sin or estrangement from God, is a manner or mode of life here and now. To take up the task of dying in this special religious sense is to become a self conscious of its fractured and sinful character. Death becomes a religious qualification of the self as spirit. To die means to exist in despair, and to exist in despair means to exist in a disrelationship with God. But to say that the "sickness unto death" is a qualification of spirit does not mean that the transitoriness disclosed in "bodily death" has no existential relevance. The very constitution of self as spirit implies a highly dialectical relationship between soul and body, which means that the self is never exhausted in either of these constitutive elements. Neither Platonic nor Cartesian dualisms are able to express the dialectical relationship of existential and biological death as it is disclosed in the "sickness unto death" as a qualification of human spirit. Death as despair contains dialectically within it the anxiety of not being able to die by "dying" a bodily death. "It is indeed very far from being true that, literally understood, one dies of this sickness, or that this sickness ends with bodily death. On the contrary, the torment of despair is precisely this, not to be able to die. So it has much in common with the situation of the moribund when he lies and struggles with death, and cannot die. So to be sick *unto* death is not to be able to die—yet not as though there were hope of life; no, the hopelessness in this case is that even the last hope, death, is not available. When death is the greatest danger, one hopes for life, but when one becomes acquainted with an even more dreadful danger, one hopes for death. So when the danger is so great that death has become one's hope, despair is the disconsolateness of not being able to die." [37] We have already seen how in Kierkegaard's phenomenology of despair the root determinant is a desire of the self to get rid of itself. The self despairs either by not willing to be itself or in a desperate attempt to affirm itself. In both cases the foundation of despair is the refusal of the self to accept itself as a dialectical synthesis of necessity and possibility, finitude and infinitude, body and soul. When the boundary limit of this despair is reached, the self stakes everything on suicide as the final possibility. Through suicide the self may dispose of itself. But in contemplating suicide the self is only plunged further into despair. Suicide provides no exit—neither the suicide in which the self succumbs to weakness nor the suicide of a defiant self-affirmation. Suicide solves only the problem of bodily annihilation, but the self is not exhausted in its mode as a living body. Suicide cannot liberate the self from itself as qualified by the "sickness unto death" which is posited in the constitution of the self as spirit. This is a death which, although in dialectical relationship with bodily annihilation, is not dependent upon it. Thus the gravest kind of despair is the despair of not being able to die as a synthetic unity of body and soul, through which the self is constituted as spirit.

Kierkegaard's theological interpretation of death in connection with the reality of sin is directly rooted in the New Testament understanding of man. Both Paul and John are clearly in the background of Kierkegaard on this point. Death, in the thought of Paul, is an ever-present reality as the consequence of sin. In his second letter to the Corinthians Paul speaks of the "despairing of life itself" in connection with receiving "the sentence of death" (1:8–9). In Romans he speaks of sin as having already killed him (7:11) and of death as the result of "living in the flesh," i.e., on one's own resources (7:5). So also John equates death with the life of sin which is defined as the religious mode of existence of fallen man (5:24). For Paul and John, as later for Kierkegaard, death in its religious qualification is a manner of existing which emerges as a constitutive element of life itself.

4. Towards an Ontology of Death

The elucidation of death as an existential theme characterizes literary and philosophical existentialism generally. We have seen how death emerges as an existential concern in the poetry of Rilke and the novels of Malraux as well as in the philosophical reflections of Kierkegaard, Berdyaev, Jaspers, and Heidegger. The position of Heidegger in this group of thinkers is in certain respects unique insofar as it was Heidegger who first attempted a conscious formulation of an ontology of death. In Heidegger's ontology the basic structure of *Dasein* is defined as concern or care. Concern is the structural unity of existentiality, facticity, and fallenness—the constitutive ontological elements of the Being of *Dasein*. The primary element of this structural unity is existentiality, by virtue of which *Dasein* understands himself as protentional or as possibility-of-being. As protentional, *Dasein* is ever ahead of himself in his projects of concern. As long as *Dasein* exists, there is that which "stands out" or which is "not yet." Thus *Dasein's* protention discloses his "constant openness" (*ständige Unabgeschlossenheit*).[38] *Dasein* is always ahead of himself, projected into his not yet actualized possibilities which are already constitutive of his Being. He is that which he can become as he actualizes his "not yet." Now it is in this protentional character of *Dasein* that the phenomenon of death is disclosed. "*Dasein*, as long as he is, stands out into that which he can become. But to this standing-out belongs the 'end' itself. This 'end' of being-in-the-world is death." [39] The end of *Dasein* is given and ontologically rooted in the care-structure which defines his being-in-the-world. Death is the final possibility of his existentiality disclosed in his protentional concern. "*Death, in reference to its ontological possibility, is grounded in concern.*" [40]

The initial point in Heidegger's ontology of death is thus the intrinsic relation of death and concern. It is only in the context of concern that death can become an existential problem. Sartre's neglect of the peculiarly existential character of death may result primarily from an undeveloped concept of concern as the basic determinant of existence. Only with a Kierkegaardian notion of passion or a Heideggerian concept of concern can death figure significantly in man's existential subjectivity. Man in his existential subjectivity becomes concerned about the possibility of the end of being-in-the-world and the problem which this poses for his attainment of wholeness. If man is unfinished as long as he exists, constantly projected into a not-yet, then it would seem that wholeness is achieved only after he has come to his end. But if this is the case, he can never experience his wholeness, for in the moment that his wholeness is achieved, he no longer exists. As long as *Dasein* exists, he has not yet attained his wholeness. Having attained it, he loses his being-in-the-world as such. It is precisely one of the tasks of an ontological analysis of death to answer this problem of wholeness as it relates to man's being-in-the-world. The clarification of this problem must proceed in light of a proper understanding of death as the *end* of *Dasein's* being-in-the-world. The concept of end can take on a variety of meanings. To come to an end commonly means to cease. We say that the rain has stopped and mean that it is no longer on hand. Or we speak of a road as having come to an end and thereby designate its termination as on on-hand object. But "ceasing to be" has different modifications. Something can cease in the sense that it is completed, as when an artist ceases to paint once he completes his painting. Or something can cease in the sense that it will never be completed, as when construction of a canal stops because the soil through which it must be cut proves too swampy. A project may end in the sense of being completed and yet be evaluated as either fulfilled or unfulfilled, as when we say that a performance ended well or ended poorly. Again, we might speak of the end in terms of change or disappearance, as when we talk about the end of summer. Or end may indicate that something is used up, as when we come to the end of the cake. All these modifications of ending apply to the region of on-hand and at-hand being. As such, they are not applicable to the unique Being of *Dasein* and hence cannot be used to characterize death as the end of his being-in-the-world. In death *Dasein* is neither completed, fulfilled, nor does he simply cease to be. Death, existentially understood, does not signify a being-at-the-end (*Zu-ende-sein*) in any of these modifications; rather, it signifies a *being-unto-the-end* (*Sein-zum-Ende*). Death is a mode of being which *Dasein* takes over as soon as he is. It is a way of existing toward the end, and hence becomes a possibility of human concern. Death, as all the other determinants of the Being of *Dasein*, must be understood through the possibilities of the existence of *Dasein* himself. Man's inner

Being remains opaque so long as it is interpreted as an extension of beings on hand or at hand.

The existentialist clarification of the meaning of end as it figures in the understanding of death as a being-unto-the-end places the problem of a possible wholeness of *Dasein* into a new light. Quite clearly man does not experience a wholeness which is defined by a coming to an end understood as an external limit of one's possibilities. Kierkegaard earlier suggested that such an external view of death is predicated on a false assumption. The assumption is that death is simply a natural and empirical happening which comes to man at the completion of his life. But death, as we have seen, is properly understood as a present possibility of existence or an existential mode of orientation. The question then becomes how man can achieve wholeness by taking over his death as a present possibility, by anticipating it. This question, we have seen, was posed by Kierkegaard when he asked whether death could be subjectively apprehended in an "anticipatory conception." Both Kierkegaard and Heidegger argue that such an anticipatory conception is involved when death is genuinely comprehended as a mode of being which man takes over as soon as he is. In his existential anticipation of death *Dasein* can assemble his possibilities and appraise himself in light of his final and irrevocable possibility. Death is existentially pre-enacted and provides the vantage point from which *Dasein* can understand the urgency of his present choices; and it is in his present choice that *Dasein* achieves wholeness. Keeping the transitory character of his being *in mente, Dasein* becomes free for the authentic choice of his concrete possibilities with the whole of his Being. Man experiences wholeness as an existential quality of choice, made in authentic awareness of his transitoriness and finitude.

As the notions of concern, being-unto-the-end, wholeness, and anticipation are central in Heidegger's ontology of death, so also is the notion of personalness (*Jemeinigkeit*). The personal as a structural determinant of existence figures most significantly in man's confrontation with the possibility of death. Death is disclosed as uniquely my own. Everyone must die his own death. One may, indeed, give his life for another, but this in no way delivers either party from the task of finally shouldering the responsibility of their personal being-unto-death. There is no dying by proxy. To a greater or lesser degree one is involved with the death of others as one participates in death scenes, wakes, burials, and wars; but in all these instances the involvement is that of a simple "being-near" (*dabei sein*), in which the personal character of death has not yet become transparent. The reality of death is disclosed only when it is taken over as a unique and personal possibility. Numerous obligations, undertakings, and tasks are transferable in man's communal world. There is much in our associations with others that can be done by proxy. But in one's being-unto-death any such transference of tasks is excluded. No substitution of roles is possible when it comes to dying. "This possibility of transference breaks down completely when it becomes a matter of replacing that possibility-of-being which constitutes *Dasein* and gives him his wholeness. *No one can take over another's dying.* . . . In each instance *Dasein* has to assume the task of his own death. Death, insofar as it 'is,' is intrinsically my own." [41] Death thus gives an unequivocal expression to the indelibly personal character of human existence and becomes significant as a principle of individuation. It calls *Dasein* back to himself and his unique possibilities which he and he alone can actualize. Kierkegaard elucidated this aspect of death when he linked death with human subjectivity. Death is indelibly my own and therefore non-transferable. Everyone must die his own death.

This death, which is the personal task of everyone, can be viewed either authentically or unauthentically. Heidegger's basic ontological distinction between the authentic and unauthentic mode of being underlies his formulation of an ontology of death. For the most part, man dies in an unauthentic mode of existence, in which he suppresses the reality of death as his personal possibility and task. He finds in the defenses of the "anonymous one" a protective support against the anxiety which reveals death as a certain and imminent phenomenon. Thus he engages in a perpetual retreat from death as an existential reality which involves him personally. He acknowledges the death of an "anonymous one," but his own death remains concealed. Both Kierkegaard and Heidegger, we have seen, develop graphic descriptions of man's constant effort to evade death as a determinant of personal existence. But if *Dasein* for the most part exists unauthentically in the mode of the "anonymous one," retreating from death by losing himself in present diversions, how is one to arrive at a characterization of an authentic being-unto-death? Heidegger develops a twofold characterization of this authentic being-unto-death in his phenomenological analysis. Authenticity involves, first of all, an adequate understanding of death, and, second, a resolute taking over or appropriation of this understanding in an anticipation which frees *Dasein* for his possibilities within the limit of his final possiblity. Adolph Sternberger in his book on Heidegger, which he has fittingly titled *Der verstandene Tod*, expresses this dual character of understanding and activity of appropriation when he describes Heidegger's notion of authentic being-unto-death in terms of a movement from existential conceptualization to anticipatory appropriation.[42] To die authentically is to live in such a way that death is constantly anticipated in one's projects.[43] This in no way implies a separation of understanding and projective activity, which for Heidegger are inextricably bound up at their very source—the care-structure. In authentic understanding *Dasein* is already anticipating his final possibility, and it is only in anticipatory appropriation that he can authentically understand his death. Understanding and anticipatory appropriation are correlated phenomena which mutually contribute to a disclosure of the existential reality of death.

Five characteristics are involved in an authentic understanding of death: (1) Death is a unique (*eigenste*) possibility; (2) Death is non-relative (*unbezüglich*); (3) Death is a possibility which cannot be outstripped (*unüberholbar*); (4) Death is certain (*gewiss*); and (5) Death is indefinite (*unbestimmt*).

Death is *Dasein's* unique possibility. All of his other possibilities can in some sense be duplicated by himself as well as by others. Death permits of no such duplication. It is incontestably unique and irreducibly singular. Only in relating myself to this possibility do I fully become aware of my existence as permeated with concern for my individual destiny. And in this way I become liberated from the bondage of the "anonymous one" in which all possibilities are levelled and generalized. Death when it shows itself in its true form defies any generalization as a possibility among other possibilities. It has a privileged status among them. It has a significance which is uniquely its own. It can be neither duplicated nor replaced.

Death as *Dasein's* unique possibility is non-relative. Not only is death unique among *Dasein's* own possibilities, but it is unique in that it is not transferable to other selves who share his communal world. It is non-relative to the world about him. Death belongs to *Dasein* not as a relative possibility but in an absolute individual manner. It addresses *Dasein* as an individual.[44] He alone can take over his death. No one can perform the task for him. Only when he shoulders his individual responsibility for death does he arrive at an authentic selfhood. In his awareness of death as a non-relative possibility he is thus individuated and brought back to himself after having lost himself in the anonymity of the impersonal one.

Death is a possibility which cannot be outstripped. As long as *Dasein* is, death is present as a future possibility. This gives death a quality of permanence which cannot characterize man's other possibilities. Other possibilities can be outstripped, but death is a possibility which is always receding. It is experienced in the present, to be sure, but not as a possibility which is surmounted. It is experienced as a future possibility hovering over the present. An authentic being-unto-death does not seek to suppress this future possibility, as does the everyday fallen existence, but resolutely faces it by becoming free for it. The anticipation of death frees *Dasein* for his death and makes possible the affirmation of his possibilities which precede his end, thus disclosing his existential wholeness. "In this anticipation of the possibility which cannot be outstripped, in which all projected possibilities are disclosed, there resides the possibility of an existential appropriation of the whole of *Dasein*, i.e., the possibility to exist as a whole in the presence of one's possibility-of-being." [45] Death remains a factor of facticity, but when resolutely faced it is interpenetrated with freedom and chosen as the final possibility which limits all preceding possibilities.

Death as the final possibility is certain. In the unauthentic being-unto-death this certainty never gets beyond an empirical probability based upon an observation of the death of others. Unauthentic existence conceals the certainty of death by viewing it in terms of fatality statistics and thus transforming it into a species of on-hand being. Authentic existence, however, courageously faces the certainty of death as this certainty shows itself in existential awareness. In an authentic being-unto-death the certainty has an existentially apodictic character insofar as death is appropriated as an interior possibility which becomes relevant in every moment of existential decision.

That man must die is certain; when he will die remains indefinite. Kierkegaard had much to say about the existential relevance of the indefiniteness of death, especially insofar as it qualifies every decision with urgency and infinite passion. The authentic self does not view death as an external event which comes to man after he has, so to speak, lived out his years. It appropriates death as an imminent reality, having become aware that as soon as man is born, he is old enough to die. This indefiniteness of death awakens in *Dasein* the anxiety of losing his possibilities of being-in-the-world. He is brought before the nothing-ness of the possibility of no longer being there. The anxiety which was suppressed by the "anonymous one" comes to the foreground in an authentic being-unto-death. Anxiety as the superlative disclosure reveals another essential determinant of man's existence—his being-unto-death.[46]

These five characteristics constitute an authentic understanding of death. The *verstandene Tod* is a death which is unique, non-relative, cannot be outstripped, certain, and indefinite. But death so understood is indissolubly linked with action. *Dasein* understands his death only in the protentional concern by which he anticipates it and thus takes it over. Understanding is always protentional. In his protentional projects *Dasein* becomes "free-unto-death" and assumes responsibility for it. Death becomes a task or a responsibility which he must assume.[47] It in-volves the task of gathering his possibilities in the anticipation of his final limit, resolutely accepting this limit, and becoming free for his possibilities in the context of his existential wholeness as defined by this limit. In each moment he becomes free to appraise himself and decide with the whole of his Being. This being free for his possibilities in each moment of choice, in an awareness of the unremovable limit which, circumscribes his being-in-the-world as an existential whole, is Heideg-ger's interpretation of man's authentic being-unto-death.

Thus Heidegger has sought to delineate an ontology of death in connection with certain basic "existentials" which arise in his interpre-tation of man: concern, personalness, being-unto-the-end, anticipation, wholeness, anxiety, unauthenticity and authenticity. These "existentials" are employed in a description of the structure of man's being-unto-death. The philosophical intention in Heidegger's analysis is to formu-late or sketch an ontology of death as part of a universal philosophy of human finitude. Heidegger makes it clear that his ontological analysis remains intentionally neutral to the material content of any special ontic interpretation of death. He has sought to clarify the ontological-existentialist foundation which is presupposed by any ontic-existential understanding, but he has not taken into his program the task of elucidating death in connection with its biological, psychological, or theological significance. The latter is not a task for ontological analysis, although its findings can and do have ontological significance after a fundamental ontology of existence has been developed. "The existen-tialist analysis," says Heidegger, "is methodologically prior to questions

concerning a biology, psychology, theodicy, and theology of death." [48]
Any theology of death, for example, which arises from man's concrete
religious experience, in which alone it finds its validation, can be clarified through existentialist concepts only after an adequate ontological
understanding of death as a human phenomenon is achieved. Kierkegaard, we have seen, analyzes death in connection with the concrete
religious experience of sin as the "sickness unto death." But in this
special theological understanding death as a mode of existence—as a
"being-unto-death" which can be phenomenologically clarified—is already presupposed. Throughout Kierkegaard's writings such phenomenological clarification is suggested. In his discussion of death in reference
to passion, individuality, certainty, indefiniteness, anxiety, the external
vs. the subjective view, he can be understood as the precursor to
Heidegger's explicit ontology of death in which similar existentialist concepts emerge. Heidegger has sought to abstract from the concrete religious experience of death so as to explicate more clearly the ontological
structures which are universally presupposed. But in this abstraction he
does not prejudice an ontic-existential self-understanding either for or
against a theological resolution. Even the question of man having some
kind of "being" after death is left open. This question falls outside the
scope of a phenomenological ontology. "The ontological analysis of
being-unto-the-end preconceives no existential position concerning
death. When death determines the 'end' of Dasein, i.e., his being-in-
the-world, no ontic decision is made as to whether 'after death' there
is a different, higher, or lower Being possible; whether Dasein lives on
or, indeed, is immortal." [49] Hence, to dismiss Heidegger's ontology of
death as crass materialism and absolute nihilism, as is done by some
interpreters, is to misread Heidegger and misconstrue his whole interpretation of the nature and task of existentialist-ontological analysis.[50]
Heidegger's interpretation of man, as ontology, remains indifferent to any
material content which may be supplied by a religious world-view or
theological conviction. There, man's concrete ethical and religious experience must constitute the court of final appeal.

V

Time and History

1. Time and Human Concern

THE PHILOSOPHY OF HUMAN finitude introduced by existentialism receives its special character through its distinctive understanding of time. The question of the nature of time has of course constituted a philosophical problem from the very beginning of Western thought. The early Greeks apprehended the paramount significance of time in their mythology. Chronos, as the most illustrious of the Titans, is in Greek mythology the first expression of the world's self-creation and the progenitor of the Olympian deities. Plato, in his discussion of the instant as a category of transition or passage in the *Parmenides*, and in his classic formulation of time as a moving image of eternity in the *Timaeus*, placed the problem of time squarely into the philosophical arena. But it was his student and successor, Aristotle, who in his *Physics* bequeathed to Western thought its standard definition of time as the measurement of movement with respect to before and after. This Aristotelian definition, which makes time a cosmological category defining the objectively measured movements of infinite recurrences in nature, became normative for philosophical thinking in the West. The discussions of time in Descartes and Spinoza and in the whole of British empiricism have no intelligibility except within an Aristotelian framework in which the "instants" or "nows" of time are correlated with movement across points in objective space. An abstracted spatio-temporal coordinate becomes the foundation for an interpretation of time. In this abstracted coordinate, temporal instants are surreptitiously identified with spatial points on the basis of which they can be objectively measured, and time becomes an infinite succession of "nows" which follow each other in a definite order of coming to be and passing away. In this objectification and quantification of time, the "nows" are rendered into discrete and isolated instants which have the character of an atomistic present. Temporality thus becomes a static temporality in which time is dissolved into an infinite "dust of instants." [1] Descartes found these discrete instants to be a source of profound embarrassment when it came to explaining the immediately experienced phenomenon of duration, and finally he had to take recourse to a doctrine of perpetual creation in which each instant was perpetually created by God. Occasionalism, as formulated by Descartes' successor, Malebranche, was an inevitable outcome of this approach to time. The "nows" which have past and the "nows" which are yet to be are unified by virtue of their status as occasions for God's creating activity. The skepticism of Hume shattered the Cartesian doctrine of perpetual creation, divested the instantaneous "nows" of their substantial character, and denied any necessary connection between the past and the future. All reality is squeezed into an isolated, present impression which then becomes the foundation for a philosophical skepticism. But in its reaction against the Cartesian doctrine of substance and its spurious theology, Hume's skepticism still moves within the framework of an atomistic understanding of time.

The existentialist interpretation, in its phenomenological description of the time of human concern or time as immediately experienced by the existing subject, has most radically placed into question the traditional understanding of time. At the very basis of the existentialist objection is the conviction that time is ontologically falsified if it is understood as an infinite, quantitative, objective succession of instantaneous "nows." The existentialists grant that this view of time may have legitimate application in the abstracted and objective ontic world of science, but they argue that it cannot characterize man's immediate experience of lived time, or the time of man's primordial being-in-the-world. Time as immediately experienced is the time of human concern. Kierkegaard had already expressed this in his penetrating existential reflections on time, which are often overlooked by his interpreters. And Heidegger has examined the phenomenon of human time in *Sein und Zeit* with a disciplined approach which is unparalleled in Western thought. Sartre and Jaspers have also made the qualitative time of human concern central in their philosophies. Although the understanding of time in relation to human concern received its first explicit formulation in the philosophy of existentialism, it finds an ancestry in the reflections of Augustine and later in the *Lebensphilosophie* of Dilthey and Bergson. Also, it has received a significant, but often overlooked, acknowledgment in the process philosophy of Alfred North Whitehead. In his *Confessions* Augustine interrogated the problem of time as a familiar but virtually inexpressible datum of human experience. If one asks me what time is, I know, says Augustine, but if asked to explain it, I know not. Time for Augustine is an inner qualification of the self in its existential concerns. Bergson, who was born four years after the death of Kierkegaard, argued that the time of human consciousness is immediately experienced as a *durée* and is falsified if it is interpreted with reference to an abstracted spatial continuum. In *The Concept of Nature*, Whitehead, following Bergson, develops a clear distinction between the intellectualized and spatialized time of science and the intuited *durée* of immediate experience. The time which characterizes the durational process of human consciousness must be distinguished, he argues, from objectively calculable or scientifically measurable time. The calculable time of science is properly defined as a series or succession of instantaneous points. This temporal series is a logical abstraction which provides a conceptual clarification for the events of nature but somehow fails to penetrate the *durée* of human consciousness. The event of consciousness is related to time in a special sense. "Mind is not in time or in space in the same sense in which the events of nature are in time. . . . Thus mind is in time and in space in a sense peculiar to itself." [2] Human time or the time of immediate experience has a character uniquely its own.

The relation of time to a human consciousness permeated with passion or concern has been suggested in our foregoing analysis of Kierkegaard's notion of the self and Heidegger's description of *Dasein*. The self as consciousness permeated with passion is understood by Kierkegaard as a structural synthesis of possibility and necessity which is rooted respectively in the temporal moments of future and past. The self is concerned about that which it has been (necessity) and that which it is yet to become (possibility). Consciousness of being a self involves arriving from a past and moving into a future. Heidegger's analysis of the structures of concern corresponds closely to the analysis of Kierkegaard. Concern is constituted by the three structural moments of existentiality, facticity, and fallenness. Existentiality defines *Dasein* as protentional, or as existing in advance of himself in his future possibilities. Facticity characterizes *Daesin* as already abandoned in a situation, and thus indicates the temporal mode of the past. Fallenness is the determinant of *Daesin* made possible through existence as presence. Temporality is thus disclosed as the ontological meaning of the structure of human concern. Concern is qualified by futurity, pastness, and presence. The temporal nature of this concern is presupposed in the immediate experience of anxiety, the reality of death, and anticipatory resolution (*vorlaufenede Entschlossenheit*). Kierkegaard had already shown that anxiety is primarily disclosed in man's confrontation with his future possibilities which call him to decision. Futurity makes possible the experience of anxiety by disclosing the "not yet" of one's existence, which holds a fascination because of its possibilities of creative self-actualization but which also threatens the self because actualization involves a loss of the self which I presently am. However, pastness is also a condition of anxiety insofar as past misfortunes, neglected opportunities, estranged relations with others, continue as repeatable possibilities for present existence. So also death as a factor in human concern presupposes a being that is qualified by time. The reality of death is experienced only through anticipatory understanding and appropriation in which temporality as the original ontological meaning of existence is made apparent. The old Latin fable which Heidegger used to elucidate the Being of man as concern now achieves its full significance. It is Saturn (time) as judge who pronounces the final verdict in regard to the original Being of the creature which concern has formed.[3]

The relation of time and concern is manifested in all of *Dasein's* everyday projects, and it is only through an examination of quotidian time, says Heidegger, that a proper or authentic understanding of time can be achieved. In his everyday existence man finds that he must cope with time and arrange his projects according to it.[4] He speaks of "having time," "taking time," "losing time," or "needing time." In his immediate practical and personal concerns *Dasein* is always planning, contriving, and reflecting as to how he can best realize his undertakings. In these undertakings time reveals itself as time *for* this or that activity. This "time for" is always related in some manner to the three modes of futurity, pastness, and presence. *Dasein*, in his everyday concerns, says: *then* this is to be done, *before* that work is finished, and *now* this has to be tried once more since it was not done *at that time*.[5] The "then" expresses concern in anticipation of the future. The "now" expresses concern in the mode of presence. And the "at that time" expresses concern in reference to the past. The practical and personal concerns of *Dasein* always have a temporal direction. Concern is grounded in time.

Sartre has developed a theory of human time in his *L'Être et le Néant* which is akin to that of Heidegger in that it binds together time and the projects of the *pour soi*. The relation of consciousness to itself, to its environmental world, and to others is always in some sense temporalized. "Time separates me from myself, from what I have been, from what I wish to be, from what I wish to do, from things, and from others. Time is chosen for the practical measuring of distance; one is half an hour from this town, an hour from another town; it will take three days to complete this work, etc." [6] But prior to the more careful and disciplined descriptions of the nature of time in relation to human concern which are found in Heidegger and Sartre, Kierkegaard had already suggested an existential view of time which could become normative for all succeeding existentialist thinkers. The subjective thinker who seeks to understand himself in his existence can properly do so only after he has become aware that he must reckon with time. Kierkegaard speaks of the existing individual as one who must "strive with time." [7] He must contend with the time of his future as well as with the time of his past. He lives in memory and in hope, and thus he experiences the whole of his existence in its temporal qualification. Existence is constituted by future possibilities which I must relate to my present projects and by past possibilities which either have been authentically chosen or which have been wasted and which are now so many phantoms that haunt my existence and cannot be driven away.[8]

Kierkegaard directs his attention, as do Heidegger and Sartre, to the time of immediate experience—time as encountered by the existential subject. This immediately experienced time, Kierkegaard argues, must be clearly and consistently differentiated from an abstract, quantitative, and measured time which has to be objectively spatialized in order to be known. The time of existence is falsified if it is visualized abstractly and placed into an objectified spatio-temporal coordinate. Time, thus understood, is transformed into an infinite succession of instantaneous "nows" that are coordinated with spatial points. Commonly we think of time as precisely such a succession, says Kierkegaard. We view it as a process of going-by, which may properly be understood as a definition of time in general. But this is not the particular time which the self experiences in its concrete immediacy. As the reality of one's death is concealed if it is thought of as "something in general," so also a proper understanding of time does not permit of a generalized standard which is external to the experience of time itself. By defining time as a general process or continuing infinite succession, we already separate time into discrete units of past, present, and future. These discrete units are then understood as constituting an infinite succession of "nows" which succeed each other in a definite order of coming to be and passing away. But such a definition of time is foreign to immediate experience. The time of immediate experience has in itself no discrete, spatialized succession of "nows." When we define time, says Kierkegaard, "it seems plausible to define it also as the present, the past and the future. However, this distinction is incorrect, if one means by it that this is implied in time itself." [9] We tend to divide time into a series of discrete units or parts because we think of time abstractly and view it in terms of a visual representation in such a way that time becomes identified with a species of spatial extensiveness. The moments of time are thus understood as having the same character as spatial points on an extended continuum. Time and space become identified. "For abstract thinking time and space are absolutely identical (nacheinander and nebeneinander), and they become so for visual representation. . . ." [10] But the time of human concern is not an abstractly visualized and spatialized time. Human time, as Augustine suggested, is time experienced concretely in the subjective reflections of the existing individual. If we divide time into a succession of discrete "nows," says Kierkegaard, this is "because we spatialize a moment, but thereby the infinite succession is brought to a standstill, and that is because one introduces a visual representation, visualizing time instead of thinking it." [11]

Kierkegaard's continuing argument against the objectification of time through a quantitative reductivism has become a distinctive characteristic of all varieties of existentialism which grew out of his new approach to human reality. Heidegger has given most rigorous attention to the distinction between objectified time and the time of human concern and has carried through the implications of this distinction for a new interpretation of man. He has shown how the objectified calendrical and clock time, based on the measurement of sequences in nature, is a restricted and limited kind of world-time insofar as it is only the temporal foundation for non-human intramundane beings—i.e., the region of tools and utensils (at-handness) and the region of objects and things (on-handness).[12] It applies peculiarly to man's environmental world (*Umwelt*). But the *Umwelt*, as we have seen, is only one horizon of man's being-in-the-world. And if the being of human existence is falsified when it is understood in terms of categories which apply to non-human reality, then it is no surprise to find that Heidegger insists that human time or the time of human concern cannot be reduced to the inner temporality of intramundane reality. Unfortunately this objectified view commonly takes precedence in our understanding of time; hence Heidegger refers to it as the common view of time. The distinguishing trait of this common view is that it understands time as an endless, passing, irreversible succession of "nows." [13] These "nows" are necessarily understood with reference to the mode of on-handness, and consequently they themselves are viewed as strange, objectified, on-hand entities. "Although not expressly stated, the 'nows' are on hand as though they were things and are thus conceived ontologically in the horizon of the idea of on-handness." [14] "Nows" become transformed into things. Those that have gone by we call the past. Those which are coming we call the future. And then there is always the present "now" which is forever slipping into the past. Thus, as Kierkegaard had already maintained, the common conception of time breaks up the temporal complex into discrete and permanent entities which succeed each other in a definite order. Each has a fixed position in the order of passing and coming. Some are in the past; some are in the future; and one is always somehow present. "Nows" are viewed as things which in their order of succession constitute an unending flowing stream. Within its restricted limits this common understanding of time has a natural validity. It loses its natural validity only when it claims to provide the one possible horizon for the understanding of time.[15] Just as the cosmological categories of substance, quantity, relation, etc. legitimately apply to the region of non-human beings, so also the common interpretation of time properly characterizes this region of beings. However, when this common view becomes normative for an understanding of the time of human concern or the time of *Dasein*, then it takes on the qualification of unauthenticity. A marine rock formation, to use an example, is a substance which "stands-in-itself" and can properly be said to occur at a point in geological time, but human reality is not a *substance* but an *ek-sistence* which "stands-out-of-itself," temporalized in its very Being. Man does not occur *in* time but rather *has* time. He exists as a temporalization. Time provides the ontological meaning of his protentional, retentional, and present concerns.

2. The Ecstatic Character of Time

The distinctive aspect of the time of human concern, in contradistinction to quantified and objectified calendrical and clock time, is its ecstatic character. Existential time is an ecstatic unity in which the future, past, and present are apprehended as inseparable phases of human existence. Future, past, and present are what Heidegger calls interpenetrating *ecstasies* rather than juxtaposed dimensions defined within an objectified spatio-temporal coordinate.[16] Or as Sartre has expressed it, they are "structured moments of an original synthesis." [17] Existing as a field of concern, man is temporalized as an interrelated complex of future, past, and present. He exists retentionally as well as protentionally and is always confronted with present choices. The ecstasies of time thus become determinants or constituents of existence itself. Therefore confusion inevitably results when one speaks of man being "in" time in the sense that one conceives of an object or utensil continuing in time without losing its self-identity. Properly speaking, man *exists as time*, temporalizing himself as future, past, and present. The structures of human concern are temporal moments. In his existentiality man is anticipating his future possibilities through his protentional understanding. Facticity, which is rooted in the past, binds man retentionally to that which he has been. Fallenness indicates man's existence as presence. Human existence is ecstatic, radiating into a future and a past, both of which interpenetrate the present. "Temporality temporalizes itself fully in each ecstasy, i.e., in the ecstatic unity of the complete temporalizing of temporality there is grounded the wholeness of the structural complex of existentiality, facticity, and fallenness, which comprise the unity of the structure of concern." [18] The original ecstatic unity of time permits no separation of the ecstasies. The past is not earlier, nor is the future later. There is no succession in a given direction. The past, present, and future are there, so to speak, all at once. The ecstasies are inseparable phases or directions of human concern. Walter Biemel in his interpretation of Heidegger speaks of a coexistence of the ecstasies as an ensemble of relations which mutually imply each other. [19] In the time of human concern the past is still present and can be projected as a future possibility. The existential past is not a now which is gone and no longer real. The past still holds significance for my practical and personal projects. It retains its reality. The existential past thus has a peculiar character. It is never "gone by" (*vergangen*). Properly speaking, it "has been" (*ist gewesen*). Heidegger's distinction between *Verganenheit* and *Gewesenheit* is not simply a semantical sleight of hand which conveys no real difference. It expresses a modal distinction in the structure of reality itself. Only artifacts and objects can be classified as having "gone by," and, as Kierkegaard had observed, commonly we think of time simply as a process of "going-by." But the time of ecstatic existence qualifies the past differently. My past is that which has been, but this past is still part of my present existence which I must appropriate and live in a certain manner.[20] As the existential past is *still* present, so the existential future is *already* present. In each decision my future possibilities impinge upon and penetrate into my present. The past is not a thing which was real once and has now ceased to be. Nor is the future a thing which will become real during the "course of time" at a later date. The future is already real, constantly calling me to decision. In the time of existence the past and the future are interrelated and intersect the present.

Interpreters of existentialist thought often overlook the fact that the concept of ecstatic time as systematically formulated by Heidegger was already made central in the philosophy of Kierkegaard. In *Either/Or*, Kierkegaard discusses the interrelatedness of the past and future with the present in connection with Hegel's teaching on the unhappy consciousness. Hegel had taught that the unhappy person is a person who is never present to himself. He is absent from himself either in the past or in the future. Hegel was right in thus circumscribing the realm of the unhappy consciousness, says Kierkegaard, but he failed to see that the phenomenon involves a relationship of existence rather than simply a relationship of thought. Hegel approached the phenomenon through objectifying categories and thus transformed the time of the unhappy consciousness into an object of pure thought. As Kierkegaard puts it, he "beheld the kingdom from afar off." [21] Kierkegaard, considering himself a native inhabitant of the realm, who has not forsaken his existential homeland for a haven in the rarefied heights of pure speculation, seeks to describe the unhappy consciousness as it shows itself in the immediacy of existence. Kierkegaard's existential phenomenology of the unhappy consciousness delineates two major types or expressions of unhappiness. There is an unhappy consciousness which cannot find itself in the future. The self is unhappy because it has nothing for which to hope. It fails to relate itself to the possibilities which it can become and which already constitute it in its present mode. The future remains unacknowledged and is thus severed from the very being of consciousness. The other type of unhappiness is when the individual is absent from himself in memory. He is unable to find himself in his past. His past becomes something which, in Heidegger's terminology, is simply "gone by" and which is no longer understood to qualify his present essence as what he is by virtue of having been. In this type of unhappiness the past has become existentially irrelevant. It is not taken over into the present concerns of the existing individual.

Thus the unhappy consciousness is a consciousness which is lost to itself either in memory or in hope. Kierkegaard's phenomenology of the unhappy consciousness in *Either/Or* reminds us of his phenomenology of despair in *The Sickness Unto Death*. In both cases there is a dissolution of the temporal interrelatedness of the structural moments of selfhood. As the self which succumbs to necessity is in despair, so the unhappy consciousness is unhappy because it is present to itself only in memory; and as the self which succumbs to possibility is in despair, so the unhappy consciousness is present to itself only in hope. For a unified consciousness to be achieved, or for the self truly to find itself, the reality of both the future and the past must be acknowledged and appropriated in their unified relevance. "In order that the man of hope may be able to find himself in the future, the future must have reality, or, rather, it must have reality for him; in order that the man of memory may find himself in the past, the past must have had reality for him." [22] In the unified consciousness the reality of the future and the reality of the past are integrated, and time is experienced as an interrelated and inseparable unity. Futurity, pastness, and presence are constitutive elements or moments of the self as such. Time as thus experienced is not a succession of instantaneous "nows." The three modes of time are ecstasies or directions of selfhood out of which and into which the self lives. This does not mean, however, that a harmonious or unified consciousness in which the temporal directions of selfhood are perfectly integrated is a historical possibility for the existing individual. Kierkegaard's insights into the ambiguous and fractured character of existential reality excludes any doctrine of mediation in which the ideal and the real are taken up in a reconciled synthesis. Hence, the moment that Hegel pronounces the doctrine of mediation in his *Science of Logic*, he becomes a comic figure by removing himself from existence as it is historically lived. Had Hegel revoked his *Science of Logic* and remained true to his initial insight that history is not the domain of the happy consciousness, Kierkegaard might well have proclaimed him to be the second Socrates of Western thought.

The existentialist understanding of time with both Kierkegaard and Heidegger constitutes a departure from the objective view in which time is spatialized and conceived as an infinite succession of "nows." The time of human concern has an ecstatic character. Man experiences the time of his existence not as a flow of instants but rather as directions of his being, held in memory and anticipated in hope. Temporality as the ground determinant of our being makes possible the remembrance of our past and the anticipation of our future in the existential present. Erich Frank cogently expresses this ecstatic view of time when he writes: "Our subjective existence is essentially that process through which the memory of the past and the anticipation of the future are fused into the sense of the present." [23] The past is not a series of "nows" which have gone by and are *no longer relevant* to my present existence, nor is the future a coming series of "nows" which are *not yet relevant* to my present existence. Whitehead with his process philosophy, although differing from existentialism on certain basic points of doctrine, also questions the traditional separation of the modes of temporality. In his *Adventures of Ideas* Whitehead assuredly approximates an existentialist approach to time when he writes: "It is evident that the future certainly is something for the present. . . . Cut away the future, and the present collapses, emptied of its proper content. Immediate existence requires the insertion of the future in the crannies of the present." [24]

The existentialist view of time as ecstatic existence grants a priority or priviliged status to the future. The future has a primal significance because man's understanding of himself as possibility, finite freedom, anxiety, and being-unto-death is conditioned first and foremost by futurity. The upsurge of the self-awareness of being-in-the-world is rendered possible only through the confrontation of a future. Both Kierkegaard and Heidegger have made the doctrine of the priority of the future central in their analysis. On this point Sartre disagrees with both Kierkegaard and Heidegger. Sartre argues that no ecstasy has any ontological priority over the other, and that if a priority of any kind is to be granted, this must be conferred upon the present ecstasy rather than on the future as Heidegger does.[25] Sartre apparently does not realize that in accentuating the present ecstasy he is falling back into a common view of time which tends to dissolve all reality into a present, defined either as an instant or as a specious present. For as Heidegger has rightly shown, a central distinction between the common view and the existentialist view is that the former ascribes priority to the present and the latter to the future.[26] Thus the common understanding of time becomes the ontological foundation for an unauthentic existence in which human life becomes solidified in its present preoccupations and concerns. Authentic existence, which acknowledges and takes over its future as its primary direction, is rooted in existential and ecstatic time.

Kierkegaard's most explicit discussion of the priority of the future in an existential understanding of time is found in *The Concept of Anxiety*. Here he writes: "In a certain sense the future signifies more than the present and the past; for the future is in a sense the whole of which the past is a part, and in a sense the future may signify the whole." [27] In its existential projects the self experiences the future as already present and apprehends the past in terms of the repeatable possibilities held for the future. One does not first experience the past and then become conscious of the future, but from the very beginning the future is already there. It is the future that posits the past. Hence it is proper to say that the future precedes the past rather than that the past precedes the future. This primal significance of the future, says Kierkegaard, never received proper recognition by the Greeks. Inasmuch as the Greeks took time seriously at all, they defined it as time past.

They understood time without "relation to the present and the future, but defined it, like the definition of time in general, as a going by." [28] The philosophical basis for this understanding of time as time past resides in Plato's doctrine of recollection. Kierkegaard, as we shall see later, replaces Plato's category of recollection with the concept of repetition.

Like Kierkegaard, Heidegger argues that the future is the primary ecstasy in the time of human concern.[29] We have already seen that existentiality is the primary structural element of concern. *Dasein* is primarily possibility-of-being. His essence resides in his "ek-sistence," which means that he is always standing out into his possibilities or into that which he can become. Man lives primarily out of the future. Quite clearly, the future as an ecstatic mode of existence has a meaning different from that of the future conceived as a moment which is not yet real. The future as an integral constituent of the Being of *Dasein* is *most* real. It expresses the "coming" (*Kunft*) character of man by virtue of which he is able to "come to" (*Zukunft*) his authentic possibilities.[30] *Dasein* is always already stretched out into a future which constitutes his primary direction of existence.

The assertion that the future is primary in no way denies the reality of the past. An existential understanding of time gives priority to the future but also affirms the reality of the past. The past is not a series of "nows" which have gone by and are no longer real. The past still holds an existential significance. We have already noted Heidegger's distinction between the common understanding of the past as vanished and the ecstatic past as having been which is part of the Being of *Dasein* as long as he is. *Dasein* holds his past in his protentional understanding and seeks to repeat its possibilities in his existential projects. John Wild in his interpretation of Heidegger has formulated a clear statement of Heidegger's view on time in the following comment: "My past is not a punctual now that was once but is finished and gone. As long as I am, I have my past as that which I have been. It is not something once there, but now finished. It is not finished because it never was all there. Even when I try to forget and evade it, it still weighs on me and limits my action. Past possibilities may be maintained and repeated by choice in this moment." [31] Again, it was Kierkegaard who first emphasized the reality of the past in connection with his concepts of anxiety and repetition. "The past over which I am supposed to be in anxiety must stand in a relation of possibility to me.

If I am in anxiety over a past misfortune, this is not insofar as it is past, but insofar as it may be repeated, i.e., become future." [32] The past as the field of my actualized possibilities constitutes the necessity of my nature. But this necessity is not irrevocably fixed. It is always qualified by possibility. This means that my past is never completed or finished. It always holds possibilities which may be repeated in the future. If I am in anxiety over a past fault or a past misfortune, my anxiety discloses the indubitable fact that the fault or misfortune is not outside my existential reality because it is past. These determinants of my having been remain as repeatable possibilities of my future as long as I am. Man could not experience remorse or any other disquietude which has a retentional direction if past experience had no relevance for the present. The past gnaws into the present via the future and conditions all my existential projects.

3. Contemporaneity, Repetition, and the Moment

The notions of contemporaneity, repetition, and the moment play an important role in an existentialist theory of time. The existential significance of these notions has already been suggested in our foregoing analysis of Kierkegaard and Heidegger. We must now examine each of these crucial concepts and discern their particular significance for the time of immediate experience, as it is contrasted with an objectified and quantified calendrical or clock time.

The notion of contemporaneity constitutes an explicit rejection of the externalization and objectification of the past. Calendrical time transforms the past into a series of objectified "nows" which in the order of succession go over into a fixed and irrevocable past. Existentially, however, past events are contemporaneous in that they continue as present possibilities. The past is held in memory not as a completed set of circumstances but as a condition for present action. The meaning of contemporaneity is discussed by Kierkegaard in the *Philosophical Fragments* in connection with the theological problem of the contemporary disciple. There is no disciple at second hand. Every disciple is contemporaneous with God's manifestation of himself in time. "When the believer is the believer and knows God through having received the condition from God himself, every successor must receive the condition from God himself in precisely the same sense, and cannot receive it at second hand; for if he did, this second hand would have to be the hand of God himself, and in that case there is no question of a second hand. But a successor who receives the condition from God himself is a contemporary, a real contemporary; a privilege enjoyed only by the believer but also enjoyed by every believer." [33] Kierkegaard develops the same theme in his book *Training in Christianity*. He defines a Christian as one who is contemporaneous with Christ. Clearly the significance of the Christ-event does not reside in an objectified past. The flow of calendrical time which has elapsed since the disciples' first encounter with Christ is existentially irrelevant. The cardinal significance of the Christ-event is that it is a contemporaneous reality in the personal decisions of the Christian. Christ's coming is not to be identified with an objectified and fixed historical incident. It expresses a religious qualification of human existence, made possible through divine revelation, which is existentially apprehended as a repeatable possibility. Christ "came" and he "comes again" in the decisive historical action of the religious consciousness. The Christ-event can become a present reality in my personal decisions.[34]

The ethico-religious significance of the phenomenon of contemporaneity is also discussed by Kierkegaard in connection with the doctrine of forgiveness in his *Gospel of Suffering*. Contemporaneity makes possible the experience of forgiveness by eliminating an objectification of the past. The melancholy man is in a state of melancholy because he is unable to forget his guilt. It has become part of his memory and weighs upon him as a *character indelibilis*. But contemporaneity continually reopens his past to new meanings. His past is not irrevocably fixed and finished. When the melancholy man becomes a believer, he still remembers his guilt, but he now can remember it as forgiven guilt. Through forgiveness a new determinant is added which transforms the meaning of the past. The guilt is taken into his present experience in such a way that its meaning is transformed into a creative possibility. This places man into a new stage of existence.[35]

The concept of repetition, like that of contemporaneity with which it is inextricably linked, occupies a central place in Kierkegaard's reflections on time. In his book *Repetition*, Kierkegaard proclaims this concept as the new category which needs to be brought to light. As the

Greeks "taught that all knowledge is a recollection, so will modern philosophy teach that the whole of life is repetition." Repetition, continues Kierkegaard, as the new category is "the interest of metaphysics," the "solution in every ethical view," and the *conditio sine qua non* of every dogmatic problem." [36]

The metaphysical import of the concept of repetition resides in its explanation of the relation between the Eleatic School and Heraclitus on the problem of being and becoming. Only through the employment of the concept of repetition can we account for becoming. The Greek concept of recollection was never able to explain this most basic fact of reality. Recollection is always directed backwards, and consequently life is understood only in terms of the past. Repetition, on the other hand, is directed toward the future. It understands life as being "recollected forwards." When the Greeks advanced their doctrine of recollection, they simply asserted that "all that is has been." When Kierkegaard describes life as repetition, he affirms that "existence which has been now becomes." [37] It is in this sense that repetition explains the fundamental dialectical relationship between being and becoming. The existing self *is* that which it has been (necessity qualified by pastness) and *becomes* that which it is not yet (possibility qualified by futurity). Kierkegaard's insight into the inherent limitations of the Greek concept of recollection, which became normative not only for Greek philosophy but literature and religion as well, is worthy of careful consideration. As interpreters of Greek thought have been quick to recognize, the concept of fate with its determinant of necessity is the very presupposition of Greek culture. This concept of fate, properly understood as necessity without possibility, has its expression in Greek religion when the gods determine the destinies of men, in Greek tragedy when the tragic hero is caught in a set of circumstances over which he has no control, and in Greek philosophy when the doctrine of recollection teaches that reality is solidified in a substantial past. For this reason the Greek view cannot account for a concrete becoming and an existential freedom. These phenomena require a new concept—repetition.

As the Greeks were unable to explain becoming or movement with their category of recollection, so also Hegel's logical categories of mediation and reconciliation are irreparably poverty-stricken in coping with this basic phenomenon of reality. Logic cannot admit of movement, because logical entities are simply states of being. They are determinations of essence which are necessary and given and hence cannot account for something becoming that which it is not yet.[38] Consequently, everything that Hegel has to say about becoming and movement in his *Science of Logic* is illusory. He interprets reality in terms of a timeless, rational process in which a logical necessity rules. Becoming for Hegel is simply a becoming in pure thought in which opposites are posited and combined into higher unities. But in this timeless and logical becoming of pure thought, the concrete temporal becoming of the existing self is lost. Hegel's system lacks the category of repetition which alone can account for the temporal movement of the self towards its future possibilities.

Repetition not only supplies the primary concept for metaphysics but also provides the conceptual clarification for ethical and religious self-understanding. Through repetition, past possibilities of action become future possibilities for the ethically existing subject and are repeated in the moment of decision. The act of choosing is the fullest expression of the ethical, for it is in the act of choice that the self achieves its unity and integrity. And choosing one's self always involves the choice of repeatable past possibilities. Through repetition, writes Kierkegaard, the "discord in my nature is resolved, I am again unified." In repetition I take up my past, project it as a future possibility, and thus am able to make an authentic choice with the whole of my being. Repetition makes authentic ethical choices possible. "He who would only hope is cowardly, he who would only recollect is voluptuary, but he who wills repetition is a man, and the more expressly he knows how to make his purpose clear, the deeper he is a man." [39]

Kierkegaard makes use of the Biblical stories of Job and Abraham as illustrations of the specifically religious significance of the concept of repetition. Through repetition the believer receives the gift of God in a new immediacy. Job had lost everything to the point of despair. Hope was about to vanish and despair to conquer. But at that very point where human understanding recognized its limitations and human striving its frailties, the action of God became manifest, and Job received double. "Job is blessed and has received everything *double*. This is what is called *repetition*." [40] Likewise, in the story of Abraham and Isaac Kierkegaard finds that repetition provides the guiding motif. Through faith Abraham miraculously receives Isaac, and by constantly repeating his faith he receives him again, after having "lost" him in the intended act of sacrifice. Abraham is contrasted with the tragic hero, who, incapable of repetition, merely renounces in an act of resignation.

This was an option which was open for Abraham. He could have sacrificed himself in an act of noble resignation and thus fulfilled the role of a tragic hero who succumbs to fate or the necessity of the past. But Abraham willed repetition through an act of faith. Believing firmly that God's promise in Isaac as the future leader of His people would be fulfilled, Abraham transformed destiny through his act of faith in which he willed repetition. "Through a double movement he had returned to his first state, and therefore he received Isaac more gladly than the first time." [41]

The significance of the moment in Kierkegaard's existentialism has already become apparent. It is in the moment that the individual unifies and integrates himself in the act of choosing, and it is in the moment that the eternal transfigures time. Throughout the whole of Kierkegaard's writings the moment has this twofold ethico-religious meaning. The moment makes possible the attainment of authentic selfhood, for which the religious condition is the manifestation of God in time. The moment is the "time" for decision. This decision receives its proper expression only in the ethico-religious stage of existence. Although the aestheticist experiences the moment in the aesthetic stage, he experiences it unauthentically. The romantic lover, Kierkegaard's prime example of the aestheticist, lives in the moment, but he can experience it only once, and he experiences it in an abstraction from existence. The moment for him becomes simply an erotic present which neither binds together a past nor anticipates a future. He seeks to squeeze all reality into the erotic present which functions as a discrete, objectified now, cut off from the past and the future. The romantic lover lives his life as though it were an infinite succession of instants, each lapsing into a past which is no longer real. In romantic love the moment is transformed into an instant which renders repetition impossible. Conjugal love, which exemplifies the ethical stage and which is contrasted with the romantic love of the aesthetic stage, is able authentically to apprehend the moment because it strives for repetition. The "ideal husband is not one who is such once in his life but one who every day is such." [42] The central determinant of the ethical stage of existence is resolute choice. The romantic lover experiments with love but does not commit himself in marriage. The married man, representing ethical existence, has made a commitment through resolute choice and has thus liberated himself from a dispersion in the immediacy of the present. In the moment of decision the self is unified and centralized. The aestheticist is always "eccentric" in that he has his center existentially outside himself. The ethical man has his center within himself. The aestheticist loses himself in the erotic present, retreating from his future and forgetting his past. The ethical man lives in anticipation and memory, projecting his future and repeating his past. He is a unified self because he holds together his future and his past in the moment of decision.

Thus the ethical significance of the moment is that it binds together the existential future and the existential past. But this ethical significance is for Kierkegaard ultimately grounded in the religious confrontation of eternity in time. The moment becomes the occasion for God's action in time and history. It is in the moment, says Kierkegaard, "in which time and eternity touch one another, thereby positing the *temporal,* where time is constantly intersecting eternity and eternity constantly permeating time." [43] In the moment eternity transfigures time. Thus the moment has both a horizontal-ethical quality, in that it makes possible the ecstatic unification of past and future, and a vertical-religious quality, in that it provides the "when" or the opportune "time" for the manifestation of the eternal in the temporal. Hence we can speak of the moment as it is qualified and transfigured by eternity as the "fullness of time." Kierkegaard has sought to elucidate this meaning of the moment in his *Philosophical Fragments.* "And now the moment. Such a moment has a peculiar character. It is brief and temporal indeed, like every moment; it is transient as all moments are; it is past, like every moment in the next moment. And yet it is decisive, and filled with the eternal. Such a moment ought to have a distinctive name; let us call it the *Fullness of Time.*" [44] It is hardly accidental that one of the most powerful Christological symbols in the history of Christian thought has been the symbol of the *kairos,* meaning in the original Greek, "right time." [45] Christ comes *en kairo,* which means that he comes at the opportune or right moment—in the moment in which time is fulfilled and eternity made present. This concept of the fullness of time appearing in the opportune moment, observes Kierkegaard, is that around which everything turns in Christianity. God enters time in the "right moment" and makes all things new through a transfiguration of man's temporality in such a manner that he apprehends the eternal meaning of his temporality as he exists it. Thus the man who passionately chooses the moment has, as Kierkegaard puts it, truly conquered time, and solved "the great riddle of living in eternity and yet hearing the hall clock strike." [46] Temporality is not annulled, as in Hegel. It is transfigured and preserved in eternity. Man remains a temporal being as long as he is, but this temporality can be qualified by the presence of eternity in the opportune moment of decision.

The moment is thus elucidated by Kierkegaard in its relation both to time and to eternity. In its relation to time it is that which binds together the past and the future, making possible a unification or centralization of the structures of selfhood. Quite clearly, the moment thus understood must be sharply contrasted with the instant conceived as a "now" within an objective time process. The moment is an *existential* presence, not an *instantaneous* presence. In its relation to eternity the moment is understood as an existential presence qualified by a transtemporal meaning. Both the concept of eternity and the concept of the moment retain an indelible existential character in Kierkegaard's thought. Eternity is neither an objectified endless succession, nor is it a dialectical timelessness. Eternity is a qualification of existence which transfigures the temporality of the self in the moment of decision. Kierkegaard has explicitly rejected the meaning of eternity as endless time, or what Hegel had called "bad infinity." Kierkegaard shares Hegel's criticism on this point. But he is equally critical of Hegel's own view of eternity as a dialectical timelessness in which eternity is simply annulled temporal succession. Driven to formulate a system in which mediation constitutes the final stage, Hegel mediated the eternal and the temporal and thus lost both. The initial impulse of this doctrine of mediation can already be discerned, says Kierkegaard, in Plato's abstract conception of the instant. In his dialogue of *Parmenides*, the instant is defined as the category of transition which lies between movement and rest, somehow accounts for their passage, but does not itself have a temporal character. The instant remains somehow exempt from the impingement or bite of time. "The instant appears now to be that strange being . . . which lies between movement and repose, without occupying any time; and to this and out of this 'the moving' passes over into rest, and the 'reposing' into movement. The instant therefore becomes the general category of transition . . . , but nevertheless the instant remains a mute abstraction." [47] Plato thus places the instant outside time and confers upon it a character which keeps it immune to transition. In another passage of the dialogue, continues Kierkegaard, we become aware of the consequences of viewing the instant as such an abstraction.

It becomes identified with the eternal. The instant as the present "now" lies between the "was" and the "will be" as the eternal present. It becomes neither "older nor younger" but remains eternally the same. Plato's abstract way of viewing the instant has reached its logical conclusion in the doctrine of mediation of Hegelianism. In modern philosophy (i.e., Hegelianism), we can see, says Kierkegaard, that "the abstraction culminates in 'pure being,' but pure being is the most abstract expression for eternity. . . ." The Hegelian mediation thus reaches its fulfillment when "eternity and the instant signify the same thing." [48] For Hegel and Plato, the instant is understood as a timeless "now." For Kierkegaard the existential moment is time bound, occurring within the temporal warp and woof of finite, human existence. The moment, understood as the concrete "time" for decisive action rather than as an abstract instant, remains within time but can also become the condition for the presence of the eternal. Eternity and time are not mediated. They are existentially experienced in their qualitative disjunction. The eternal remains qualitatively distinct from the temporal but enters the temporal in the opportune moment for decision. Eternity is a qualification and transfiguration of temporal existence. This transfiguration of time cannot be expressed through the rational categories of a science of logic. Its expression demands the use of paradox. The advent of the eternal in time is paradoxical in that it is contrary to the opinions of pure reason. The paradox of the eternal intersecting temporality in the existential moment has its fullest expression in Christ as the "Supreme Paradox." [49] In Hegel's philosophy of mediation the paradoxical character of the relation of time and eternity is removed. Kierkegaard places the paradox back into existence and makes it the pivotal notion of the religious consciousness.

We have been examining the significance of contemporaneity, repetition, and the moment in Kierkegaard's theory of human time. These same concepts also play an important role in the philosophies of Jaspers and Heidegger. Existence for Jaspers has its most vital center in the historically lived moment. To exist means to deepen, penetrate, and involve one's self in the moment in such a manner that the past and the future become relevant components of a fulfilled present.[50] So also in Heidegger's analytics of *Dasein* the moment is given a central place. The moment is the crucial time of decision in which *Dasein* resolutely shoulders his responsibility and unifies the temporal ecstasies of his existence. "In resolve the present is not only extricated from its dispersion in the proximate concerns of *Dasein* but is held in unity with the future and the past. This present, held in an authentic temporality and, therefore, an *authentic present,* is called the moment." [51] This authentic present (*Augenblick*), Heidegger cautions us, must not be confused with the unauthentic solidifying present (*Gegenwärtigen*), which is still bound to a common understanding of the present as a discrete, on-hand "now." The moment is not to be confused with a "now." The "now" as a temporal phenomenon belongs only to the inner temporality which characterizes non-human intramundane beings. And to understand the temporality of *Dasein* in terms of a succession of instants is, again, to deprive *Dasein* of his distinctive human and existential character. The moment of authentic temporality is never simply "now"; rather, it is the existential bond between past and future possibilities which are anticipated in a protentional understanding and realized in resolute choice. What Heidegger has done in his distinction between the authentic and unauthentic present is to ontologize Kierkegaard's ethical distinction between the erotic present, exemplified by the undecided and uncommitted romantic lover of the aesthetic stage, and the decisive moment as it figures in the life of the committed, married man who has made the transition to the ethical stage.

Authenticity and unauthenticity, however, are not merely possible modes of relating one's self to the present. This all-important distinction in the Heideggerian analysis applies equally to the other two ecstasies of human temporality. For the most part *Dasein* exists unauthentically in his projects of concern. Fallenness is an original condition of being-in-the-world, and in his state of fallenness man has forfeited his existential uniqueness to the everydayness, mediocrity, levelling, and publicity of the "anonymous one." This forfeiture involves not only an unauthentic attitude toward the present but an unauthentic attitude toward the past and future as well. The unauthentic attitude toward the past is one of oblivion (*Vergessenheit*).[52] In unauthentic existence the past is no longer held in memory. Man exists as though he had no facticity, as though he were pure possibility. This unauthentic attitude toward the past receives its conceptual clarification through the common understanding of time, in which the past is viewed as a series of objectified instants which have gone by and are no longer real. The authentic modification of this original unauthenticity has its ontological foundation in the concept of time as ecstatic existence, in which the past remains as a continuing direction of human existence and can be appropriated in an act of repetition. As Kierkegaard earlier maintained, in repetition I take over my past as that which I have been and still in a sense am. In authentic choice I must choose with the *whole* of my being, and this involves choosing in the light of my past. Thus, as there is both an authentic and an unauthentic way of relating myself to the present, so there is an authentic and unauthentic way of relating myself to the past.

Finally, the future can be apprehended and appraised authentically or unauthentically. In unauthentic existence the future is simply expected or awaited (*Gewärtigen*). Unauthentically understood as a "now" which is not yet real, the future is made peripheral to *Dasein's* existential projects. *Dasein* awaits the future but does not seek to penetrate it and discern its relevance for his present decisions. Indeed, he may seek to escape or avoid it, as is made apparent in his unauthentic being-unto-death. Only when the future is brought into the present in an existential anticipation (*Vorlaufen*) is authenticity achieved. This authentic attitude toward the future is a necessary prior condition for an authentic appraisal of one's present and one's past, insofar as the future constitutes the primary directionality of human existence. One can choose one's self authentically in the moment only when one has existentially anticipated one's future, and repetition is made possible only when the past can be projected as a future possibility. Again, the ontological basis for an unauthentic attitude toward the future is the common view of time. One of the central contentions of the common view is that time is endless. Applied to human existence, this common view of time conceals man's being-unto-death by mistaking the finite character of existential time for an endless succession of "nows." In this unauthentic view the urgency for choice never arises because the unavoidable limit to man's future possibilities remains unacknowledged. Thus is suppressed man's authentic future which discloses the indelible transitoriness of his being-unto-death. "In the retreat of human concern there resides a retreat from death, i.e., an evasion of the end of being-in-the-world. . . . The unauthentic temporality of the fallen, everyday *Dasein* in his evasion of his transitoriness misapprehends his authentic futurity and thereby temporality itself." [53]

In summary, the temporality of human concern can be qualified either authentically or unauthentically. In unauthentic temporality the past lapses into oblivion, the present is subject to solidification, and the future is approached by waiting. In authentic temporality the past is taken over in repetition, the present is chosen as the decisive moment, and the future is pre-enacted in existential anticipation. It is necessary to keep in mind that Heidegger's phenomenological description of unauthenticity and authenticity remains on the level of a pure ontological analysis and as such remains neutral to any specific concrete ethical and religious experience in which the ontic-existential self-understanding of the authentic and the unauthentic is set forth. The religious experience of the concrete presence of eternity in the moment cannot be taken into consideration (with respect to its validity or non-validity) in an ontology of human finitude. Nor can the experience of the contemporaneity of Christ and the experience of faith as a repeatable possibility for the future be given a final justification. Nor can a decision be reached on the proper definition of sin as a form of unauthenticity. A philosophy of human finitude, by its very nature and program, can provide no assertions on the validity or non-validity of religious experience. Every religious experience, however, presupposes certain universal human possibilities which arise from the nature of existence itself. It is the task of an existentialist ontology to clarify these universal human possibilities, presupposed not only in religious experience but in other regions of ontic experience as well. Such an ontology, already suggested in the existential reflections of Kierkegaard, has received one of its most powerful contemporary expressions in the philosophy of Heidegger.

4. The Historicity of Existence

Hegel's criticism of all previous modes of thought was that they had not made history a central theme of philosophy. Greek and medieval philosophers, as well as Decartes and Spinoza, he argued, took as their primal category the category of substance, which they applied to reality with the help of a formal logic. But Hegel found that neither the category of substance nor a formal logic would explain the movement which characterized all historical becoming. Thus he undertook to convert "substance" into "subject" and formal logic into dialectical logic, which alone, he believed, could furnish the indispensable conditions for the explanation of an historical reality which was in the process of realizing a universal freedom. Possibly one of the reasons why Kierkegaard was so scathing in his attack upon Hegel was that Hegel had come so close to the truth of historical existence and then fantastically distorted this truth through the erection of a system of logic in which historical existence is ultimately taken up into a timeless and non-historical concept.

Kierkegaard is assuredly at one with Hegel in his emphasis on becoming, movement, and freedom as they are implied in man's historicity. We have already examined Kierkegaard's criticism of the Greek doctrine of recollection, which never succeeded in explaining the immediately experienced phenomenon of becoming, so central to Kierkegaard's analysis of the self. "A self, every instant it exists, is in process of becoming," writes Kierkegaard in *The Sickness Unto Death*.[54] This becoming self is a polar unity of necessity and possibility. It is always on the way, taking over that which it has been, and becoming that which it is not yet. Repetition is the phenomenon which makes possible this becoming character of the self. In the *Philosophical Fragments* and the *Postscript* Kierkegaard has submitted a careful analysis of becoming as a reality of historical existence. He agrees with Hegel on the initial point that becoming is the movement from possibility to actuality. "A being of this kind, which is nevertheless a non-being, is what we know as possibility; and a being which is being is actual being, or actuality; so that the change involved in becoming is the transition from possibility to actuality." [55] But whereas Hegel, because of his final rationalism, was driven to formulate this movement from possibility to actuality in terms of a logical necessity, Kierkegaard, following the injunction of Nietzsche's Zarathustra, remains "true to the earth" and places the movement squarely into the horizon of man's existential freedom. The transition from possibility to actuality is for Kierkegaard a movement within existence and not within a timeless system of logic. It is a movement disclosed and apprehended in the self's actualization through historical decision. Freedom and choice, not the dialectical procession of logical categories, are the determinants of this movement. Why cannot logical necessity account for becoming? The answer for Kierkegaard is obvious. "In logic no movement can *come about*, for logic *is*, and everything logical simply is." [56] Logical entities are determinations of timeless essences which are necessary and fixed, and so they cannot account for something becoming that which it is not yet. Thus, "a becoming by necessity is simply a state of being." [57] The becoming of which Hegel speaks is ultimately an abstract becoming in the realm of timeless essences in which logical necessity has the final word. For Kierkegaard becoming is a *concrete* historical becoming, grounded in existential freedom. Kierkegaard has placed becoming back into existence. "The change involved in becoming is an actual change, the transition takes place with freedom. Becoming is never necessity. It was not necessary before it came into being, for then it could not come into being; nor after it came into being, for then it has not come into being." [58] Kierkegaard has indissolubly linked becoming with freedom and both of these with history. Everything that comes into being, he says, is *"eo ipso* historical."* [59] This inner connectedness between existential freedom and history remains unacknowledged in Hegel's rational system, where the historical process is ruled by reason's necessity. In such a view there can hardly be any talk about process or becoming at all. The iron-clad necessity of logic transforms all real becoming into illusion, and the concrete individual who apprehends his becoming in relation to his decision-demanding historical possibilities is comically ejected from the all-inclusive system. We must conclude, then, says Kierkegaard, that "everything said in Hegel's philosophy about process and becoming is illusory. . . . In spite of all that Hegel says about the process, he does not understand history from the point of view of becoming, but with the help of the illusion attaching to pastness understands it from the point of finality that excludes all becoming." [60] Hegel's system makes it impossible to understand history in relation to personal existence. It excludes the concrete, decision-demanding historical possibilities which call man to action. Thus it has "no answer for the living when the question of becoming is raised in earnest, in the interest of action." [61] For Kierkegaard, on the other hand, history begins only when man confronts his future, and thus his freedom, and actualizes himself in passionate choice. History is the movement of human decisions. History, in short, becomes existential and bursts through the essentialist shell in which Hegel ultimately confined it.

Kierkegaard was not alone in voicing discontent with Hegel's interpretation of history. Marx pointed to its irrelevancy for the concrete socio-economic situation in which man is abandoned. Feuerbach sensed its limitations for the understanding of man in his concrete biological existence. Later Croce and especially Dilthey made man, in his lived concreteness (*Erlebnis*), the subject of history. This concrete man stands within history and must understand himself in the historicity which qualifies his very existence. Both Croce and Dilthey have far-reaching reservations about the possibility of achieving a standpoint outside of history, as Hegel attempted, from which history can be understood in its finality or completeness. It was largely these two thinkers along with Troeltsch who were responsible for the inauguration of the subjective historical consciousness which called into question the objectified and "progressive" attitude of late nineteenth-century historism. Historism had advanced an interpretation of history, based upon analogies drawn from nature, which sought to eliminate the subjectivity within the historian and within history itself. Its approach toward the past was expressly theoretical, geared to an objective analysis of the casual interconnection of "historical" facts. Its approach toward the present was thoroughly relativistic. And its approach to the future was characterized by an unqualified belief in progress. Carl Becker, in his *Heavenly City of the Eighteenth-Century Philosophers*, has shown how historism transplanted the kingdom of God from its celestial abode into man's historical future. This melioristic attitude toward the future received the kiss of death through the advent of the historical philosophies of Croce, Dilthey, Troeltsch, and twentieth-century existentialism. It was this group of thinkers, particularly the existentialist Heidegger, who sought for a fundamentally new approach to the nature of historical reality—an approach already suggested, but not further developed, by Kierkegaard. The notion of a future moving progressively toward perfection was rejected. The objective attitude toward the past was replaced by an attitude of existential involvement and concern. And efforts were made to proceed beyond the relativistic present of historism. The problem of historical relativism was taken most seriously by Troeltsch and Dilthey, but it is questionable whether either succeeded in overcoming it. Indeed, Dilthey concludes with a blanket denial that such a venture is possible, affirming that the relativity of every human apprehension and project is the last word in an historical world-view.[62]

It is this all-important problem of historical relativism which Heidegger has inherited from Dilthey and Troeltsch and which he has sought to resolve in his ontology of historical existence. Heidegger's contention, in questioning the nature of history, is that the question can be answered only when it is simultaneously pursued with the question, "What is man?" Man is not only the subject of history but *is* history insofar as history "historicizes" itself. Man is not an event among other events which occur "in" history. He is historical by virtue of the temporal fabric of his existence. History becomes a constitutive structure of man's being-in-the-world. Karl Löwith in his critical interpretation of Heidegger has maintained that "Heidegger presses Dilthey's historical relativism to its ultimate conclusion in that he carries it back to the unconditioned historicity of a unique, finite *Dasein*. A *Dasein* who is not only 'in' time and 'has' history, but who is temporal and historical in his essence, is no longer relative to world-time and world-history." [63] Historical relativism, according to Heidegger, can be overcome only by going *through* the historical itself. Any appeal to non-historical, cosmological categories and essences results only in a reduction of the historical to the natural and hence evades the problem. Dilthey, of course, recognized this. But Dilthey had not pursued the possibility of a phenomenological penetration and description of the structures of the historical as they are disclosed in man's temporal existence. Dilthey stopped short of an ontology of history. Heidegger seeks to delineate such an ontology with the tools of phenomenology.

The central "existential" in Hiedegger's ontology of history is time. Time as the original meaning of concern is also the foundation of man's historicity. "The analysis of the historicity of *Dasein* attempts to show that this being is not 'temporal' because he 'stands in history,' but rather that he exists historically because he is temporal in the ground of his Being." [64] Time in its ecstatic directionality constitutes the original structure. History presupposes time. Indeed, historicity is time in one of its modifications. Heidegger discusses the temporality of *Dasein* in three different horizons: the temporality of everydayness, the temporality of non-human intramundane beings, and the temporality of historicity. We have examined the former two horizons of time and seen their relevance for the distinction between authentic and unauthentic existence. We shall now focus our attention on Heidegger's description and structural analysis of historical time.

The ontological question of historical time is asked, says Heidegger, when we inquire about the structural unity of the care-projects which define human existence between birth and death. The analysis of time has shown us that *Dasein* as ecstatic existence is stretched out into a past which he *still* is and a future which he *already* is. Futurity and pastness are disclosed as existentially present in the authentic time of human concern. The future limit of this temporal stretching is death; the past limit is birth. Man exists as a being-unto-death but also as a being-toward-birth. [65] The specific movement of this temporal stretching between birth and death is the "event" (*Geschehen*) of *Dasein*. The explication of the structural unity of this event (and the existentialist possibilities which underlie it) is the task of an ontology of historicity.[66]

As a preliminary clarification it is important to keep in mind the distinction between the lived reality of history (*Geschichte*) and the scientific study of history (*Historie*). Unfortunately, the English language has no terms which distinguish the subject matter of history from the scientific discipline which seeks to describe it. Quite clearly, Heidegger's ontological analysis is concerned with the former and not the latter. His task is to elucidate historical reality as a determinant of immediate experience. The scientific or objective study of history, he says, can only be understood in regard to its proper methodological principles after the meaning of historical reality has been illuminated and clarified. The science of history should be based on an analysis of historicity, and not the reverse. "The scientific-historical disclosure of history is in itself, whether fully realized or not, ontologically rooted in the historicity of *Dasein*." [67] The historicity of the historian himself must be taken into consideration, and the significance of this historicity for the understanding of literary documents and the interpretation of the significance of past social, economic, and political events must be investigated. On the level of scientific analysis the subject-object distinction cannot be avoided; hence its particular applicability to the study of history relative to the possibility of an objective historical knowledge must be examined.[68]

Likewise, the ontological understanding of history must be marked off from other common views as to what history is. Commonly, history is identified simply with that which has gone by. We express this view in everyday fashion when we say that something is of *mere* historical concern, suggesting that one is dealing with facts which are no longer on hand, which are devoid of existential relevance for the present. We immediately detect this common view to be rooted in the common understanding of time as a succession of "nows" in which the past disappears from the present. Another common view is that history is the totality of man's cultural achievements through the course of time. Here history is understood as a region of being, i.e., culture, which is contrasted with another region of being, i.e., nature. And finally, history is commonly identified with tradition as such, either as historically acknowledged or simply taken over without questioning.[69] All these views are significant in helping us to understand the everyday *Dasein's* views on history, but as such they do not arrive at the heart of the matter. We only arrive at the heart of the matter when history is understood as historicity, which is to say, as a constitutive structure of the "events" between man's birth and his death. An ontological analysis will have performed its function when it has clarified this constitutive structure as it shows itself in the events themselves.

The events of existence reveal an historical becoming which is qualified by destiny. To be historical means to have a destiny. This destiny makes its appearance as both a personal destiny (*Schicksal*) and a communal destiny (*Geschick*). Man's being-in-the-world as essentially a being-with-others, when understood in light of its historicity, supplies man with a communal destiny which from the very beginning penetrates his personal destiny. This double-aspect destiny has its primary temporal condition in the past, and in this mode constitutes man's heritage (*Erb*).[70] Not only are the events of *Dasein's* historical existence qualified by destiny, but they are also qualified, primarily so, by possibility, which has its foundation in the future. And it is possibility which keeps destiny from being solidified into an ontological determinism. It is possibility which keeps history open and reveals the inner connection between history and freedom. Heidegger is here certainly following (probably without explicit knowledge) the understanding of history already suggested by Kierkegaard when he criticized Hegel for transforming the freedom of historical becoming into a logical necessity. The formal structure of historicity is thus disclosed as a retentional-protentional field, providing the context for the events between *Dasein's* birth and death. We are thus able to comprehend the structural elements of the care-structure as directions of historical time. Facticity is historically understood as destiny, and existentiality discloses man's historical freedom which calls him to decision. This decision takes place in the moment, the third structural determinant of concern. History is thus understood by Heidegger, as by Kierkegaard, as an arriving from an existential past in which one is already confronted with an existential future, which makes possible man's self-actualization through choice.

Historicity thus defines man as an historical event between birth and death as qualified by destiny, possibility, and decision. What remains unanswered thus far is how man's destiny or heritage is itself taken over in the moment of decision. How does destiny enter the domain of responsibility? The answer to this question is supplied by the notion of repetition—a central concept for both Kierkegaard and Heidegger. Man can take over his destiny, his personal and communal history, in the act of repetition. "Repetition is the expressed deliverance from the past, i.e., the return to the possibilities of *Dasein's* having been." [71] The past still holds historical possibilities that can be repeated in the future. Thus historical time, through the introduction of repetition, is oriented toward the future. In our analysis of the ecstatic character of time, we were made aware that the future has priority. The historical past must be understood in light of the future. It is a repeatable possibility. This repetition of the possible, cautions Heidegger, must not be confused with a re-enactment of a *completed* past, because the past is never completed as long as there is history. Nor does repetition involve tying the present to that which has occurred in the past. "Repetition *returns* to the possibilities of an existence which has been." [72]

The paramount importance of repetition for man's historicity was clearly stated in Kierkegaard's distinction between external and internal history. "As it is related to the individual life, history is of two kinds: external and internal." [73] The basic distinction of content involved is that external history is history as observed from the outside, whereas internal history is history as experienced by the existing individual, or history as lived and apprehended from within. To illustrate the distinction between the two kinds of history, Kierkegaard suggests that we think of a knight who has fallen in love with a princess. To possess his love he slays five wild boars, four dragons, and rescues three brothers of the princess whom he loves. For external history the significance of this adventure resides in the chronology of the external events which lead up to a present "now" in which the succession of events is completed. For internal history the significance resides in the lived history of the knight through which he acquires his possession in every moment. Every moment holds existential import for the knight, and his ethical task is to repeat the moment through resolute decision. Thus internal history characterizes the genuine history of the self, or what Heidegger would call authentic historicity. "Internal history is the only true history; but true history contends with that which is the life principle of history, i.e., time," says Kierkegaard. "But when one contends with time, then the temporal and every little moment of it acquires for this fact immense reality." [74] Internal history as man's genuine history is vitalized by the time of immediate experience in which the reality of the past is recovered through a repetition which projects the past as a possibility to be chosen time and again. This distinction between external and internal history is also expressed in Frater Taciturnus' psychological experiment, "Guilty?/Not Guilty?", which Kierkegaard develops in *Stages on Life's Way*. Judged by the norms of external history, the lover who breaks his engagement with his beloved is accused of infidelity. Externally, the breaking of the engagement is proof that he never loved her, or if he loved her once, this love has evaporated into a solidified past. From the standpoint of internal history, however, the lover is not guilty. He breaks the engagement and leaves her precisely because he loves her, realizing that he could never provide her with the happiness which she so innocently desires. This love, which was a reality in the past, each moment recovers its past reality through the possibility of repetition.[75]

The relation of Kierkegaard's distinction between external and internal history to his discussion on time readily becomes apparent. External history is based on a spatialized and measured time, understood as a succession of instants. External events happening successively in time are affirmed to embody full reality. In such a view the moment passes and lapses into an objectified past and loses its contemporary existential significance. Internal history is rooted in the existential time of immediate experience in which the future, past, and present are held in an integrated unity. The past is never emptied of its existential reality. It holds future possibilities which can be repeated in the authentic moment. Past history becomes contemporaneous in the act of repetition and is never past in the sense of a completed series. In its historical existence the self lives out of the past and into the future. Temporally and historically qualified, it unifies itself by taking over both its past and its future in the moment of decision.

Heidegger in his analysis of the historicity of *Dasein* proposes a distinction which evinces, at least in one of its aspects, a remarkable similarity to Kierkegaard's distinction between internal and external history. This is the distinction between primary and secondary history. Primary history designates the historicity of *Dasein* himself. Secondary history refers to the region of intramundane beings, including the world of tools as well as the natural environment.[76] From secondary history arises the common understanding of history as world-history, which includes all regions of non-human being. Primary history, then, is a unique determinant of human existence. Secondary history applies to the modes of at-handness and on-handness. This history is secondary because it is derived from man as the primary historical. Heidegger seeks to elucidate this secondary quality of the historical through an investigation of the historical significance of antiquated artifacts which have become museum pieces. For example, household utensils which were used in a previous age, if preserved in a museum, can still be observed as being on hand. Now wherein resides the historical character of these outdated utensils? These utensils have a history, says Heidegger, only insofar as they disclose an instrumental system which was once used by *Dasein* to order his world through practical concern. But the *Dasein* which used the utensils and the world in which they were used is no longer extant. What remains is only the utensils which have become converted into on-hand objects and have historical significance only insofar as they disclose the primary history of a *Dasein* which has been. What, however, can be said about the historical character of on-handness as a determinant of nature? Tools, books, buildings, institutions have their history, but in what sense can we speak of the world of nature as having a history? Heidegger never pursues this question with the disciplined thoroughness for which one might hope, but he does suggest that there is a sense in which nature is historical. Provinces, settlements, and battlefields have a secondary historical significance, as do utensils, in that they receive their definition through the historical projects of *Dasein*. But nature in the sense of geological, astronomical, and physico-chemical process has no history for Heidegger. Happenings in nature are qualified by the inner temporality characterizing intramundane beings, but they fall outside the domain of the historical. Kierkegaard has also emphasized the distinction between historical and natural time. The time of nature is quantitative and spatialized, but historical time has a mode of being uniquely its own. "Now there is, of course, much in nature that takes place in time. Thus when a brook ripples and continues to ripple, there seems to be in it a qualification of time. However, this is not so, and insofar as one may wish to insist that we have here a qualification of time, one would have to say that the time is indeed present, but present as if spatially qualified." [77] The time of physical nature, as a special ontic region of on-handness, is consistently differentiated from historical time, by both Kierkegaard and Heidegger. However, according to Kierkegaard, there is a peculiar sense in which one can speak even of nature as participating in historical time. "The difficulty comes from the fact that nature is too abstract to have a dialectic with respect to time in the stricter sense. This is nature's imperfection, that it has no history in any other sense; but it is a perfection in nature that it nevertheless has this suggestion of a history, namely that it has come into being." [78] Nature, insofar as it has a beginning and end, at least analogously partakes of the finite time of historical existence. The dualism between history and nature, although acknowledged by both Kierkegaard and Heidegger, is more sharply drawn and more emphatically maintained by the latter.

The final structural determinant or "existential" in Heidegger's ontology of history is the old familiar one—authenticity vis-à-vis unauthenticity. Authentic historicity is historical self-understanding in which *Dasein* properly apprehends himself as qualified by the primary historical, which is founded upon the ecstatic time of human concern. Unauthentic historicity arises when *Dasein* abandons his unique existential history through a reductivism of the primary historical to the secondary historical, which finds its ontological meaning in the common understanding of time as an infinite succession of on-hand "nows." Again, this does not mean that the secondary historical nor the common understanding of time are *in themselves* unauthentic. Unauthenticity permutates human existence when *Dasein's* unique mode of being is dissolved through a subordination to modes which characterize regions of non-human being. Authentic historicity designates the existential self-understanding of man through the very historicity in which he is involved and the ecstatic time which conditions it. This makes possible the recovery of the historical past through the movement of repetition, and it allows man to attain an integrated wholeness in the moment of decision. Anticipating the future, which is the primary direction of authentic historicity, *Dasein* takes up his past historical possibilities in resolute choice and achieves his integrity. His future is authentically confronted in anticipation; his destiny or his heritage is appropriated in repetition; and his ecstasies of historical time are unified in resolution. This is authentic historicity. [79]

Thus Heidegger has sought to formulate an ontology of history through the delineation of a set of cardinal existentialist concepts: destiny, historical possibility, repetition, decision, primary and secondary history, and authenticity and unauthenticity. These concepts point to the structure of historical reality. In his delineation of the structures of historicity Heidegger has proceeded beyond the historical relativism which Dilthey and Troeltsch never succeeded in overcoming. Heidegger has shown that human history is not simply an unknowable, relative, and discontinuous succession of lived experiences (as it was ultimately for Dilthey) but that in its radical historicity it is grounded in constitutive structures which provide the ontological condition for its concrete becoming.

VI

Conscience and Guilt

1. Conscience and Concern

THE PHENOMENON OF CONSCIENCE has been given disciplined attention by various thinkers in the Western tradition. Augustine formulated a theology of conscience in connection with his voluntaristic understanding of man. Aquinas advanced an intellectualized view of conscience which later played a dominant role in the ethical theories of Butler. Mill and contemporary positivists have argued for an emotivism in which conscience is a simple determinant of feeling. Existentialists have re-examined this basic datum in an attempt to clarify its peculiar quality and status in man's immediate experience. Dissatisfied with previous endeavors to define conscience as localized in one or another of the abstracted faculties of the human psyche (reason, will, and emotion), the existentialists have sought to describe the movements of conscience as it shows itself in the immediate concerns of lived experience. The existential subjectivity of Kierkegaard had already undercut traditional faculty psychology with its cumbersome distinctions between the intellectual, the volitional, and the emotional. Heidegger's concept of concern, an ontological formulation of the passion of Kierkegaardian subjectivity, rendered explicit the level of existential disclosure in which the reified distinctions of the tradition become questionable. Conscience as a total response of the concerned self in existence is not primarily an intellectual, volitional, or emotional activity. It is a manner of self-relatedness, a *comportement* which precedes any objective psychic trichotomies.

The interior of the self, in Kierkegaard's analysis, exhibits a structural self-relatedness. The self is a relation which relates itself to itself. The primary factor in this self-relatedness, we have seen, is the factor of consciousness understood in terms of existential passion. To this primary factor we must now add the determinant of conscience, for consciousness and conscience are for Kierkegaard inextricably bound up at their very source. Consciousness and conscience are modalities of the same self-relation. The self which is conscious of itself as finite freedom becomes conscious of its possible concrete ways of existing through the activity of conscience. Thus conscience becomes a constitutive element in the self's immediate lived experience. In his *Journals* Kierkegaard writes: "It is really the conscience which constitutes a personality. . . . For the conscience may slumber, but the constitutive factor is its possibility." [1] Conscience contributes to self-awareness the revelation of the hiatus between what the self is and what it might have been and might be. Conscience thus performs, as does anxiety, with which it is closely related, a disclosing or revealing function. Conscience further elucidates the orientations of man's being-in-the-world. In this disclosing capacity it has both a negative and positive aspect. On the one hand, it discloses the estrangement of the self from its genuine possibilities and thus brings to light the reality of guilt; and on the other hand, it opens the way for authentic or committed existence.

Heidegger's analysis of conscience proceeds along similar lines. Like Kierkegaard he describes conscience as a fundamental factor in the reflexivity of existential concern. *Dasein* is that being who is concerned for his Being and who strives for an authentic relationship to his Being. Concern, rooted in the ecstasies of temporality, provides the foundational structure of *Dasein's* being-in-the-world. Conscience shows itself as an intrinsic element of this concern. It summons *Dasein* out of his unauthentic preoccupations in his world to his authentic possibility-of-being. To analyze conscience, therefore, is to carry further the analysis of *Dasein* as being-in-the-world and arrive at a clarification of his authentic Being. *Dasein* is fallen as long as he exists, suppressing his unique possibilities in his everyday concerns. But even in this mode of fallenness his authentic possibilities are still present as possibilities and can be courageously affirmed. The primary goal of the analysis of conscience is an elucidation of this transition from the unauthentic to the authentic.

The inner relatedness of conscience and concern is expressed in Heidegger's characterization of conscience as the "call of concern" (*Ruf der Sorge*). Conscience, properly understood, is a call, a mode of speech through which *Dasein* is addressed and summoned to the responsibilities of authentic concern.[2] In conscience as the call of concern, man is addressed not in generalities, ambiguities, and pointless platitudes, which characterize the talk of flattened and everyday existence, but in an unequivocal and decisive voice which speaks to his particular and concrete situation. It unmasks his contentment with his everyday fallenness and dispersion in the movements of the "anonymous one," and it points the way to a life of resolve and commitment. The voice in the call of conscience is not audible. Conscience does not express itself in words; it speaks constantly and uniquely in the mode of silence. Silence is itself a mode of speech and can disclose the truth of one's existence as forcefully and incisively as the spoken word. To *Dasein* in the contentment, trust, and false security of his everyday existence, the voice of conscience seems startling. The call of conscience to an authentic concern seems strange and foreign to *Dasein* because he has fallen to the conventionality and publicity of the "anonymous one," in which all genuine possibilities are levelled. For the most part *Dasein* heeds the voice of the public conscience, which is simply the pronouncements of the "anonymous one," voicing the conventional standards of behavior and tempting *Dasein* to abdicate his unique responsibilities. Hence the voice of conscience which summons him to his authentic possibilities awakens and disturbs him (as it repeatedly awakened Socrates throughout his philosophical mission in ancient Greece).

Kierkegaard and Heidegger agree that the external view of conscience, rooted in the heteronomous directives of institutionalized laws and principles, involves a fundamental denial of its irreducibly personal character. "The qualification 'conscience' is so inward that it requires the very finest filters in order to discover it. But if it is found, if it really is conscience, conscience alone, then your regulations be blowed—I should only laugh at them," writes Kierkegaard.[3] Seeking refuge in the authority of heteronomous constraints and regulations constitutes a retreat from subjectivity—a refusal to acknowledge the inwardness of conscience and to assume the responsibility of this inwardness. Man places himself under laws and constraints, says Kierkegaard, because he is unable to face the freedom, risks, and possible failures which are part and parcel of the inwardness of conscience. Heteronomy provides a convenient escape from the responsibilities of personal freedom. The man who stands alone in his inwardness and subjectivity, obedient only to the counsel of his conscience, has reached the pinnacle of ethical existence.[4] Only he can authentically understand his guilt and learn the ways of authentic self-being. The individual who seeks to understand his guilt by analogy to external juridical proceedings or police enforcements never really comprehends that he is guilty.[5] The courtroom analogy of conscience, rooted in an ethical heteronomy, simply breaks down. Conscience has to do with inward counsels rather than external demands. But as Kierkegaard rejects ethical heteronomy, so also he rejects ethical autonomy. It is ethical autonomy, he argues, that constitutes the primary weakness of Kant's moral philosophy. "Kant held that man was his own law (autonomy), i.e., bound himself under the law which he gave himself. In a deeper sense that means to say: lawlessness or experimentation."[6] Heteronomy leads to legalism, autonomy to lawlessness, which is simply a reaction against legalism. The weakness of an ethical autonomy is the lack of a compelling factor which arouses the self to its freedom in which it can become itself. For the self to become itself in a genuine self-reduplication, a third factor which provides the commanding element is required. "Real self-reduplication without a third factor, which is outside and compels one, is an impossibility and makes any such existence into an illusion or an experiment."[7] Thus in conscience, which calls one to authentic self-being, both heteronomy and autonomy are transcended by a third factor which provides a compelling quality without sacrificing freedom. One might say that in this third factor the constraints of heteronomy and the freedom of autonomy are both retained and transfigured. The third factor does not deny man's freedom; rather it deepens and fulfills it by providing the inner directives for authentic existence. This third factor in the structure of self-relatedness, in Kierkegaard's view, receives a specifically religious expression in the divine-human encounter in which God is disclosed as the Power that sustains and directs the self. "God's power is in the conscience," he writes in his *Journals*.[8] Thus, on the one hand, Kierke-gaard rejects a heteronomous view of conscience in which the directives of conscience are rooted in a legalism of rules and laws, whether of the state, church, or society; on the other hand, he rejects ethical autonomy in which man is his own lawgiver. The directives of conscience reside neither in external and alien laws, nor are they derived from the au-tonomous legislation of human reason. They are rooted in an existential or inward freedom which transcends both law and reason and is ulti-mately grounded in God.[9]

Heidegger rejects with equal vigor any externalization and ob-jectification of the voice of conscience. "Conscience as a phenomenon of *Dasein* is not an external and passing on-hand factuality." [10] Such an external view of conscience characterizes only the "public conscience" which seeks its norms and standards outside itself. But the public conscience, which expresses an unauthentic orientation, neglects the fundamental fact that conscience, like all the other determinants of existence, bears the imprint of personalness. Conscience is my very own, and the call proceeds from the Being which I myself am. The call comes not through some external source but through myself. Yet the call is neither planned, nor prepared, nor voluntarily realized by myself. Con-science calls one contrary to expectations and wishes. It has something to say about me. Thus it must properly be said that the call comes *through* myself, but at the same time it is *about* myself.[11] In this way Heidegger also proceeds beyond the alternative of heteronomy or au-tonomy. The call of conscience has neither an external source, nor does it arise from the legislation of an autonomous reason. As a pure phe-nomenologist, however, Heidegger does not specify any religious ground for the directives of conscience as does Kierkegaard (although the pos-sibility of such a religious ground is not denied in Heidegger's analysis). Heidegger makes it clear in defining the scope of his analysis that it is a strictly ontological analysis, which precedes any psychological descrip-tion, remains outside a biological explanation, and abstracts from any possible theological interpretation. The relevance of psychological, biological, and theological enquiries is not called into question, but rather an attempt is made to delineate the ontological structures of conscience which are presupposed in such enquiries.

2. The Ontological Foundations of Conscience

The impulse which propelled the whole of Kierkegaard's writing, if we are to take seriously his literary self-evaluation in his book *The Point of View*, was a passionate pursuit of the question concerning the task of becoming a Christian.[12] Thus one must never lose sight of the fact that Kierkegaard's reflections arise from an interrogation of the concrete and existential dialectic of ethico-religious experience. Yet, of equal importance, we maintain, is his recognition and implicit delineation of the finite ontological structures which show themselves in all existential becoming and comprise the universally human, whether the universally human is given a religious expression or not. Such an ontology of human finitude we have found to be suggested in Kierkegaard's examination of the phenomena of self-relatedness, anxiety, death, time, and history. So also in his discussion of the correlative phenomena of conscience and guilt a possible ontology is suggested. This possible ontology has received its most rigorous formulation in the philosophical investigations of Heidegger. Kierkegaard, we have seen, has defined conscience as that which constitutes personality. Whether latent or active it is a "constitutive factor" of personal existence. This central constitutive factor, Kierkegaard has argued, can be viewed in terms of external sanctions and constraints, or it can be understood as being intrinsically qualified by inwardness or existential subjectivity. Heidegger has assumed the task of making clear the ontological factors which give rise to an external and unauthentic view of conscience and differentiate this view from an authentic existentialist understanding of conscience. In *Sein und Zeit* he presents a fourfold phenomenological description of the external or "common" view of conscience, which he argues is *rooted* in an ontology of on-handness and which thus conceals the phenomenon of authentic conscience.

First, the common view is based primarily upon the moral categories of good and evil, censure and warning. The meaning of conscience is thus restricted at the very outset, limited by moral categories and a formulation of the question in terms of these categories. Conscience, in short, is understood morally rather than ontologically, as a matter of "right" and "wrong" action rather than a matter of relatedness to Being. In this moralistic interpretation of conscience the category of evil is given priority. Conscience, says the common view, is primarily concerned with that which is evil. The inadequacy of such an interpretation is that the voice of conscience is oriented exclusively to the succession of on-hand experiences for which the individual is censured or pronounced guilty. The existentialist understanding of conscience proceeds beyond the individual moral misdeeds to an ontological determinant of being guilty which is prior to every guilty act. The conscience of the common view judges according to moral constraints. The existentialist interpretation advances a transmoral view which extends beyond the ken of moral categories.

Second, the common view fails to see that the call of conscience is rooted in the Being of *Dasein* himself. It conceives conscience as a kind of on-hand being which plays the role of an external judge who censures and condemns *Dasein*. Conscience is understood as something coming from the outside. Its locus is in the mode of on-handness and therefore external to the unique Being of *Dasein*. The analogy used by the common view is that of a court scene. Conscience is a court which judges whether *Dasein* is guilty or not. This interpretation, contends Heidegger, found its most significant exponent in Kant, for whom it was an immediate implication of the idea of the moral law.

Third, conscience is understood in the common view as relating only to specific completed or intended acts. Conscience judges the isolated acts of the individual. Man's motives and intentions and the specific acts which are consequent to these motives and intentions are either censured or approved, but the very Being of man somehow remains immune from the pronouncements of conscience. Guilt is localized in the particular act, which in some strange way is violently wrested from the existential context out of which it emerges. Just as Hegel had abstracted the intellect from the dialectic of existence, so the common view of conscience abstracts the particular acts of will from the Being of *Dasein* and then applies to these abstracted entities the moral categories of good and evil.

Fourth, the common view interprets conscience as having essentially a critical function and thus ignores any positive significance which might attach to the phenomenon. Here also the fundamental fallacy resides in preoccupation with individual moral acts. The existentialist-ontological interpretation seeks to correct this fallacy by advancing a transmoral view. A transmoral conscience makes no pronouncements on the negative or positive moral content of specific motives, inclinations, desires, and acts. Its function is to disclose the irreducible character of existential guilt and to summon *Dasein* to his authentic possibilities. "The call discloses nothing positive or negative which can become the object of my practical concerns; an ontologically different Being is under consideration—existence. In the existentialist sense, the properly understood call presents something 'positive,' i.e., the unique possibilities presented to *Dasein* in a calling back and a calling forward to his ever present possibility-of-being." [13] Conscience calls man to an authentic existence which transcends the realm of moral categories. Authentic existence is a modality of being or a manner of existence which drives beyond the confining strictures of the "good" and "bad" conscience. Heidegger's predecessor in the formulation of the notion of the transmoral conscience was Nietzsche, with his attempted transvaluation of values. The affirmation of life as life, for Nietzsche, demanded the exercise of a will-to-power which placed man "beyond good and evil." In this way man could remain "true to the earth" and achieve his primordial unity with the dynamism of life universal. But Nietzsche's vitalistic and tragic naturalism, as Heidegger keenly points out, is still predicated on the metaphysical and moral categories which have shaped the Western tradition. Heidegger (and existentialism in general) has sought to reinterpret and understand human existence through its own and unique mode of Being—a task for which the traditional metaphysical and moral categories remain philosophically impoverished. Although Nietzsche succeeded in destroying the old altars of Western metaphysics and morality, he was unable to erect the promised new ones and thus unable to proceed beyond nihilism. He marks the end of an old era and the transition to a new.

The common view of conscience, indicated by the foregoing four characteristics, is contrasted by Heidegger with the existentialist interpretation of conscience as the call of authentic concern. This existentialist interpretation is then clarified with regard to the structural elements which constitute it. Conscience as the call of concern, coming through myself and yet making pronouncements about myself, can be analyzed relative to a threefold structure: the "caller," the one who is "called to," and the one who is "called forth." It becomes evident that these three structural elements arise from the care-structure itself, which has its final ontological clarification and meaning in the three ecstasies of temporality. The "caller" is *Dasein* in his facticity or original abandonment in the world, which we have seen is grounded primarily in the ecstasy of pastness. The one who is "called to" is *Dasein* in his existentiality, by virtue of which he is protended into his possibility-of-being. This existentialist structure is ontologically rooted in the ecstasy of futurity. The one who is "called forth" is *Dasein* in his mode of fallenness, lost in the "anonymous one," sacrificed to the present. The structural elements of conscience are thus rooted in concern as it is qualified by temporality. Conscience as the call *in* man's facticity, *out* of his fallenness, *to* his authentic possibility-of-being is phenomenologically clarified in the context of man's Being defined as finite and temporal concern.[14]

Corresponding to the call, in an existentialist understanding of conscience, there is the phenomenon of hearing. What is indicated by conscience, says Heidegger, is only fully determined when one is made aware of the hearing which corresponds to the call. The call of conscience is consummated only in the hearing and the understanding of this call. The voice of conscience speaks to man that which he can understand, and only when this voice is authentically heard and understood is the task of conscience completed. Authentic hearing and understanding are integral aspects of the phenomena-complex of conscience.[15]

The call of conscience proceeds from *Dasein*, is directed to *Dasein*, and is heard by *Dasein*. But this does not mean that conscience is "merely subjective." Conscience speaks with a universal and obligatory voice. It tells man something about the universally human—his universal guilt and the universal possibility of authentic being. Nor does this mean that any religious interpretation of God's "voice" in the conscience is precluded. The charge of atheism against Heidegger rests upon a glaring misconception of the intention and delineation of his ontology of finitude. Heidegger states clearly and unambiguously that the *existentialist* interpretation of conscience does not, and cannot, take the *existential* religious question into consideration. "As concrete existence is not necessarily and directly prejudiced through an ontologically inadequate understanding of conscience, so also the existential understanding of the call is not validated through an adequate existentialist interpretation of conscience." [16] On this point there is not the slightest contradiction between the existentialism of Heidegger and that of Kierkegaard. Kierkegaard's assertion that "God's power is in the conscience" is neither validated nor denied by an existentialist understanding; however, the ontic-existential possibility of the former presupposes the latter. But the latter can make neither positive nor negative assertions concerning the validity of religious experience.[17] The ontological-existentialist description of conscience gives *Dasein* neither moral ideals nor religious directives. This cannot be its task. Its task is to elucidate the structures in the phenomenon of conscience which are presupposed in every ontic-existential situation. In every concrete and existential encounter with conscience, there is a "caller," there is one who is "called to," and there is one who is "called forth." But the existentialist elucidation cannot provide the concrete content of ethical and religious experience.

3. Freedom, Guilt, and Sin

Prometheus became guilty when he stole fire from Zeus, the sovereign god of Mt. Olympus, bringing to mankind self-consciousness, knowledge, and *techne*. In this powerful Greek myth we have a dramatic expression of the reality of guilt as a determinant of human becoming. Greek tragedy arrived at the insight that guilt is an inevitable accompaniment in the self-actualization of human freedom. Shakespearian tragedy likewise exemplified the correlative phenomena of conscience and guilt as components in the human condition. King Richard, in Shakespeare's tragedy, exclaims in Act V:

> My conscience hath a thousand several tongues,
> And every tongue brings in a several tale,
> And every tale condemns me for a villain.
> Perjury, perjury, in the high'st degree:
> Murder, stern murder, in the dir'st degree;
> All several sins, all us'd in each degree,
> Throng to the bar, crying all, "Guilty! guilty!"

The modern novel has also powerfully portrayed the experience of guilt in its manifold forms. Franz Kafka's *The Trial* and Albert Camus' *The Fall* are cases in point. These literary expressions of the phenomenon of guilt have of course never remained without their philosophical counterparts in the history of thought. It was not, however, until the advent of existentialism that the notion of guilt became a central philosophical concept. Kierkegaard, Jaspers, and Heidegger in particular have given careful attention to this most basic phenomenon of human experience. Kierkegaard has described guilt as "the most concrete expression of existence." [18] Jaspers has analyzed the concept in connection with his doctrine of the "boundary situations" which constitute the unsurmountable limits of man's existence. Heidegger has made the concept central to his ontology of human finitude.

Conscience discloses guilt. The call of conscience, says Heidegger, "reveals *Dasein* in his original possibilities as being guilty." [19] The reality of guilt is indissolubly linked with possibility and freedom as determinants of existence. "Insofar as I know myself as being free," says Jaspers, "I acknowledge myself as being guilty." [20] When man turns toward his subjectivity, says Kierkegaard, he discovers freedom, and "there comes into being along with this *Ansich* of freedom another figure, guilt." [21] The consciousness of guilt as the failure of the self to relate itself to its possibilities, disclosed by conscience, accompanies the awareness of freedom or the awareness of selfhood. Conscience speaks to man in his finite freedom and brings him to the self-awareness that in his freedom he has not become that which he might have become. It points to an irremovable estrangement of the self from itself—a hiatus between the possibility which it might have become and the actualized possibility which it in fact is.

One of Kierkegaard's most penetrating discussions on the nature of guilt and its relation to freedom is presented in his essay "On Ancient Tragical Motive as Reflected in the Modern," which appears in *Either/Or*.[22] In this essay Kierkegaard discusses the difference between ancient and modern tragedy on the question of tragic guilt. Aristotle, he says, saw that authentic tragedy requires guilt. This guilt was understood with the help of the categories of activity and passivity or action and suffering. Only when both of these factors are taken into consideration can a tragic theme emerge.

It is well known that Aristotle requires the tragic hero to have guilt. But just as the action in Greek tragedy is intermediate between activity and passivity (action and suffering), so is also the hero's guilt, and therein lies the tragic collision. On the other hand [in modern tragedy] the more the subjectivity becomes reflected, the more one sees the individual left Pelagianally to himself, the more his guilt becomes ethical. The tragedy lies between these two extremes. If the individual is entirely without guilt, then is the tragic interest nullified, for the tragic collision is thereby enervated; if, on the other hand, he is absolutely guilty, then he can no longer interest us tragically.[23]

Tragic guilt is the result of the tension between the self's ethical activity in freedom and its passivity in the presence of given and insurmountable conditions. Here again we see the significance of Kierkegaard's analysis of the self as *finite* freedom—a freedom constituted by the polar synthesis of possibility and necessity, or a freedom conditioned by the factor of destiny. Also, we see how these existential notions of Kierkegaard are related to the Aristotelian categories of activity and passivity. Kierkegaard has, in effect, existentialized these cosmological categories of Aristotle as they apply to the phenomenon of guilt. Guilt is always present as a possibility in one's freedom, and thus it becomes a matter of individual responsibility. But guilt also has a hidden necessity which is part of the self's destiny. The phenomenon of guilt has an active and a passive side. One acquires guilt through one's actions, and one suffers guilt in the given situationality of one's destiny.

Kierkegaard argues that Greek tragedy overaccentuated the factor of necessity involved in guilt and, consequently, tended toward a fatalistic world-view. Individual freedom and action were submerged. The categories of state, family, and destiny were given priority. "Even if the individual moved freely, he still rested in the substantial categories of state, family, and destiny. This substantial category is exactly the fatalistic element in Greek tragedy, and its exact peculiarity." [24] Modern tragedy, on the other hand, "strives to let the whole tragic destiny become transubstantiated in individuality and subjectivity." [25] It makes the hero accountable for everything. The hero's actions become the sole determinants of the tragic outcome. His past decisions, his past history, his environmental and social world are affirmed to be of no significance. The whole of life rests upon his own shoulders. His guilt is the result of his own acts alone. In such a view the necessity of universal destiny is dissolved by the possibility of individual freedom. Freedom becomes "infinitized" and is wrested from the context of its irreducible existential finitude. Thus guilt receives its proper clarification only when the polarity of necessity and possibility as the fundamental structural constitution of the self is kept in view. Guilt is related to both necessity and possibility. The phenomenon, says Kierkegaard, expresses a peculiar dialectic in which the guilt of the state, the family, and the race (hereditary guilt) is posited in relation to the individual. [26] The self *is* guilty because of its necessity or destiny (rooted primarily in its past). The self *becomes* guilty through the actualization of itself as possibility (rooted primarily in the future). Thus, we see how the structures of selfhood, the phenomenon of time, and the factor of guilt are inter-related in Kierkegaard's analysis.

The element of necessity or destiny, or what Heidegger calls facticity, gives to guilt the qualification of inevitability and universality. Kierkegaard speaks of the self as being "essentially and unconditionally guilty." [27] Guilt is posited in the very process of existential becoming. It is a "power which spreads abroad everywhere" and "broods over existence." [28] Guilt is understood as an inevitable and universal determinant of human existence. Man is always arriving from a past in which he has already chosen possibilities, and this has entailed an inevitable sacrifice of other possibilities which might have been but are not. Thus the very charter of his being has become infused with an irremediable partiality, and guilt is understood as being eminently present. "The fact that he discovers guilt so profoundly shows that to him this concept is present *sensu eminentiori*." [29] Jaspers develops the same viewpoint in his discussion of guilt as an unavoidable boundary situation. My projects, he says, inevitably involve me in guilt. All my actions have consequences which bear the stamp of guilt. So also my refusal to decide and act has consequences through which I become guilty for not acting. In the final analysis, not choosing is simply a privative form of choosing. I have to "choose" not to choose, and this privative choice partakes of universal guilt. Jaspers has given specific attention to the guilt involved in my dealing with others. Existential reality inevitably excludes from the reach of my personal concerns others for whom I remain nevertheless responsible. I cannot strive for communication with all. I must select from the outreach of my communal world the single individuals who are to be included in my interpersonal projects. But in this very selection, others are inevitably excluded, and again I gravitate into an unavoidable guilt.[30] Heidegger, more emphatically then even Kierkegaard or Jaspers, has proclaimed guilt as universal and unavoidable. "*Dasein as such is guilty*," he writes in *Sein und Zeit*. This concept of an unavoidable guilt is analyzed and described by Heidegger in connection with the disclosure of nothingness. We have already examined the significance of nothingness relative to the phenomenon of anxiety. Now we must see how nothingness forms the background for the understanding of guilt. Nothingness, contends Heidegger, is always implied in the concept of guilt. "The formal existentialist idea of guilt is determined as follows: the fundamental modality of a being determined through nothing, i.e., *grounded in nothingness.*" [31] Now how is this nothingness which permeates *Dasein* and constitutes the matrix of guilt to be understood? Clearly, it is in no way a simple "not-on-handness" (*Nichtvorhandenseins*). As we noted in our earlier discussion, nothingness is a constituent of the Being of *Dasein* himself. *Dasein*, in his care-structure, is basically a structure of possibilities. He holds within his Being a field of possibilities which he is free to actualize in his concrete choices. These possibilities, although primarily rooted in the future, are not limited to the future. The past is laden with possibilities that can be repeated. Human existence is stretched out both into the future and into the past, and in the moment of choice relates itself to the present. Existing into these three ecstasies of time, *Dasein* is constantly projected in one or another of his possibilities, choosing one and excluding another. The exclusion of some possibilities is inevitable because of the very nature of existential reality. In the choice of one possibility *Dasein* is always foregoing another. Hence he carries within the charter of his Being, so to speak, an accumulation of non-chosen possibilities. Insofar as he *is* his possibilities, these non-chosen possibilities are structurally a part of his Being. They constitute the nothingness of his care-structure. "The nothingness which we have in mind belongs to *Dasein's* being-free for his existential possibilities. This freedom *is* only in the choice of one, which means not having chosen and not being able to choose the other." [32] Nothingness, in its relation to guilt, thus has reference to the sacrificed choices in *Dasein's* field of existential possibilities, which structurally belong to him as long as he is. Nothingness is indelibly stitched into the very warp and woof of human existence or human concern. In every choice I am "cutting off" (*ent-scheiden*) other possible choices which are constitutive of my Being. I become guilty in not affirming all my possibilities. Conscience calls me to my possibilities, but I must always sacrifice some in choosing others. In actualizing one, I am not actualizing another, and thereby I become guilty. Every action implies guilt, and it is impossible to exist and not to act. Thus, guilt is an unavoidable phenomenon in human existence. "*Dasein as such is guilty.*"

Guilt, like the phenomenon of death, has the peculiar character of being both a universal determinant and a principle of individuation. It defines an aspect of the universally human and at the same time calls the individual back to his unique self with its unique responsibilities. "The concept of guilt," writes Kierkegaard, "posits precisely the single individual as the single individual." [33] Guilt is a reflexive phenomenon which brings the self back to itself, making it aware of a discontinuity in its innermost experience, which marks it as the self which it is. Just as the death which the self must die is its own death, so also the guilt in which the self is involved is uniquely its own. The guilt which I exemplify is *my* guilt. The universal is posited as the individual or the particular. The self, existentially understood, is not an abstract individual, individuated by some underlying signate matter, as was the view of traditional metaphysics, but an historical event which emerges concretely as universal humanity. " 'Self' signifies precisely the contradiction of positing the general as the particular." [34]

Guilt can be understood as a general discontinuity of human experience in which the self experiences estrangement within itself as possibility-of-being, or guilt can be qualified by religious experience in which case it becomes sin, understood as estrangement of the self from God. Kierkegaard has formulated the distinction between guilt and sin in his distinction between religiousness A and religiousness B. Guilt properly understood is a determinant of religiousness A, the religion of immanence; sin is a determinant of religiousness B, or the "paradoxical religiousness." In the *Postscript*, where Kierkegaard most clearly discusses this distinction, he writes: "The totality of guilt-consciousness is the most edifying factor in religiousness A." [35] Insofar as religiousness A is still the religion of immanence, one is led to conclude that "the consciousness of guilt still lies in immanence, in distinction from the consciousness of sin." [36] In dealing with the phenomenon of guilt we are dealing with the self as a "human self." Consciousness of sin is a qualification of the self as a "theological self." "In sin-consciousness the individual becomes conscious of his difference from the human in general which becomes itself conscious of what it is to exist *qua* man." [37] Guilt as a determinant of existence is disclosed through an analysis of what it means to exist *qua* man. This is the self in terms of its human possibilities in abstraction from any possible relation to a divine ground. It is, in short, the self as the subject of phenomenological description independent of theological interpretation. Consciousness of guilt can thus be understood as "an alteration of the subject within the subject himself." [38] To be conscious of guilt is to be conscious that the self in its becoming is always estranged from some of its possibilities. Consciousness of sin places the individual into a new "existence-medium" which marks the transition from religiousness A to religiousness B. The latter is defined by Kierkegaard as the paradoxical religiousness which "places the contradiction absolutely between existence and the eternal." Consciousness of sin first becomes a possibility in religiousness B, of which Christianity with its teaching of the "Absolute Paradox," i.e., God's action in time and history, is the supreme expression. "The relation to that historical fact (Deity in time) is the condition for sin-consciousness." [39] Whereas the individual can acquire a guilt-consciousness in becoming aware of himself as actualized finite freedom, sin-consciousness requires an encounter with a divine power in relation to whom the individual has entered a state of estrangement. Sin is posited only in the divine-human encounter. The pagan can have no consciousness of sin. Sin-consciousness emerges only in the self's awareness of itself as existing before God. The self as human self apprehends itself as guilty through an awareness of the unavoidable estrangement with itself. The self as theological self apprehends itself as sinful through an awareness of its primordial estrangement from God. Apart from sin-consciousness, to exist means simply that the individual has come into the world and is made guilty through the process of existential actualization. With the new determinant of sin-consciousness, having come into the world means having become a sinner.

This sin which constitutes the new existence-medium must be contrasted with the Socratic definition of sin as ignorance. Socratic intellectualism, argues Kierkegaard, failed to recognize the determinant of freedom in the phenomenon of sin. It thus left undetermined the origin of both ignorance and sin. "Sin must properly have its ground in something else; it must have its ground in the activity with which a man has labored to obscure his intelligence." [40] In ascribing the origin of sin to an activity and a freedom which precedes intellect, Kierkegaard expresses a theological position which had already been advanced by Augustine. Augustine had argued that sin is a consequence of man's actualization of an original freedom. In his original freedom man is free to sin (*posse peccare*) or not to sin (*posse non peccare*), but in his first choice he chooses to sin, and every succeeding choice bears the mark of his original act of rebellion. Thus, both Kierkegaard and Augustine (and the whole Augustinian-Franciscan-Scotus-Lutheran tradition) find the origin or source of sin in a primordial freedom which accounts for both ignorance and sin. Freedom is given priority over intellect. Sin is posited in the actualization of human freedom.

As sin is never simply the result of ignorance, so also it is never the result of individual sinful acts which accumulate sin through a species of quantitative progression. This, Kierkegaard points out, would lead to the absurd conclusion that there are degrees or quantitative levels of sinfulness among the human race. "It surely would be a very ludicrous abracadabra if one were to say that the mathematical average is 3⅜ inches of sinfulness for each man, that in Languedoc it comes only to 2¼, but in Brittany to 3⅞." [41] Sin is a condition of human existence from which sinful acts follow. Every particular sin is simply an expression of an original state of being sinful. Man is sinful not because he commits sinful acts, but he commits sinful acts because he is sinful. Sin as a new existence-medium is a religious qualification of the self as spirit or freedom. It is not an act but a condition of existence.

4. *Unauthentic and Authentic Guilt*

Guilt is an unavoidable phenomenon in existential reality. But for the most part man refuses to accept it as a determinant of his existence, or he seeks to mitigate or reduce it through various unauthentic conceptions. It is first in Jaspers and Heidegger that the distinction between unauthentic and authentic guilt becomes explicit, but the roots of this distinction go back to the Danish existentialist. In the *Postscript* Kierkegaard elaborates what he considers three lower or less genuine conceptions of guilt. There is the conception of guilt by which the self considers itself as guilty only momentarily—probably on Sunday or New Year's morning. The universal and pervasive character of guilt is suppressed. The self considers itself guilty only at certain times. But such a self has not yet penetrated to the heart of its existence, where it finds guilt as a decisive determinant of its very being. There is also the conception of guilt under the category of mediation. But this is to view guilt abstractly and externally. "Every mediation is a lower conception of guilt. . . . Mediation dispenses man from absorbing himself in determinants of totality and makes him busy outwardly, his guilt being external." [42] Mediation thus suppresses the existential reality of guilt. The self that mediates guilt avoids the consciousness of guilt by "existing" abstractly. Another lower conception of guilt is the comparative view of guilt. In this view man compares himself to various external standards in terms of which he judges himself guilty, and the degree of

guilt consciousness becomes dependent upon the austerity of the standard. Guilt becomes a matter of degrees which can be quantitatively
determined with the help of external norms. "The comparative consciousness of guilt is recognizable by the fact that it has its standard outside itself, and when on Sunday the parson employs a very high standard (without, however, employing that of eternity), it seems dreadful to
the comparer to think what he has deserved; in good company on
Monday it does not seem to him so bad, and thus the outward relationship suffices to determine an entirely different conception, which in
spite of fine variations always misses one thing: eternity's determinant." [43] Closely allied with the comparative consciousness of guilt is the
judicial conception of guilt. In this view man recognizes his guilt only
by analogies drawn from civil courts or civil standards of justice. But as
Kierkegaard had already argued in *The Concept of Anxiety*, the individual "who learns to recognize his guilt by analogy with the decisions
of the police justice or the supreme court never really comprehends that
he is guilty." [44] The common denominator of all these lower conceptions
of guilt is that guilt is externalized and objectified. They constitute a
flight from the reality of guilt experienced in inwardness and existential
subjectivity. Only by turning toward himself does man encounter genuine guilt. He then discovers that guilt is not a matter of degrees externally determined but is basically and fundamentally a matter of
being guilty.

Heidegger in his existentialist analysis has clarified the ontological foundation of this externalized and objectified conception of guilt
by showing how it arises from an application of the categories of on-
handness. The everyday understanding of guilt, in the realm of common
and conventional interpretations, tends toward an unauthentic view in
making the external conception of guilt normative. A common and
conventional view of guilt is that guilt has to do with debts. One owes
something to another person for which that person has a claim. One
speaks of being indebted to someone for something—for financial aid,
help with some undertaking, or a deed of kindness. [45] This conception of
guilt, quite clearly, arises from our dealings with others in our common
practical concerns. Being guilty may have a broader significance in the
common view whereby it means "to be guilty of . . . ," i.e., being the
cause, author, or occasion for the occurrence of something. [46] In this
sense one can be guilty without owing anything to another, and one
can owe something to another without himself being guilty. Another

can incur guilt for one. The common denominator of both of these views on guilt is the idea of "making debts" or making one's self liable. Guilt then becomes a defect for which one must make amends. This everyday view of guilt clearly moves solely within the confines of a framework of moral demands. The authentic existentialist understanding of guilt drives beyond a moral interpretation and describes guilt as a modality of existence. The existentialist interpretation separates the phenomenon of guilt not only from the realm of everyday conceptions of practical calculating concern but from the categories of "ought" (Sollen) and law (Gesetz) as well. Through an application of these categories guilt is understood as a moral or juristic defect, or a lack of something which ought to be and which can be. Guilt, in the final analysis, is still conceived in the common and conventional view as a moral category rather than a mode or manner of existing. So also the notion of guilt as it is associated with the idea of evil is excluded in an existentialist interpretation. All these views of guilt are based on the use of categories and modes of thought which apply only to the region of on-hand being. Guilt is conceived to have its source in some external, on-hand reality, which means that it has its source outside the unique Being of Dasein himself. The clearest expression of such an external view of guilt is the court-scene analogy in which man is pronounced guilty by an external judge. Kierkegaard, we have observed, defined as a lower conception of guilt that view which recognizes guilt only by analogies drawn from the decisions of the police justice or the supreme court. Through this process of externalization and objectification man surreptitiously places the phenomenon of guilt outside himself. Guilt becomes localized in the region of on-handness, and remains only adventiously related to the unique mode of human existence. But the application of on-hand categories and concepts to the concrete historicity of human becoming renders man's understanding, and his projects which are inextricably bound up with this understanding, unauthentic. The everyday conception of guilt thus leads invariably to an unauthentic view.

Jaspers has also undertaken an analysis of the various unauthentic approaches to guilt which are devised so as to conceal the reality of guilt as a boundary situation in human existence. Man may develop an attitude of indifference to his guilt, proclaiming that it is unavoidable and thus outside the reach of responsibility. But guilt authentically understood and appropriated, argues Jaspers, is a matter of both personal responsibility and situational unavoidability. Man's freedom and his situation interpenetrate each other. Guilt arises from man's freedom, which is always a freedom-within-a-situation. Another way of suppressing the reality of guilt is through a neglect or refusal to acknowledge its presence at all—neither as an expression of freedom nor as an implication of situationality. Again, the boundary situation of guilt is concealed through various moralistic interpretations, whereby it is held that man can rid himself of guilt through the attainment of a moral purity. Finally, guilt is unauthentically conceived when it is viewed as a consequence of a particular action which could have been avoided, a view that opens the door to superficial moral optimism.[47] Jaspers contends that the foregoing views directly contribute to a concealment of guilt as an unavoidable boundary situation. Authentic existence must accept guilt as an implication of existential freedom and pursue its responsible projects while aware that guilt is unavoidable. "It is a matter not of becoming guiltless but rather of actually avoiding that guilt which can be avoided, so as to arrive at that guilt which is authentic, profound, and unavoidable." [48]

Heidegger agrees with Jaspers that authenticity involves taking over guilt as unavoidable and irremediable. Guilt is not an attribute which man may or may not possess. Man, according to Heidegger, does not *have* guilt; he *is* guilty. John Wild states Heidegger's concept of guilt most clearly when he writes: "This guilt is not conceived as something that may be added or subtracted from man. It attaches to his finite being as such. He is inevitably guilty, not because he has violated some law, but his existence is necessarily pervaded with negation." [49] Guilt is part and parcel of the existential finitude of man. It attaches to man's Being by dint of the nothingness which is present in every act of choice. It is for this reason that man in the Heideggerian understanding can never become fully sovereign over his Being. He pursues his projects on grounds of an existential freedom, but this existential freedom always includes the element of facticity, which circumscribes all the non-chosen possibilities of his past through which he has become guilty. The ontological nothingness of his non-chosen possibilities permeates his Being as long as he exists. This authentic existentialist guilt implied in every action is the original condition for the ontic possibility of moral guilt in irresponsible decisions. One becomes guilty in some particular act because one's total being is pervaded by guilt. Any ethical or ethico-religious understanding is made ontologically possible only through the acknowledgement of guilt as a determinant of human finitude as such. Both conscience and guilt in an ontology of human finitude are transmoral concepts.

The distinctive role of conscience, we have seen in this chapter, is to call man to his authentic possibility-of-being. This call, which proceeds from man himself and at the same time makes pronouncements about him, discloses an intrinsic state of being guilty. The task of *Dasein* then becomes that of an authentic understanding and appropriation of his guilt which is unavoidable in existential actualization. Guilt must be taken over in authentic choice. To hear and understand the call of conscience is to choose.[50] Authentic existence is consummated in decision or resolute choice. Anxiety, death, and guilt are unavoidable phenomena in human experience, but they do not for that matter remain outside the purview of freedom. Human existence *is* finite freedom, through which anxiety, death, and guilt are taken up in the final resolute decision of the "courage to be."

VII

Decision and Integrity

1. Freedom and Choice

THE PARAMOUNT SIGNIFICANCE of the phenomenon of choice for an existentialist understanding of the self has become apparent in the preceding analysis. Choice is implied in the very structure of the self as finite and actualized freedom. The self as finite freedom is a polar synthesis of possibility and necessity (Kierkegaard) or of existentiality and facticity (Heidegger). These structural moments of the self, we have seen, are rooted respectively in the temporal ecstasies of the future and the past. Anxiety discloses man's possibilities and confronts him with a future. And in this confrontation with his future, man is called to decide in the moment. "As truly as there is a future, just so truly is there an either/or." [1] Kierkegaard also expresses this implicatory relation of existence, possibility, future, and decision in a passage in the *Postscript*. To exist means to be in a process of becoming; in the process of becoming man faces a future; in facing a future he is summoned to action. [2] In the preceding chapters we have seen how the phenomena of anxiety and death disclose the priority of the future and how conscience reveals guilt and summons the self to decisive action. The self is called to a choice—namely, to a choice of itself as finite self. Anxiety, death, and guilt must be taken up in an act of existential resolve. The self must choose itself as mortal and guilty and in its act of decision translate necessity into freedom and thereby attain authentic selfhood. Thus the reality of choice is disclosed in the very structure of the self which constitutes it as finite freedom, qualified by the determinants of anxiety, death, time, history, conscience, and guilt. Choice is the indispensable condition for an attainment of an authentic awareness and acceptance of one's finitude. One is hardly surprised, therefore, to find Kierkegaard asserting that "the most tremendous thing which has been granted to man is: the choice, freedom." [3] In *Either/Or* Kierkegaard speaks of choice as his primary category—that which lies closest to his heart and thought. "But I return to my category. I have only one, for I am not a logician, but I assure you that it is the choice both of my heart and of my thought, my soul's delight and my bliss—I return to the importance of choosing." [4] Again, he speaks of freedom and choice as the greatest treasure which man can possess.

> For freedom, therefore, I am fighting. . . . I am fighting for the future, for either/or. That is the treasure I desire to bequeath to those whom I love in the world; yea, if my little son were at this instant of an age when he could thoroughly understand me, I would say to him, "I leave to thee no fortune, no title and dignities, but I know where there lies buried a treasure which suffices to make thee richer than the whole world, and this treasure belongs to thee, and thou shalt not even express thanks to me for it lest thou take hurt to thine own soul by owing everything to another. This treasure is deposited in thine own inner self: there is an either/or which makes a man greater than the angels." [5]

All varieties of existentialists agree with Kierkegaard that freedom and choice are pivotal concepts in the description and interpretation of human existence. Jaspers speaks of freedom as the very "being" of existence.[6] For classical rationalism, man is the bearer of an abstract and cosmological reason; for Jaspers and Kierkegaard, man is understood as the bearer of a concrete and historical freedom. Freedom is given priority to reason and is apprehended as the original image of man. This does not mean that reason is vitiated. It means only that reason is placed back into existence, from which it had been so violently abstracted by the rationalistic tradition. If freedom is the original being of man, then it is through choice that man drives toward historical and existential actualization and achieves self-awareness and self-integration. This is what Jaspers means when he speaks of decision as constituting the "substance" of man.[7] "Insofar as I choose, I am; by not choosing I lose my self."[8] Through choice I affirm my being. Indecision involves a loss of being and the victory of non-being. I constitute myself through my decisions and through these decisions seek to wrestle successfully with the threat of non-being. Selfhood is achieved, never simply given. Kurt Reinhardt in his book *The Existentialist Revolt* has appropriately suggested that Jaspers translates Descartes' *cogito ergo sum* into an *eligo ergo sum*.[9] Resolute choice becomes the touchstone for authentic self-hood. "Resolve and self-being are one," concludes Jaspers in his *Philosophie*.[10]

Berdyaev is at one with Kierkegaard and Jaspers on the centrality of freedom. In his book *The Destiny of Man*, Berdyaev develops a theo-andric ethics which, in its phenomenological aspect, is founded upon a radical view of freedom. Man's being, argues Berdyaev, springs from a primeval, uncreated, meontic freedom, which provides the ontological condition for an ethics of creativity. Classical teleology with its concepts of substance and fixed ends could never proceed beyond the restricting confines of a deterministic world-view and hence remained impoverished in accounting for the creative act. Only a philosophy of freedom, argues Berdyaev, can do justice to the creativity which man exhibits as he molds his destiny. In his book *Freedom and the Spirit*, he develops the concept of freedom within the context of the opposition between nature and spirit. As with the early Hegel, spirit and freedom become for Berdyaev convertible terms. However, unlike the later Hegel, Berdyaev does not advance a dialectical synthesis in which nature is *aufgehoben* through a cunning of reason. Berdyaev proposes an ontological dualism in which there is a determinism of nature and a freedom of spirit.

Sartre and Marcel, although disagreeing as to the meaning of freedom, particularly in its theological expression, nevertheless are united in their appeal to a philosophy of existence in which freedom provides the guiding motif.[11] Sartre has elucidated the theme of freedom not only in his major philosophical work, *L'Être et le Néant*, but also in his novels and plays. Freedom for Sartre is indistinguishable from human reality. Existence and freedom are identified. There is no difference between man's being and his being-free.[12] Man is condemned to freedom. He cannot cease being free. Freedom, quite clearly, cannot be understood as a quality or property which is somehow attached to man's being. Freedom is the very stuff of human reality. Man does not *have* freedom; he *is* freedom.

Traditionally the question of freedom has been discussed in connection with the so-called "freedom of the will." The problem then becomes that of determinism vs. indeterminism. Is the will determined by motives, inclinations, and ends, or does it possess an autonomy on the basis of which it can act contrary to these motives, inclinations, and ends? The existentialists, particularly Jaspers, Sartre, and Heidegger, have insisted on a re-examination of the traditional formulation of the problem. The traditional formulation is rooted in an ontology of on-handness in which the will is objectified as a thing which may or may not have freedom. The determinist objectifies the will and defines it as an expression of necessitated mechanistic functions and thus denies freedom, but the freedom which he denies is only a phantom or a "straw man." The indeterminist is intent upon defending freedom, but by transforming the will into an object he surreptitiously denies that which he wishes to affirm. "In every case determinism and indeterminism lead to a false level. They make the existential source (*Ursprung*) dependent," says Jaspers. "The one makes freedom falsely objective and in spite of his constant affirmation dissolves it; a defense of freedom which is not genuinely freedom leads only to an unconscious negation of freedom. The other denies freedom but actually never strikes it, for what he denies is an objectified phantom. Both are wrong because they transform all being into objective being and thus forfeit freedom."[13] Although certain individual volitional acts may be objectified for psychological analysis, freedom as the original source of these acts eludes any objectification. The moment that freedom and existence are objectified, both are lost. At best, the indeterminist may muster evidence for the presence of chance and arbitrariness, as in the proverbial story of the donkey who opts for one of two bundles of hay placed equidistant from him. But chance and arbitrariness are not freedom, and in the final analysis to speak of freedom of the will, when the will is understood as an object or a thing, is to speak of the freedom of a thing, which is blatantly contradictory. It is for this reason, argues Tillich, that determinism is always right when the problem is objectively posed. It is right, however, only because in the final analysis it expresses nothing more than the tautology that a thing is a thing.[14]

Sartre has also given careful attention to the phenomenon of will as it relates to the freedom of man. The will, he argues, should not be understood as a privileged manifestation of freedom. It is a psychic event among other psychic events, and like all psychic events it presupposes an original freedom which provides the foundation through which it constitutes itself as will. Both passional and volitional action follow from the primary project of a for-itself whose essence is freedom. Freedom is thus not an expression of the will, but rather the will is an expression of freedom. The will, writes Sartre, "is determined within the framework of motives and ends already posited by the for-itself in a transcendent projection of itself toward its possibles." [15] Properly speaking, there is a freedom of man but not a freedom of the will. The will is a consequent psychic phenomenon. It emerges as a reflective decision in relation to the ends which the for-itself has projected. The will is thus supported by an original, ontological freedom.

Closely connected with the traditional discussions of the doctrine of free will is the doctrine of an inner teleology. Combined with the idea of free will, the teleological point of view affirms that there are certain fixed ends in human nature, made known to the intellect, which the will can then choose either to realize or not realize. As the existentialist view of freedom rejects the concept of free will, so also it rejects the doctrine of an inner teleology—at least in its application to human existence. Man has no inner *telos* which directs him to a given end. As Bergson pointed out, the teleological view is simply determinism in an attenuated form. Finalism is simply the inversion of mechanism. Both views lead to the conclusion that all is given. Man in his primordial freedom, the existentialists maintain, *chooses* his ends. He projects, appraises, questions, and modifies his ends in the moments of decisive action throughout his personal history. Teleology as a strictly cosmological category can make no place for history, and thus it excludes freedom and decision, for decision as we have seen is the very stuff of history.[16] The teleological point of view has its basis in an ontology of on-handness, but such an ontology can never penetrate the interior structures of the lived experience of the historical self. Or it does so only at the expense of transforming man's unique personal existence and historical freedom into an object or a thing. Existentialism, in all its varieties, is a continuing protest against any such objectification and depersonalization of man.

2. The Unauthentic Mode

Freedom provides the ontological basis for unauthenticity and authenticity as possible modes of existence. Man can affirm his freedom through resolute choice and thus attain integrity, or he can abdicate his freedom, neglect to choose, lose his existential centeredness, and succumb to unauthenticity. Although Heidegger was the first to formulate an ontological clarification of the distinction between the authentic and the unauthentic, the reality of these two possible modes of existence was earlier set forth in Kierkegaard's doctrine of the stages —and indeed has historical roots in the whole Judaic-Christian tradition. Kierkegaard's doctrine of the stages is as crucial for an understanding of his analysis and interpretation of human existence as is his description of the self as a synthesis of possibility and necessity. These two schemata of analysis, as we shall show in our discussion, are basically interrelated, and each must be understood with the help of the other.

The word, "stages," insofar as it suggests successive levels of development, does not do justice to the intended meaning of Kierkegaard's threefold characterization of the human self. In the last half of his book *Stages on Life's Way*, Kierkegaard uses the word "existence-spheres" instead of the word, "stages." The former clearly comes nearer to the intended meaning. "There are three existence-spheres: the aesthetic, the ethical, the religious. . . . The aesthetic sphere is that of immediacy, the ethical is that of requirement . . . , the religious is that of fulfillment." [17] The doctrine of the existence-spheres underlies the whole of Kierkegaard's thought; however, it is most systematically and most explicitly presented in *Either/Or* and *Stages on Life's Way*. In *Either/Or* Kierkegaard sets forth what he calls an outline of the territory of the aesthetic view of life. Aesthetic existence, defined in its broadest terms, in contrast to ethical existence, is existence determined by immediacy. "What is the aesthetical in a man, and what is the ethical? To this I would reply: the aesthetical in a man is that by which he is immediately what he is; the ethical is that whereby he becomes what he becomes." [18] But the aesthetic sphere is itself not a simple phenomenon. It is multi-dimensional in that it expresses itself through various modifications. Although these various modifications within the aesthetic sphere are nowhere systematically delineated by Kierkegaard, we can discern at least two main varieties of the aesthetic point of view: romantic hedonism and rationalistic speculation.

Romantic hedonism receives its most vivid exemplification in Kierkegaard's portrait of the young lover, portrayed in his essay "Diary of a Seducer." It soon becomes apparent that Kierkegaard's young lover is a prototype of Mozart's Don Giovanni. The life of the young lover is basically an experiment. He experiments with numerous possibilities but never chooses any of these possibilities with an inward passion. He experiments with love but never commits himself in marriage. As Kierkegaard explains in the *Postscript*, "The aestheticist in *Either/Or* was an existential possibility, a young, richly gifted, partly hopeful human being, experimenting with himself and with life." [19] The aesthetic sphere is thus represented as the sphere of indecision. The aestheticist is unable to make a choice. He flounders in possibility. Or to express it in terms of the analysis in *The Sickness Unto Death,* the self becomes volatilized and "tires itself out with floundering in the possible." [20] It lacks necessity or relatedness to its past. Living in the aesthetic sphere the self is unable to define itself because it neglects to choose itself. It seeks to exist as pure possibility and refuses to take on concrete determinants through which it alone can achieve centeredness and integrity.

The guiding principle for the young lover in the aesthetic sphere is enjoyment or pleasure. "Its teaching is, 'enjoy life,' and it explains it thus: 'live for your pleasure.' " [21] Physical beauty and health are exalted as the principal internal conditions of this life of pleasure; wealth, glory, and high status are viewed as the principal external conditions. In this life of pleasure the aestheticist lives in the moment. But he lives in an unauthentic moment, because the moment has no permanent relevance for the whole of his life. After the moment passes, all is over, all lapses into an objectified past. The moment, for the aestheticist, is a successive "now" which loses its significance as soon as it goes by. He lives in an illusory moment which is merely an erotic present. In this erotic present he seeks to escape from the future which demands responsible decision. As he retreats from the future, so also he forgets his past. He disperses himself in the unauthentic present, losing the continuity with his existential past and the relevance of his existential future. His self has no unity, no continuity, and no centeredness. He chooses but not with the whole of his being, which always includes the future and the past. Thus his choice, in the last analysis, is no choice at all. "Therewith you have chosen . . . not, to be sure, as you yourself will admit, the better part. But in reality you have not chosen at all, or it is in an improper sense of the word you have chosen. Your choice is an aesthetic choice, but an aesthetic choice is no choice." [22]

In the above description of the aesthetic sphere we immediately recognize the ethical significance of Kierkegaard's existential analysis of time. The life of the aestheticist exemplifies an unauthentic view of time as a succession of "nows" which are real only in the erotic present. The past consists of instants which are gone and have no more relevance for his existence. The future holds instants which may become relevant for the erotic present when they arrive, but as yet they are not real. In aesthetic existence there is no repetition of the past and no facing of the future which always already belongs to the self. The aestheticist strives to squeeze all reality into the present. But in this attempt he sacrifices his unity or integrity. He becomes a "multifarious" self, striving to fulfill all his present desires which demand satisfaction. "When an individual regards his self aesthetically, he becomes conscious of this self as a manifold concretion very variously characterized; but in spite of the inward diversity, all of it taken together is, nevertheless, his nature, each component has just as much right to assert itself, just as much right to demand satisfaction. His soul is like a plot of ground in which all sorts of herbs are planted, all with the same claim to thrive; his self consists of this multifariousness, and he has no self which is higher than this." [23]

Kierkegaard finds in Nero another exemplification of this aesthetic dispersion of the self.[24] Surrounded by ministers of pleasure Nero demands satisfaction of his immediate lusts. He craves for pleasure in each successive moment but is never fully satisfied. There are always some desires which remain unsatisfied, and those which have been momentarily satisfied return in various disguises. In this respect Nero and the young lover express the same view of existence, and both lose themselves in a frustrating cycle of pleasure-seeking.

The rationalist, the detached speculative thinker, like the romantic hedonist, belongs in the aesthetic sphere of existence. The principal representative of this variety of aesthetic existence is Kierkegaard's favorite opponent—Hegel. Hegel is for Kierkegaard the embodiment of speculative rationalism *par excellence*. The rationalist shares the aesthetic sphere with the hedonist because both express immediacy as the common denominator. "All of the stages [within the aesthetic sphere] have this in common, that what one lives for is that whereby one immediately is what one is; for reflection never grasps so high that it grasps beyond this." [25] The hedonist is immediate in his pleasure; the rationalist is immediate in his thought. In this immediacy of thought the rationalist or speculative thinker comically forgets that he exists. He seeks to understand reality through the logic of pure thought for which the individual existent really does not matter. Hegelian rationalism mediates existential reality and essential reality in the pure thought of immediate reflection. But in the region of pure thought the Hegelian can find no place for existential and historical becoming. To be sure, he advances theories about the nature of movement and process, but this is a movement within the confines of a logical necessity, which is no movement at all. In the rationalistic understanding of the historical process there can be no question of an either/or. Everything is viewed under the category of a cosmological necessity. Historical becoming, existential freedom, the reality of the future, and decisive action are of no account for the speculative thinker. Thus both the hedonist and the rationalist evade the responsibility of decision. The hedonist evades choice by dispersing himself in momentary pleasures; and the rationalist evades choice by playing the role of the detached observer, who views world history through the interplay of logical categories but never participates in existence with passion and inwardness. The speculative philosopher makes no resolute choices. "To the philosopher world history is concluded, and he mediates. Hence, in our age as the order of the day we have the disgusting sight of young men who are able to mediate Christianity and paganism, are able to play with the titanic forces of history, and are unable to tell a plain man what he has to do in life, and who do not know any better what they themselves have to do." [26] The speculative thinker reduces existence to thought, sacrifices involvement for detachment, and substitutes a logic of universal history for concrete decision. In such a mode of existence the self has not yet authentically found itself as an historical self which must concretely face its future through decisive action.

The indecision which characterizes the life of the aestheticist is also the distinctive mark of the public conformist, who is for Kierkegaard another example of unauthentic existence. The public conformist, like the hedonist and the rationalist, suppresses the urgency and retreats from the responsibility of decision. The task of every man is to choose himself as an individual. This task, however, is made singularly difficult because of the levelling tendencies of the public and the crowd. The public levels man to the average, the mediocre, and the general. Especially with the help of the press, the public is able to reduce man's interests and actions to a common denominator. The public, according to Kierkegaard in *The Present Age*, has virtually made the category of the individual extinct. The public as that "monstrous abstraction" assumes the function of making decisions for the individual, and there results a stultifying standardization and conventionalism in which "everyone is undecided." [27] If the individual does not assume the responsibility for decision, then he will sooner or later find that his choices have been made for him. Jaspers expresses this Kierkegaardian theme when he writes: "It is of the very essence of the appearance of existence in its temporal being that a decision must be made. Either I decide (existentially), or a decision will be made for me (whereby I am transformed into material for another and thus lose my existence). Nothing can remain undecided." [29]

Kierkegaard singles out the crowd as a contributory factor to unauthenticity, both in its ethical and religious expression. Public conformity and levelling culminates in the view that the crowd is the criterion of truth. To have truth you must have the crowd and the public on your side. This involves, says Kierkegaard, a most fantastic distortion of truth. This is just the opposite of truth. Where the crowd is, there is untruth. It was the crowd under the guise of Athenian democracy that killed Socrates. It was the crowd under the guise of the church that crucified Christ. "The crowd is untruth. Therefore was Christ crucified, because, although He addressed Himself to all, He would have no dealing with the crowd." [29] Kierkegaard's incisive and oft bitter *Attack on Christendom* was penned in protest against a formalized religion which had virtually identified itself with convention and public opinion. In the state church of Denmark Kierkegaard saw an externalization and conformity which contradicted everything that Christ preached. Indeed, the most difficult religious task with which Kierkegaard challenges the individual is that of becoming a Christian *in Christendom*. The crowd has sucked the church into its orbit and has transformed it into a depository of prevailing conventions. The Holy Spirit has been bartered for the spirit of the times. To appeal to the crowd as the criterion of truth is thus in the last analysis an act of irreligion.

Nowhere in the scriptures does Kierkegaard find the commandment, "Thou shalt love the crowd." It reads: "Thou shalt love thy neighbour as thyself." [30]

This levelling tendency of the crowd, whether in its social or religious aspect, has produced a fractional, depersonalized, and irresponsible man. The crowd divests the individual of his unique responsibilities and confers upon him at best a numerical significance. It reduces him to a fractional man who is identified with his functions and is thereby replaceable. This does not mean that the crowd possesses some kind of a group substance through which it can act. Crowds never act. They are abstractions which have no hands. Action is always the action of individuals within a crowd. Socrates was killed and Christ was crucified through the corporate actions of individuals. No one single individual had the courage to condemn Socrates or to lay hands upon Christ. But in corporate action each individual could do what he was unable to do alone. Hence, when one is sacrificed to the crowd, one is sacrificed to the actions executed by the individuals who constitute it. To take refuge in the crowd is to take refuge in the decisions of others. It is in this way that the individual flees in cowardice from affirming his authentic self. He wants others to make his decisions, so he thinks what others think, he feels what others feel, and he does what others do. When this is fully accomplished, he has lost his self. He has, in Heidegger's terminology, given himself over to *Das Man.*

The common denominator of the various modifications of unauthentic existence as sketched by Kierkegaard is a retreat from the responsibility of choice. The self exists unauthentically because it has not yet earnestly and passionately chosen itself in its concrete existence. The either/or is a matter of indifference for the romantic hedonist, for the detached rationalist, and for the public conformist. "There comes at last an instant when there no longer is any question of an either/or, not because he has chosen but because he has neglected to choose, which is equivalent to saying, because others have chosen for him, because he has lost his self." [31] The unauthentic self is always deferring the moment in which a passionate choice must be made.

Heidegger, directly or indirectly influenced by Kierkegaard, has sought an ontological clarification of unauthentic existence in his descriptive concepts of the "anonymous one" and fallenness. We have previously examined the concept of the "anonymous one" in connection with the structural determinant of communality (*Mitsein*), and the concept of fallenness in connection with the care-structure and the three modes of temporality.[32] We must now investigate the bearing of these concepts upon the specific question of unauthenticity. The "anonymous one" succumbs to the false security of everydayness by moving within the realm of approved habits, accepted customs, and current conventions of everyday life. In this everydayness he falls victim to a way of life in which the average becomes the measure or standard of his existence. This leads to a levelling of his original possibilities and to a publicity through which he expresses only the opinions of the public and the masses and divests himself of his personal responsibilities. The unauthenticity of the "anonymous one" thus involves a flight from *Dasein's* unique possibilities, a sacrifice of his personal freedom to the will and the whims of the public. These movements of the "anonymous one" are disclosed by talk, curiosity, and ambiguity, which are specific expressions of superficial concerns. Talk is a degenerate form of communication which simply expresses the accepted, average, everyday interpretations of the public. No real content is communicated, and nothing is genuinely understood. All attention is focused on the talking itself, which always uses the conventional clichés and simply repeats what someone else has said. Curiosity reveals the tendency to explore things, not for the purpose of arriving at truth, but simply for the sake of discovering novelty. Man is always "on the move," searching for something which can provide a momentary distraction and diversion. But this leads to a dispersion of the self in which integrity and unity of purpose are lost. Ambiguity expresses the vascillation of the "anonymous one" between that which is genuinely comprehended and that which is only talk. The trivial and superficial is never clearly separated from the important and significant. This existential ambiguity pervades all thought and action of the "anonymous one."

This threefold structure of talk, curiosity, and ambiguity, which reveals the manner in which the "anonymous one" exists, constitutes the existentialist structure of fallenness. Fallenness, properly defined, is "an absorption into a being-with-others insofar as this absorption is induced by talk, curiosity, and ambiguity." [33] For the most part *Dasein* exists in this fallen condition, fallen from his unique and original possibilities. Heidegger delineates six constitutive elements in his phenomenological description of fallenness: (1) temptation (*Versuchung*), (2) contentment (*Beruhigung*), (3) self-estrangement (*Entfremdung*), (4) self-entanglement (*Sichverfangen*), (5) the fall itself

(*Absturz*), and (6) the "whirl" (*Wirbel*). In his talk and receptiveness to the appeals of the public, the "anonymous one" prepares for himself a constant temptation to fallenness. He is tempted or invited to surrender his unique individuality and personal freedom. In this temptation, talk is always there with its words of contentment, assuring the "anonymous one" that everything is in the best of order. This contentment, however, is not a passive contentment. It leads to uninhibited pursuits (*Hemmungslosigkeit des "Betriebs"*)—the investigation of strange cultures, a curiosity about everything imaginable, and an unceasing craving to know everyone and everything. But in this striving to know everything about everything, man forgets himself and becomes estranged from his own unique self.[34] Kierkegaard had already shown in his polemic against Hegel how a knowledge of world history may provide us with voluminous details pertaining to the rise and fall of ancient empires but at the same time leave us impoverished concerning knowledge of ourselves. In this estrangement the "anonymous one" entangles himself, locking himself up in a prison of everyday concerns (*Verfängnis*). This movement through temptation, contentment, estrangement, and self-entanglement culminates in the "whirl" or gyration in which man "falls" to an uprooted and baseless existence. In this terminologically complex and philosophically strange language, Heidegger has sought to describe the primary movements in the phenomenon of fallenness. It is through these movements that *Dasein* disperses himself and loses his integrity, failing at each moment to grasp those authentic possibilities which structurally always belong to him.

In the second half of *Sein und Zeit* Heidegger discusses the phenomenon of fallenness in connection with the notion of time as ecstatic existence. The unauthentic dispersion of the "anonymous one" is now defined as a dispersion of the ecstasies of temporality. "The original possibilities of existence, authenticity and unauthenticity, are ontologically rooted in the possible temporalizing of temporality." [35] We remember that existentiality, facticity, and fallenness, as the three structural moments of concern, are grounded in the future, past, and present respectively. *Dasein*, in his unauthentic, fallen mode exists simply as present, to the neglect of his future and past possibilities. In Kierkegaard's analysis the structures of selfhood are disrupted when the self fails to relate itself to itself as a synthesis of possibility (future) and necessity (past); in Heidegger's analysis unauthentic existence results from a refusal to face the future in one's existentiality or protential understanding and from a consequent inability to take over the facticity of one's past. Existing unauthentically, *Dasein* exists piecemeal as a queer kind of present entity, separated from his future and his past. As simple presence he is reduced to the mode of on-handness and is depersonalized. He succeeds in transforming himself into an object or a thing.[36] His rich personal history, in which he has a remembered and repeatable past and a projected future, is suppressed. The ecstasies of time, which are integral aspects of the structural whole of *Dasein*, are separated and dispersed. The very Being of *Dasein* is fractured. He has lost the centeredness and integrated unity of his temporal modes.[37]

Unauthenticity as a possible mode of existence thus achieves its final clarification in the "existentials" of the "anonymous one" and fallenness, both of which indicate the retreat from the urgency of choice. Now it is necessary to underscore Heidegger's repeated reminder that the concept of fallenness is strictly an ontological structure and must not be confused with an ethico-religious concept of sin. The ontological analysis remains neutral to any special ontic possibilities, whether theologically, sociologically, or psychologically defined. "The existentialist-ontological interpretation makes no ontic pronouncements as regards the depravity of human nature, not because the necessary means of verification are lacking, but because the problem *precedes* every assertion about depravity or innocence. Fallenness is an ontological concept. No ontic decision is made as to whether man is 'drowned in sin,' in the *status corruptionis*, or whether he exists in the *status integritatis*, or whether he finds himself in a state between the two, *status gratiae*." [38] Philosophy cannot provide a justification for the truth or falsity of religious experience—as it did in Hegelian rationalism, for example.[39] Heidegger makes it crystal clear that religious faith is its own foundation and cannot be judged by any criterion external to itself. Theology, he writes, "seeks for an original interpretation of the Being of man in relation to God which proceeds from and remains within the meaning of faith itself." [40] At no point does Heidegger's philosophy deny the religious as a possible concrete mode of experience. The charge of atheism against Heidegger is wholly without foundation. His philosophy is neither theistic nor atheistic. It is a philosophy of human finitude in which any assertion concerning the existence or non-existence of God is pure and simple philosophical presumption. Philosophy, properly understood, seeks a clarification of the structures of Being in abstraction from any concrete relation between man and God. Heidegger states his position clearly when he writes in his essay *Wom Wesen des Grundes:* "In the ontological interpretation of *Dasein* as being-in-the-world neither a positive nor a negative decision as regards the possible Being of God is made. Rather an adequate concept of *Dasein* is first achieved through an elucidation of transcendence, after which the question relative to *Dasein's* relationship to God may properly be asked." [41] The concrete experience of sin as an ontic modification of fallenness in no way receives its justification through an ontological analysis. This is why Heidegger insists that fallenness not be confused with an ethico-religious concept. The specific relation which obtains between the ontological and the ethico-religious is that the former provides the conceptual clarification of the regions in which the latter receives its concrete expression. The self which concretely experiences sin is a self which is so structured that authenticity and unauthenticity are possible modes of existence. When we thus argue that Heidegger has ontologized Kierkegaard, we mean that he has rendered explicit the ontology of human finitude (already implicit in Kierkegaard) which is presupposed by any ontic self-understanding of man, whether this be a physico-biological, socio-psychological, or ethico-religious self-understanding.

3. *Resolve and Authenticity*

The aestheticist in Kierkegaard's doctrine of the "stages" personifies the unauthentic mode of existence. He exists unauthentically because he is unable to make a choice and thus fails to apprehend himself in his unique, historical freedom. The ethical thinker personifies the authentic mode. The peculiar and distinguishing characteristic of the ethical sphere is that it is the sphere of decision and resolute choice. To exist ethically is to exist in full awareness of one's freedom and to choose one's self within the conditions of this freedom. "The act of choosing is essentially a proper and stringent expression of the ethical." [42] The transition from the aesthetic to the ethical thus marks the transition from the unauthentic to the authentic. In the ethical sphere the accent falls upon the urgency of choice, and this choice becomes a matter of infinite concern. The ethical choice, in Kierkegaard's language, is a choice permeated with passion. In its infinite passion or concern the existing self strives to become itself by resolutely choosing itself in an act of inward freedom. In this way it achieves its genuine or authentic selfhood. "Even the richest personality is nothing before he has chosen himself, and on the other hand even what one might call the poorest personality is everything when he has chosen himself; for the great thing is not to be this or that but to be oneself, and this every one can be if he wills it." [43] Choice is the *conditio sine qua non* for the attainment of authentic selfhood. Choice liberates the self from the bondage of immediacy, both of pleasure and pure reflection, as well as from the anonymity and levelling tendencies of the public. Through decision the self is able to "collect itself, as it were, out of this dispersion and become in itself transformed." [44] Decision unifies and centralizes the self. The aestheticist is always "eccentric" in that he has his center in the periphery, which means that he has lost his self. The ethical man, on the other hand, has his center within himself; he has integrated his various moods and projects. "When a man lives ethically his mood is centralized." [45] The ethical man strives for the unity and integrity which comes with resolute choice. In the act of choosing man "becomes himself, consciousness is unified, and he is himself." [46] The unity and integrity of the self are not "given" in some residual ego or abiding substratum. The self must *gain* or *achieve* its unity through choice. The self is not an object or thing. The self is an historical being, anticipating a future and remembering a past which must be unified through resolute choice in the opportune moment. Whereas the aestheticist loses himself in the unauthentic present, neither anticipating a future nor repeating a past, the ethical man lives in anticipation and memory. The future, for the ethical man, is prior to the other directions of time insofar as an authentic life is lived primarily into the future. Yet the past retains its existential relevance, for the past always stands in a relation of possibility to present choices. In a unified self the past is rendered present through the phenomenon of repetition. Through repetition the "discord in my nature is resolved, I am again unified." [47] A self is unified or integrated when the future, past, and present are held together in the moment of decision. Hence, time existentially understood becomes of paramount significance for the ethical sphere. The ethical thinker "emphasizes particularly the category of time and its significance." [48]

Authenticity is made possible through resolute choice, and choice presupposes freedom. As the self gains its integrity by establishing a temporal and historic continuity, it is ever in the process of transforming necessity into freedom. "For man's eternal dignity consists in the fact that he can have a history, the divine element in him consists in that fact that he himself, if he will, can import to this history continuity, for this it acquires only when it is not the sum of all that has happened to me or befallen me but is my own work, in such a way that even what has befallen me is by me transformed and translated from necessity to freedom." [49] Choice translates necessity into freedom. This does not mean, however, that necessity is dissolved. The self still remains a synthesis of necessity and possibility, but it takes on a new qualification. In every act there is a hidden necessity or a factor of facticity. If necessity were dissolved, finitude would vanish, and the self would become an infinite or absolute freedom. But as long as it exists, the self remains a finite and actualized freedom, which means that it has a destiny, or as Heidegger would say, it "exists factically." Through its freedom it can translate or transform this necessity by giving it a new meaning. The past decisions and the past history which constitute the self's destiny can be infused with new existential import. They cannot be forgotten, for they remain as intrinsic limits of the being of the self, but they are remembered or recollected in a new light. They are recollected as possibilities which can be repeated and transformed through creative and responsible decision. The past can be translated from a burden into a creative possibility. Kierkegaard discusses this transformation of the past in connection with the phenomenon of forgiveness. Through forgiveness a past guilt loses its destructive quality and becomes the occasion for a new attitude toward one's self and one's relations with others. The guilt is still remembered, but it is no longer remembered as a fixed and on-hand trait of one's personality. It is remembered as forgiven guilt, or as guilt which has undergone a translation into freedom. In the same way the possibility of psychiatric healing presupposes a freedom over one's past. Healing could not occur if the patient's past were irrevocably fixed. If one's past were forever closed, life would be ultimately tragic. Psychiatric healing is made possible because of the patient's ability to transcend his past, redefine himself, and accept himself as the new self which he has now become. In every ontic situation—whether theological or psychological—it is choice which keeps the self from being swallowed by necessity.

The touchstone of the decision through which the self achieves its unity or integrity is pathos, passion, or earnestness. Authentic choice is choice made in passion. In making a choice, says Kierkegaard, "it is not so much a question of choosing the right as of the energy, the earnestness, the pathos with which one chooses." [50] This does not mean that the distinction between right and wrong action has no significance for Kierkegaard; it only underscores the fact that authenticity as a mode of existence precedes any question concerning the specification of particular moral norms or standards. "It is therefore not yet a question of the choice of something in particular, it is not a question of the reality of the thing chosen, but of the reality of the act of choice." [51] The ethical stage designates a way of existence rather than a set of moral prescriptions. Moral principles, values, and norms take on ethical validity only within the context of the ethical as a mode of existence. Being precedes value, and ontology precedes normative ethics.

Choice always involves an act of will. The crucial determinant in decision is not the deliberation, important as it might be, but what Kierkegaard calls "the baptism of the will." [52] This voluntaristic emphasis becomes apparent also in Kierkegaard's discussion of the structures of self in *The Sickness Unto Death*. "The more consciousness, the more self; the more consciousness, the more will, and the more will, the more self." [53] The same theme is elaborated in Kierkegaard's discourses. "Purity of heart" is to will one thing.[54] Yet this voluntaristic emphasis must not be understood as an anti-intellectualism or as a denial of the role of imagination. The subjective thinker seeks for a unification of imagination, thought, and will in the medium of existence. James Collins aptly characterizes Kierkegaard's position on this point when he states that "Kierkegaard does not advocate that we *suppress* imagination and intellect, but only that we *integrate* them with will and the sense of concrete conditions of action which it heightens." [55] Will, intellect, and imagination are later manifestations of an original project of the self, namely, a project of the self as freedom. Freedom, which constitutes the very existential being of the self, is ontologically prior to any reasonings of the intellect, inclinations of the will, and representations of the imagination. As Jaspers has expressed it, existence is the source from which reason, volition, and sentience spring.

The religious sphere constitutes the culmination or final stage of unified and integrated existence. Although in tension with the ethical, "the religious sphere . . . lies so close to the ethical that they are in constant communication with one another." [56] Thus Kierkegaard often brackets the two spheres and speaks of the ethico-religious sphere. The new determinant added in the religious sphere is suffering. Suffering is the highest intensification of subjectivity. It expresses the most profound movement of inwardness. In the phenomenon of suffering the breach of the religious sphere with aesthetic immediacy is clearly made manifest. The sufferer is neither immediate in pleasure nor immediate in reflection. To suffer is qualitatively different from reflecting about suffering.

There is a twofold modification which characterizes the religious sphere—religiousness A and religiousness B. Religiousness A is the religion of immanence. Religiousness B is the "paradoxical religiousness" in which the new existential determinants of sin and faith are posited.[57] Consciousness of sin discloses the estrangement of the self from God. But sin always points to the existential possibility of faith, in which the discontinuities of sin are overcome. In this encounter with faith, as a distinctive determinant of religiousness B, the self confronts a teleological suspension of the universal-ethical with its external moral demands. This teleological suspension is most sharply set forth in Kierkegaard's existential exegesis of the story of Abraham and Isaac in *Fear and Trembling*. Judged in terms of the universal-ethical, or the ethical understood as an obligatory moral demand with the sanctions of objectivity and rational intelligibility, Abraham's intended act of sacrifice of his son made him guilty of murder. Understood in terms of the subjective and inward movements of faith, his intended sacrifice was a superlative expression of religious commitment. To avoid possible misinterpretation of Kierkegaard's teleological suspension of the ethical, it is necessary to underscore the distinction between the ethical as a universal moral requirement and the ethical as a sphere or mode of existence. In the former we have to do with an ethical heteronomy which ultimately leads to a moral legalism; in the latter we are dealing with a quality of existence determined by passionate and resolute choice. Abraham's act of faith was discontinuous with external moral standards but was a most profound expression of resolute choice, which for Kierkegaard is the definitive mark of the ethical stage.[58]

The religious sphere, which encompasses both religiousness A and religiousness B, is the sphere of religious commitment. But in this religious sphere, as we have already suggested, the ethical is not destroyed; nor is the aesthetic sphere excluded. The religious commitment of the third stage of existence in no way annihilates the preceding two. Instead, it restores them in a new perspective. In *Either/Or* Kierkegaard speaks of the three existence-spheres as three great allies: "If you cannot reach the point of seeing the aesthetical, the ethical, and the religious as three great allies, if you do not know how to conserve the unity of the diverse appearances which everything assumes in these diverse spheres, then life is devoid of meaning." [59] The ethical sphere does not annihilate the aesthetical but, rather, transforms it. So also the religious preserves both the aesthetical and the ethical. Concerning the relation of the aesthetic sphere to the other spheres, Kierkegaard writes: "All of the aesthetical remains in a man, only it is reduced to a ministering role and thereby precisely is preserved. Yes, it is true that one does not live in it as before, but from this it by no means follows that it has been lost; it may perhaps be employed in a different way, but from this it by no means follows that it is gone." [60] The existence-spheres are thus not to be understood as temporally successive stages or levels of development in which each is left behind through the advancement of the other. Properly understood, the existence-spheres define possible modes of existence which are always in some sense present and which penetrate the personality in its process of self-actualization. They constitute the cross-section of the self, and coexist interdependently throughout the history of the self. No sphere is sufficient by itself. All spheres play their proper roles in a unified and integrated existence. The aesthetic sphere is never excluded from authentic selfhood. It is preserved and taken up as a dependent and relative phase of personality. "The whole of the aesthetical comes back again in its relativity." [61] In authentic existence the aesthetic sphere is no longer absolutized as the final and sovereign mode of existence (as in the case of Don Giovanni, for example) but is transformed through an ethical inwardness and religious commitment. The self thus takes on a new direction or a new orientation. The concrete and existential decisions which ultimately unify and integrate the self are grounded in the experience of faith in religiousness B. The fullest concrete expression of authentic selfhood is reached via faith in the religious sphere, which then restores the aesthetical and the ethical as inseparable and interdependent phases of existence.

These three existence-spheres, representing interdependent phases of the history of the self, include irony and humor as transitional stages or "boundary zones" between the aesthetical and the ethical and the ethical and the religious, respectively. "There are thus three spheres of existence: the aesthetic, the ethical, the religious. Two boundary zones correspond to these three: irony, constituting the boundary between the aesthetic and the ethical; humor, as the boundary that separates the ethical from the religious." [62] Kierkegaard himself was a master of irony and humor and saw clearly their existential relevance. His first writing, which was submitted as a dissertation for the Master's Degree, deals specifically with the concept of irony as it was used and taught by the Athenian Socrates.[63] He devotes further attention to the phenomena of irony and humor in his *Postscript* and *Stages*. The purpose of irony is to rouse man from his unauthentic concerns to an ethical consciousness. To this end the method of irony was used by Socrates. Fulfilling his role as the "gadfly of Athens," Socrates pricked the complacent conscience of the conventional Athenian so as to elicit an awareness of the ethical. The irony of Socrates, writes Kierkegaard, "has a tendency towards the ethical, seeking to rouse the man to win self-assurance." [64] To attain ethical existence one must first become aware of the incongruity between the inward and the outward, between the subjective and the objective, as they are expressed in one's life. Irony elicits this awareness. Hence the ironist uses irony precisely "because he grasps the contradiction there is between the manner in which he exists inwardly and the fact that he does not outwardly express it." [65] The ironist apprehends the discrepancy between the inward lack of wisdom and the outward manifestation which conceals this lack. He apprehends the discrepancy between the inward lack of virtue and the outward claim of its possession. These cross-currents of incongruities and discrepancies define the ironical situation. The aestheticist remains happily unaware of these incongruities and seeks to suppress the conditions which bring them to the light of consciousness. The ironist, who is in the "boundary zone" between the aesthetical and the ethical, poignantly expresses these incongruities and thus drives beyond the aesthetical to the ethical.

As irony lies between the aesthetical and the ethical, so humor lies between the ethical and the religious. The humorist, although he has become aware of the contradiction between the outward expression and the inward movement of faith, like the ironist, is still unable to affirm the higher. He "protests against the assumed commensurability of the external" but at the same time is not yet able to "maintain a relationship to God in terms of religious passion *stricte sic dictus*." [66] His commitment remains incomplete and partial. But he is an "awakened" individual who is on the threshold of wresting religion from its externality and infusing it with the determinant of inwardness.

Heidegger and Sartre follow closely Kierkegaard's central insight that the authentic life is the life of resolute choice and commitment. However, for the most part, Sartre's reflections on the subject remain undeveloped, and consequently it never becomes clear what Sartre means by authenticity and to what extent it is possible in his tragic view of life. Yet there are suggestions by Sartre that man is capable of authentic choices which provide at least provisional meaning for an existence which is somehow incurably fractured. A man is that which he wills to be and that which he makes of himself through his existential projects. This presupposes an awareness of freedom, and freedom, for Sartre, as for Kierkegaard and Heidegger, is the foundation for any possible authentic selfhood. For Sartre, authenticity is achieved when man emancipates himself from the "bad faith" (*mauvaise foi*) through which he has transformed himself into the mode of objective being (*en-soi*) and seeks for a radical affirmation of himself as subjective freedom (*pour-soi*). He seeks to affirm a freedom over his destiny or facticity as well as a freedom over his situation in general, which includes the Other (*Autrui*), his environmental world, and his instrumental world. The situation with its coefficient of adversity is itself chosen, and thus brought into the orbit of my free projects. I am born a bourgeois or a proletarian but remain responsible for my social status. Through my freedom I either deny the existence and reality of social classes and thus choose myself as a bourgeois, or I affirm their reality and choose myself as a proletarian. Social conditions, environmental factors, my past, my death, and the existence of other selves, remain neutral until I have given them a place in the world of my projects and chosen them either as obstacles to be overcome or opportunities which I find advantageous. Hence for Sartre there is no final limit to freedom, save the limit which freedom imposes upon itself. Freedom becomes total and infinite.[67] But in Sartre's radical view of freedom, the question remains whether freedom does not cancel itself. When Sartre writes that even the individual who is subject to the executioner's tools is free, it would seem that the freedom of which he speaks is no more than a freedom to accept one's fate, which, to be sure, still has the earmarks of freedom but can hardly be understood as total and infinite. It is a freedom which has been trammeled by the facticity of existence and remains incurably partial and finite.

Kierkegaard and Heidegger take more cognizance of finitude than does Sartre. For Kierkegaard the self remains in tension between necessity and possibility, and for Heidegger *Dasein*, as long as he exists, is a complex of facticity and existentiality. This means that man's freedom is always a *finite* freedom. And authentic existence must be understood within the context of this irremovable finitude. The pivotal "existential" or structural concept in Heidegger's description of authentic existence is that of resolution (*Entschlossenheit*). Through resolute choice *Dasein* emancipates himself from the unauthentic "anonymous one" and achieves his integrity or authenticity. Heidegger's notion of resoluteness must first be understood in relation to the "existentials" of anxiety and guilt. Anxiety isolates *Dasein* from his unauthentic present preoccupations, breaks up the illusion of his everyday contentments, throws him back upon his solitude, and makes him free for the choice of the authentic possibilities which are always structurally a part of his Being. Conscience then discloses the guilt which is indelibly a part of the existential actualization of *Dasein* and summons him to the original possibilities revealed by anxiety. *Dasein* responds to this call of conscience by choosing. To understand the call of conscience is to choose. Conscience calls *Dasein* out of his unauthentic fallenness, in the mode of the "anonymous one," to his authentic possibilities, and *Dasein* responds to this call with resolution.

Now resolution as an ontological-existentialist concept must not be confused with the ontic-existential choice (*Wahl*) which determines the concretion of authenticity. The existentialist structure of resolution does not specify any concrete existential possibilities. It is charactrized by an existential indefiniteness of the particular psychological and theological possibilities which are open to the existing *Dasein* in every concrete situation. For example, the concrete achievement of faith described by Kierkegaard is a religious existential possibility which the self confronts in its concrete history and through which it may attain integrity and wholeness. But the existentialist concept of resolution remains consciously neutral in regard to the question of ultimate meaning. A radical atheistic self-affirmation may equally strive to answer the question of meaning. The concrete religious question cannot be decided on the level of ontological analysis. What Heidegger's ontology provides is a conceptual clarification of resolution as an existentialist structure of human being, which defines the universal possibility of authenticity within which all concrete and specific choices must fall. Now this ontological analysis, Heidegger reminds us, although designating another level, retains its intimacy with the concrete. Indeed, it has significance *only* insofar as it leads *Dasein* to an awareness and understanding of his existential and ontic possibilities.[68]

Dasein is brought to his unique possibilities through the intentional disclosure of anxiety, which places him in confrontation with his future and thus specifies the demand for choice. He then resolutely chooses himself in his irremovable finitude. As *Dasein* is ever projected ahead of himself in anticipating the future, authenticity or resolute choice is properly understood as "anticipatory resolution" (*vorlaufende Entschlossenheit*). *Dasein* chooses authentically only when he is projected into his future, for only then does he relate himself to the possibilities which lie ahead of him, appraise himself in light of these possibilities, and choose with the whole of his Being. In his anticipatory resolution *Dasein* comes to himself through choice and in his choosing achieves his unity and integrity.[69]

Heidegger agrees with Kierkegaard and Jaspers that decision constitutes the "substance" of selfhood. "A decision becomes the substance of the man," writes Jaspers.[70] In existentialist thought the classical concept of substance is "existentialized" in its application to the historical self. Heidegger, however, has suggested that one avoid altogether the use of the term "substance," as well as "subject," in an existentialist analysis. These are categories which apply to the mode of non-human being (at-handness and on-handness) and must be sharply contrasted with the "existentials" which are the peculiar structural concepts of human being. A proper understanding of selfhood is made impossible from the very start if man is understood with the aid of the categories of substance and subject, cosmologically defined. "The ontological concept of subject characterizes *not the selfhood of the I* qua *self but the sameness and permanency of something on-hand.*" [71] Here we see the ontological basis for Heidegger's persistent "dualism" of selfhood and thinghood, or *Dasein* and non-*Dasein*. Heidegger continually emphasizes that human existence cannot be reduced to the mode of non-human being, and thus it remains immune to any categorial definition. The "permanency" of *Dasein* resides not in some self-identical substantial ego but in the unity, self-continuity, and integrity achieved through resolve. "*Dasein* is ontologically fundamentally differentiated from all on-handness. His 'stability' is grounded not in the substantiality of a substance but rather in the integrity of the existing self, whose Being is known as Care." [72]

Here also we see the inextricable relatedness between ontology and ethics in the philosophy of Heidegger. Depersonalization and dehumanization have their roots in an inadequate ontology, consciously or unconsciously appropriated, in which man is understood as an in-

stance of non-human substance or as an on-hand being and consequently reduced to an object or thing. It has been the error of all
traditional metaphysics, asserts Heidegger, to interpret the self by recourse to a supporting ground or residual ego on which the individual
characteristics of personality are founded. The care-structure of *Dasein*
rests on no such supporting ground or substance. *Dasein* has no such
self-identical essence and static permanency as one finds in the substantial structure of an object or a utensil. The concepts of both a pre-
fabricated nature and an inner teleology are rejected by Heidegger because they conceal rather than reveal the unique personal freedom of
authentic existence. Man is not a ready-made substance. He is a protentional field of possibilities, and he achieves integrity in his choice of
these possibilities through resolution. The self is unified and integrated
in resolute choice. "The integrity of the self, understood in an existentialist sense, means nothing other than anticipatory resolution." [73] In
this anticipatory resolution *Dasein* achieves or "wins" his authentic selfhood. "The phenomenon of an authentic possibility-of-being opens the
view for the *integrity* of the self in the sense of having 'won his stand'
[*Standgewonnenhabens*]." [74]

Unauthentic existence, we have seen, receives its final clarification in the notion of temporality. *Dasein* exists unauthentically when the
temporal ecstasies, which define the retentional and protentional qualities of his care-structure, are disrupted. The reality of his past is suppressed, and his future remains unacknowledged. The authentic mode,
as the converse of the unauthentic, is also finally rooted in the phenomenon of time; but in authentic existence the ecstasies of temporality
are unified in resolute choice. *Dasein* takes over his past in repetition,
anticipates his future from which he evaluates himself as a whole, and
chooses in the moment with the entirety of his Being. An authentic
choice is a choice made with the whole of one's Being, in which past
possibilities are held in memory and the future is courageously faced.

Authentic existence involves a new attitude toward fallenness,
death, and guilt. Fallenness is not overcome in *Dasein's* resolution but is
transformed by freedom into an existential project which can be authentically taken over. Authenticity, properly understood, is a modification of fallenness.[75] It does not involve its obliteration. Authenticity and
unauthenticity are possible qualifications of the Being of *Dasein* as always already fallen to his world. Likewise authenticity does not cancel
the reality of death. The transitoriness of existence cannot be sur-

mounted, but the authentic self courageously affirms itself in the awareness of its having to die by appropriating its death as a determining
factor in the urgency of choice. An awareness of the irremovable limit of
one's being-in-the-world drives one to a passionate affirmation of one's
self through resolute choice in the opportune or privileged moment. In
authentic existence *Dasein* liberates himself from the evasive mecha-
nisms and false protections of the "anonymous one," the self which is
unable to accept the reality of its transitory existence. "The anticipatory
resolution is not a means by which death is 'overcome' but is rather the
response of the understanding to the call of conscience in which death
makes *Dasein* free to assimilate his resources and reject every retreat
from and concealment of death." [76] Guilt is courageously faced and
taken over by the resolute *Dasein*. Guilt is accepted as an indelible character of existential reality, disclosing the nothingness which threatens
existence as long as it is. There are always possibilities in the projects
of *Dasein* which remain unactualized but for which he is nonetheless
responsible. In choosing one possibility he is always excluding others.
Partiality is an implication of every choice. *Dasein* can never become
wholly sovereign over his Being, because he is always in some sense constituted by the non-being of his sacrificed possibilities which have been
excluded in his decisions. And insofar as he is responsible for the whole
of his Being, he becomes inevitably guilty in every act of choice. This
guilt is taken up in resolution. *Dasein* resolutely chooses himself as being-
guilty. "The existential taking over of guilt in resolution is authentically
consummated only when *Dasein* discloses himself in this resolution, becomes transparent to himself, and understands himself as *permanently*
guilty." [77] Resolution liberates *Dasein* from the unauthentic concealing
of guilt, characteristic of the "anonymous one," and makes possible the
affirmation of Being within the bounds of finitude.

4. *Authenticity and Community*

Critics of existentialism repeatedly level their attack against the
apparent individualism which existentialists affirm to the neglect of the
social and communal character of existence. It is argued that the existentialist has viciously abstracted the individual from his social context
and abandoned altogether any interest in authentic communal exist-

ence. Such a criticism can muster only feeble support. To be sure, certain existentialists such as Kierkegaard and Sartre, in their fear of public conformity and the possible loss of freedom involved in being with others, have placed such a premium upon individual decision that the solution to the problem of authentic communality becomes most difficult. But even Kierkegaard and Sartre have intermittently offered suggestions which point in the direction of authentic communal awareness. Furthermore, it is necessary to keep in mind the distinction between individuality and individualism. The accentuation of the reality of the individual does not necessarily entail such an existential solipsism as is implied in the use of the terms "individualism" or "individualistic." Ultimately, if he is to achieve authentic existence, the individual must make his decision alone, but this decision, made in solitude, at the same time reaches out into the social context which determines the self's concreteness. Kierkegaard clearly expresses this when he writes: "He who has ethically chosen and found himself has himself as he is determined in his whole concretion. . . . But although he himself is his aim, this aim is nevertheless another, for the self which is the aim is not an abstract self which fits everywhere and hence nowhere, but a concrete self which stands in reciprocal relations with these surroundings, these conditions of life, this natural order. This self which is the aim is not merely a personal self but a social, a civic self." [78] Sartre also gives priority to the individual. A man is what he wills to be. Man constitutes himself through the projects which he chooses in his personal freedom. But this involves a responsibility, not only for oneself but for the whole of mankind. "I am responsible for myself and for everyone else. I am creating a certain image of man of my choosing. In choosing myself, I choose man." [79]

Kierkegaard further elaborates his concept of the "social self," particularly its ethico-religious significance, in his *Edifying Discourses* and his *Works of Love*. In the latter he examines love as the primary religious directive for authentic communal life. The commandment, "Thou shalt love thy neighbour," when freely appropriated and divested of any vestigial legalism or heteronomy, defines the authentic relation between men which transforms mere sociality into religious community. In the last analysis, then, Kierkegaard does emerge with a positive doctrine of community, at least insofar as it takes on a religious definition. In Sartre there are suggestions of a creative being-with-others, but these suggestions remain undeveloped. Sartre certainly does not offer a religious doctrine of community, nor does he explicitly develop a positive resolution non-religiously defined. The Other (*Autrui*) is depicted for the most part only as a contributory factor to the negativities of existential estrangement. The Other becomes a threat to my personal freedom as he seeks to transform me into an *en-soi*.[80] This means that the relationship of love, as a basis for authentic communality, can never reach fruition or fulfillment. By transforming the loved one into an object, love brings about its own destruction, degenerating either into sadism or turning back upon itself in the movement of masochism. Both Freud and Sartre have expressed penetrating insights with regard to the destructive possibilities within love, but they have said little indeed about its creative possibilities.

Marcel, Berdyaev, Jaspers, and Heidegger offer in various ways a corrective to some of the individualistic tendencies which recur in the thought of Kierkegaard and Sartre. Marcel has formulated a philosophy of participation which is intentionally critical of Sartre on this point. Central to Marcel's view on authentic community is the distinction between being and having, as well as the notions of fidelity and love. The relationship of "having" designates an external relationship in which there is an object outside me, over which I am sovereign and which I can in some sense manipulate and mold. The relationship of "being" is a relationship of immediate involvement or participation. The former underlies the unauthentic attitude which one develops toward his body as well as toward other selves. As long as I conceive of my body only as an object or an entity which I have or possess, then I remain alienated from it and ultimately from myself. Only when I understand my body as something which I *am* do I authentically grasp its significance. I not only *possess* a body, but I *exist* as body. I am incarnated as body. The applicability of this distinction between having and being to the interpersonal relationships of the self becomes evident. As long as my dealings with another self express the mode of having, I depersonalize him and reduce him to an object. He becomes an external entity which I can possess and manipulate through my free projects. But fidelity and love make it possible for me to break through this estrangement of self from other selves by opening myself to a participation in their being and the Being which transcends us all. In authentic love the other self is no longer an object for my projects. He now fulfills an ontological need for me, and I fulfill an ontological need for him. We mutually complete each other's being through creative intersubjectivity. We make promises and seek to remain faithful to these promises. We establish bonds of loyalty and love. We acknowledge each other as a "Thou" rather than simply a "He." [81] In these ways the path is opened to authentic community.

Jaspers, probably more than any of the other existentialists, has made the problem of community and communication central to his philosophy. Indeed, communication is the guiding motif upon which his philosophy rests. "The thesis of my philosophizing is: The individual cannot become human by himself. Self-being is only real in communication with another self-being. Alone, I sink into gloomy isolation—only in community with others can I be revealed in the act of mutual discovery." [82] As for Fichte, so for Jaspers, self-knowledge involves *acknowledgement* of others. Only through communication does man arrive at genuine knowledge of himself and achieve authenticity. Such existential communication presupposes freedom, and the very task of philosophy is to strive to disclose this freedom and make communication possible. Jaspers' philosophy thus becomes at the same time a philosophy of communication and a philosophy of human freedom.

Jaspers' discussion of communication renders explicit the distinction between sociality and community. Sociality is an empirical concept which specifies certain psychological and sociological relationships which can be objectively studied and described through scientific investigation. Communication, on the other hand, remains opaque to the methods of science and must be elucidated through philosophy.[83] Sociality as an empirical concept is existentially neutral. It takes on existential import when the concept of philosophical freedom is introduced and sociality expresses itself either as a denial of this freedom (conformity) or an acknowledgement of it (community). In a sense we can speak of conformity and community as the two possible existential modifications of sociality. Conformity is an existentially destructive way of being with others. Community is an existentially creative way of being with others. Jaspers' writings are filled with illuminating descriptions of the depersonalizing and dehumanizing forces at work in conformity. Conformity reduces man to an anonymous entity and transforms him into something impersonal and replaceable.[84] *Man in the Modern Age* is devoted specifically to an analysis and description of the threat of conformity and to an interrogation of possible means for achieving a sense of community. The masses have become our masters, and we have become as automatic as ants.[85] At the root of this automa-

tion and depersonalization we find a blindness to man's essential freedom and an abdication of the personal responsibility which it entails.
Unauthentic *Mitsein*, like unauthentic *Selbstsein*, is an implication of
human bondage. Conversely, authentic *Mitsein* and authentic *Selbstsein* are made possible in and through existential freedom. Communication becomes a reality when interdependent selves mutually acknowledge the personal freedom of each other and seek to ferret out the forces
which undermine it.

Heidegger's phenomenological ontology gives a place to communication but does not make it central as does the philosophy of
Jaspers. In Heidegger's structural analysis of the phenomenon of being-
in-the-world, *Mitwelt* is delineated as one of the "existentials." Communality belongs to the very Being of *Dasein* insofar as his world is
always a world that he shares with others. To exist is always to exist in
interdependence with other selves. In Heidegger's view, man's projects
in his *Mitwelt*, or communal world, have a special character. They are
projects of personal concern (*Fürsorge*) and must be clearly contrasted
with the projects of practical concern (*Besorgen*) which constitute
man's *Umwelt*, or natural and instrumental environment.[86] Heidegger's
concept of an authentic being-with-others is already suggested in this
distinction between personal and practical concern. For the most part
Dasein exists in an unauthentic relation to others because he transforms persons into objects or uses persons as utensils which have some
kind of practical cash value. In the mode of the "anonymous one" he
apprehends both himself and the other self as either an on-hand or at-
hand being. The other self is sucked into the orbit of his practical concerns, becomes material for manipulation, and is deprived of his existential freedom.

Resolution, we have seen, is the movement elicited by the call of
conscience which brings *Dasein* to his authentic existence by confront-
ing him with the choice of his possibilities, which are always pervaded
with finitude and guilt. This resolution is the touchstone for authentic
self-being, but it also becomes the condition for authentic community.
"Out of the authentic self-being emerges an authentic being-with-
others." [87] Indeed, an authentic self-being cannot be fully achieved until
resolution sets the other self free for the choice of himself. In resolution
the totality of *Dasein's* being-in-the-world is re-evaluated, and the various
horizons of the world are placed in their proper perspective. *Dasein's*

authentic choice of himself in resolution has consequences for his being-in-the-world as such. "*Authentic* resolution modifies simultaneously the uncovering of the 'world' and the disclosure of the coexistence with others." [88] Both *Dasein's* practical and personal concerns are qualified by authentic understanding and authentic projective activity. In no sense does *Dasein* become an isolated "I," severed from the world, in which heretofore he has been lost in the mode of the "anonymous one." [89] Rather, resolution drives him to assume responsibility for his world and reorder his practical and personal projects of being-in-the-world through his newly acquired consciousness of freedom. "Resolution brings the self to a practical concern for that which is at-hand and directs it to a personal concern for others." [90] Thus authenticity for Heidegger involves a fundamentally new attitude of world-orientation. Being-in-the-world is no longer that of a depersonalized, levelled, and conventional existence; it has been transformed into a creative possibility.

The decisive movement of authentic community is initiated when *Dasein* becomes the conscience for the Other in the call to authenticity. Authentic self-being is achieved only when the resolute *Dasein* transforms the *Mitwelt* in such a way that he can be a conscience for the Other and help emancipate him from his bondage to the "anonymous one" and free him for his unique possibilities. "Only the resolution taken on by himself brings *Dasein* to the possibility of freeing the Other for his possibilities. . . . The resolute *Dasein* can become the conscience of the Other." [91] It is in this way that *Dasein* becomes responsible to and for his fellow men who share his world. Having freed himself from the unauthentic dispersion of the "anonymous one," *Dasein* must assume the responsibility of aiding another in the achievement of his integrity by becoming the voice of conscience for him.

Heidegger's doctrine of authentic community does not prescribe any concrete program of social action, nor does it specify any religious directives and commitments. As an ontological and existentialist designation it remains intentionally neutral to any and all ontic and existential experience. However, it points to the set of conditions and the authentic attitude which must permeate all concrete existential decisions if authenticity is to become a possibility for one's concrete lived experience. The concrete expression of this authenticity relative to religious and psychological dispositions depends upon the special character of the situation in which the self discovers itself. This cannot be forthcoming from an ontological analysis. Thus we see again how Heidegger has rendered explicit the ontology of human existence which is presupposed in any psychological, ethical, and religious self-understanding. With Kierkegaard such an ontology was suggested and foreshadowed. With Heidegger it becomes explicit.

Notes

NOTES/INTRODUCTION

1. Binswanger's book was published in Zurich (Niehans) in 1942. For a discussion of Binswanger's views and a clear statement on the relationship of existentialism to psychotherapy, the reader is referred to a book of essays and case histories edited by Rollo May, Ernest Angel, and Henri F. Ellenberger, *Existence: A New Dimension in Psychiatry and Psychology* (New York: Basic Books, Inc., 1958).

NOTES/CHAPTER I

1. Søren Kierkegaard, *Concluding Unscientific Postscript*, trans. David Swenson and Walter Lowrie (Princeton, N. J.: Princeton University Press, 1944), p. 313. Cited hereafter as *CUP*.

2. G. W. F. Hegel, *Science of Logic*, trans. W. H. Johnston and L. G. Struthers (New York: Macmillan Co., 1929), Vol. I, p. 51.

3. *CUP*, pp. 111, 256.

4. Cf. *CUP*: "One must therefore be very careful in dealing with a philosopher of the Hegelian school, and, above all, to make certain of the identity of the being with whom one has the honor to discourse. Is he a human being, an existing human being? Is he himself *sub specie aeterni*, even when he sleeps, eats, blows his nose, or whatever else a human being does?" (p. 271).

5. Kierkegaard, *The Sickness Unto Death*, trans. Walter Lowrie

(Princeton, N. J.: Princeton University Press, 1951), p. 68. Cited hereafter as *SUD*.

6. Martin Heidegger, *Einführung in die Metaphysik* (Tübingen: Max Niemeyer Verlag, 1953), pp. 142–43. Cited hereafter as *EM*. Cf. *Was Heisst Denken?* (Tübingen: Max Niemeyer Verlag, 1954), p. 127. Cited hereafter as *WHD*.

7. *CUP*, p. 311.

8. "Pure thought is altogether detached, and not like the abstract thought which does indeed abstract from existence, but nevertheless preserves a relationship to it. . . ." Again, "the relation which abstract thought still sustains to that from which it abstracts . . . is something which pure thought innocently or thoughtlessly ignores," *ibid.*, pp. 278–79.

9. *The Journals of Søren Kierkegaard*, ed. Alexander Dru (New York: Oxford University Press, 1938), entry 733. Cited hereafter as *Journals*.

10. *CUP*, p. 184.

11. *WHD*, p. 52.

12. *CUP*, p. 35.

13. *Journals*, entry 584.

14. *EM*, p. 143.

15. *CUP*, p. 182.

16. *Journals*, entry 22.

17. John Wild, *The Challenge of Existentialism* (Bloomington: Indiana University Press, 1955), p. 53.

18. "Das beständige Wetzen der Messer aber ist langeweilig, wenn man nichts zu schneiden vorhat." Quoted in *Die Kategorien und Bedeutungslehre des Duns Scotus* (Tübingen: Mohr Verlag, 1915), p. 9. Cited hereafter as *Scotus*.

19. *Journals*, entry 676. Cf. entry 1376: "Take Socrates! . . . he has an objective attitude to his own personality, and when he is about to be condemned to death speaks of his condemnation like a third person. He is subjectivity raised to the second power, his attitude is as objective as that of a true poet to his poetic works; he is just as objective to his own subjectivity. . . . The task is to have an objective attitude to one's own subjectivity."

20. "Philosophie ist universale phänomenologische Ontologie, ausghened von der Hermeneutik des Daseins, die als Analytik der *Existenz* das Ende des Leitfadens alles philosophischen Fragens dort festgemacht hat, woraus es *entspringt* und wohin es *zuruckschlägt*." Heidegger, *Sein und Zeit* (Tübingen: Max Niemeyer Verlag, 1953), p. 38. Cited hereafter as *SZ*. (Because of the inherent difficulty of finding an English correlate for the German word *Dasein*, we shall use the original German throughout.)

21. *Ibid.*, pp. 27–28.

22. Nicolas Berdyaev, *The Destiny of Man*, trans. Natalie Duddington (London: Geoffrey Bles, 1957), p. 1.

23. SZ, p. 38n.

24. Edmund Husserl, *Ideen zu einer reinen Phänomenologie und phënomenologischen Philosophie* (*Husserliana*, Vol. III [Den Haag: Martinus Nijhoff, 1950]), p. 6.

25. *Ibid.*, p. 17.

26. This point is discussed by Alphonse de Waelhens in his book *La Philosophie de Martin Heidegger* (Louvain: Éditions de l'Institut Supérieur de Philosophie, n.d.). He concludes as follows: "Nous pouvons donc conclure que si Husserl fait de la neutralité vis-à-vis de l'existence la condition sine qua non de la phénoménologie, Heidegger regarde cette neutralité comme la négation même de l'attitude philosophique" (p. 17).

27. Manuskript BI 5 IX, pp. 8, 10, as quoted in Gerd Brand, *Welt, Ich und Zeit; Nach unveröffentlichen Manuskripten Edmund Husserls* (Den Haag: Martinus Nijhoff, 1955), p. 18.

28. "Die Welt ist uns gegeben als Weltgeltung, oder Welthaftigkeit, oder Weltbegriff, oder Weltgesetz, nicht also als ein Seiendes, sondern als das, worin und woraufhin alles Seienden verstanden wird, und als solche ist sie fur das Seiende 'bodengebend' " (*ibid.*, p. 18).

29. William Barret, *Irrational Man: A Study in Existential Philosophy* (New York: Doubleday & Co., 1958), p. 11.

30. Kierkegaard, *The Concept of Dread*, trans. Walter Lowrie (Princeton, N. J.: Princeton University Press, 1946), p. 65. Cited hereafter as CA, for reasons explained in chap. iii, n. 2.

31. SZ, pp. 38, 39.

32. Heidegger, *Vom Wesen der Wahrheit* (Frankfurt: Vittorio Klostermann, 1943), p. 16. Cited hereafter as WW.

33. See Karl Löwith, *Heidegger: Denker in Dürftiger Zeit* (Frankfurt: S. Fischer Verlag, 1953), p. 46.

34. WW, p. 16.

35. See particularly Dilthey's work, *Die geistige Welt, Einleitung in die Philosophie des Lebens* (*Gesammelte Schriften*, Vol. V [Leipzig: Verlag von B. G. Teubner, 1924]).

36. SZ, p. 44.

37. SZ, pp. 12–13.

38. Walter Biemel, *Le Concept de Monde chez Heidegger* (Paris: J. Vrin, 1950), p. 90.

39. "*Phänomenologische Wahrheit* (*Erschlossenheit von Sein*) *ist veritas transcendentalis*," SZ, p. 38. Also cf. pp. 44, 50, 53, 199; and WG, p. 20.

40. Jean-Paul Sartre, *L'Être et le Néant* (Paris: Gallimard, 1943), p. 350.

41. Karl Jaspers, *Philosophie* (Heidelberg: Springer-Verlag, 1948), Vol. I, p. 15.

42. Gabriel Marcel, *The Mystery of Being* (London: Harvill Press, 1950), Vol. I, p. 88.

43. *L'Être et le Néant*, pp. 16–23.

44. *CUP*, p. 281.

45. *Ibid.*, p. 169.

46. SZ, p. 24.

47. "Die erste Aussage ist dann: 'sum' und zwar in dem Sinne: ich-bin-in-einer-Welt" (*SZ*, p. 211).

48. In his interpretation of Kant, Heidegger argues that the primary significance of the *Critique of Pure Reason* resides in providing the foundation for the possibility of a phenomenological ontology by grounding the meta-physical question in anthropology. The place where Kant erred, Heidegger maintains, was in his own attempt to develop an ontology which was based on pure intuition and pure reason alone. In thus giving priority to reason and logic, Kant prepared the stage for the identification of logic and metaphysics in the thought of Hegel. See his *Kant und das Problem der Metaphysik* (Frankfurt: Vittorio Klostermann, 1929, pp. 186, 220. Cited hereafter as *KPM*).

49. *SZ*, p. 62.

50. *Scotus*, pp. 129–30.

51. *Husserliana*, Vol. I, p. 79.

52. "Als Ausgang nehmen wir das Bewusstsein in einem prägnanten und sich zunächst darbietenden Sinne, den wir am einfachsten bezeichnen durch das Cartesianische *cogito*, das 'Ich denke' " (*ibid.*, p. 75).

53. Brand has shown that intentionality in Husserl's later manuscripts, besides in some passages in his earlier writings, is understood not as a static consciousness *of* something but as a dynamic, functioning intentionality (*fungierende Intentionalität*), which is continually in the process of transcending itself in a world of lived experience. "Die Intentionalität ist somit nicht ein statisches Bewusstsein-von sondern ein dynamisches, kontinuerliches Ubersteigen ihrer selbst. Sie ist nicht schlechthin, sondern sie fungiert. Deswegen nennt Husserl sie 'fungierende Intentionalität' " (*ibid.*, p. 23). "Welt-erfahrendes-Leben ist anonym fungierende Intentionalität" (*ibid.*, p. 25).

NOTES/CHAPTER II

1. Martin Heidegger, *Sein und Seit* (Tübingen: Max Niemeyer Verlag, 1953), p. 365. Cited hereafter as SZ. Cf. Heidegger's *Vom Wesen des Grundes: "Zur Selbstheit gehört Welt"* (4th ed.; Frankfurt: Vittorio Klostermann, 1955), p. 37. Cited hereafter as WG.

2. Jean-Paul Sartre, *L'Être et le Néant* (Paris: Gallimard, 1943), p. 149.

3. See Rollo May *et al.*, *Existence* (New York: Basic Books, Inc., 1958), pp. 61–65, 191 ff.

4. "Das In-sein meint so wenig ein räumliches 'Ineinander' Vorhandenes, als 'in' ursprünglich gar nicht eine räumliche Beziehung der gennanten Art bedeutet; 'in' stammt von inan—, wohnen, habitare, sich aufhalten . . ." (SZ, p. 54).

5. *Ibid.*, pp. 56–57.

6. ". . . le *dans* de l'être-dans-le-monde se réfère à une attitude de familiarité. Il signifie 'être familier avec . . . ,' *être-auprès* (*Seinbei*). . . . La différence qui existe entre la proximité purement spatiale et la proximité au sens de familiarité s'exprime en francais par la différence qu'il y a entre les termes *près* et *auprès*" (Walter Biemel, *Le Concept de Monde chez Heidegger* [Paris: J. Vrin, 1950], p. 12).

7. *The Journals of Søren Kierkegaard*, ed. Alexander Dru (New York: Oxford University Press, 1938), entry 426. Cited hereafter as *Journals*.

8. WG, p. 23. (Reference cited: Diels, *Fragmente der Vorsokratiker: Melissos*, Frag. 7; Parmenides, Frag. 2).

9. WG, pp. 24, 25.

10. In his book *Holzwege*, Heidegger speaks of Kierkegaard as being a "religious writer" rather than a "thinker" ([Frankfurt: Vittorio Klostermann, 1950], p. 230). Though in *Sein und Zeit* Heidegger credits Kierkegaard with a most penetrating elucidation of the existence problem, he says that existentialist and ontological considerations remain foreign to Kierkegaard's thought (SZ, pp. 235 n., 338 n.).

11. "This self is no longer the merely human self but is what we would call, hoping not to be misunderstood, the theological self, the self directly in the sight of God" (Søren Kierkegaard, *The Sickness Unto Death*, trans. Walter Lowrie [Princeton, N. J.: Princeton University Press, 1951], p. 127; cited hereafter as *SUD*).

12. SZ, p. 138.

13. SZ, p. 64.

14. Biemel, *op. cit.*, p. 32.

15. SZ, p. 207.

16. Sartre, *op. cit.*, p. 586.

17. "Die 'Umwelt' richtet sich nicht in einem zuvorgegeben Raum ein, sondern ihre spezifische Weltlichkeit artikuliert in ihrer Bedeutsamkeit den bewandtnishaften Zusammenhang einer jeweiligen Ganzheit von umsichtig angewiesenen Plätzen" (SZ, p. 104).

18. Cf. Heidegger's essay, "The Way Back into the Ground of Metaphysics," trans. Walter Kaufmann, *Existentialism from Dostoevsky to Sartre* (New York: Meridian Books, 1956), pp. 206–21.

19. Heidegger, *Über den Humanismus* (Frankfurt: Vittorio Klostermann, 1947), p. 35. Cited herafter as *Humanismus*.

20. See particularly Rollo May, *op. cit.*, pp. 108–14.

21. *Phénoménologie de la Perception* (Paris: Gallimard, 1945), p. 337.

22. See particularly Henri Ellenberger's discussion of spatiality in Rollo May, *op. cit.*, pp. 108–14.

23. See *L'Être et le Néant*, p. 318.

24. *Humanismus*, p. 14.

25. Kierkegaard, *Either/Or* (Princeton, N. J.: Princeton University Press, 1949), Vol. II, p. 269. Cited hereafter as *EO*.

26. *Ibid.*, pp. 219–20.

27. *Works of Love*, trans. David Swenson and Lillian Swenson (Oxford University Press, 1946), p. 111.

28. *Journals*, entry 719.

29. *SZ*, p. 125.

30. "Selbstsein und In-Kommunikation-Sein ist Untrennbar," *Von Der Wahrheit* (Munich: Piper & Co., 1947), p. 546. Jaspers insists that his "elucidation of existence" not be construed as an existentialist ontology. He argues that because of man's inevitable "shipwreck" in passing from one situation to another, a unifying perspective of existence is impossible. "Existenz gewinnt *keine Rundung* als Bild, weder für andere noch für sich selbst; denn der Mensch muss in der Welt *scheitern*" (*Philosophie* [Heidelberg: Springer-Verlag, 1948], Vol. II, p. 647).

31. *SZ*, p. 121.

32. Gabriel Marcel, *The Philosophy of Existence* (New York: Philosophical Library, 1949), p. 2.

33. *The Present Age*, trans. Alexander Dru and Walter Lowrie (Oxford University Press, 1940), p. 28.

34. *The Point of View*, trans. Walter Lowrie (New York: Oxford University Press, 1939), p. 112.

35. *SUD*, p. 51.

36. *Journals*, entry 1293.

37. *Ibid.*, p. 724.

38. *The Present Age*, p. 59.

39. *Ibid.*, p. 57.

40. *Stages on Life's Way*, trans. Walter Lowrie (Princeton, N. J.: Princeton University Press, 1941), p. 44. Cited hereafter as *SLW*.

41. *SZ*, p. 126.

42. *Ibid.*, p. 128.

43. Jaspers pungently elucidates the experience of this phenomenon when he writes: "Im naiven Dasein tue ich was alle tun, glaube, was alle glauben, denke, wie alle denken" (*Philosophie*, Vol. II, p. 339). Both Jaspers and Heidegger have accepted and developed Kierkegaard's theme of the levelling and depersonalizing influence of the public. Jaspers acutely expresses this theme in his book which bears the translated title *Man in the Modern Age*. "The masses are our

masters; and for everyone who looks facts in the face his existence has become dependent upon them, so that the thought of them must control his doings, his cares and his duties. Even an articulated mass always tends to become unspiritual and inhuman. It is life without existence, superstitution without faith. It may stamp all flat; it is disinclined to tolerate independence and greatness, but prone to constrain people to become as automatic as ants" (trans. Eden and Cedar Paul [London: Routledge & Sons, 1933], p. 43).

44. SZ, p. 169.

45. Cf. Biemel's explication of the phenomenon of curiosity in his study of Heidegger. "Alors que l'instant ouvre le présent et permet ainsi au *Dasein* d'être en même temps dans l'avenir et le passé-présent et, par lā, de comprendre ce qui est véritablement présent, la présentation est la curiosité insatiable qui se nourrit continuellement du présent, sans le comprendre" (*op. cit.*, p. 134).

46. SZ, p. 298.

47. *Philosophie*, Vol. II, p. 344.

48. *Ibid.*, p. 356.

49. Marcel, *Metaphysical Journal* (Chicago: Henry Regnery Company, 1952), p. 322.

50. "Das Dasein ist ein Seiendes, das nicht nur unter anderem Seiendem vorkommt. Es ist vielmehr dadurch ontisch ausgezeichnet, das est diesem Seienden in seinem Sein um dieses Sein selbst geht." Cf. SZ, pp. 12, 14, 52, 143, 191, 333.

51. SUD, p. 17.

52. *Training in Christianity*, trans. Walter Lowrie (Princeton, N. J.: Princeton University Press, 1941), p. 159.

53. *Journals*, entry 1376.

54. *Philosophie*, Vol. II, p. 324. Sartre submits a basically similar statement on the reflexivity of the self in *L'Être et le Néant*: "Le *soi* ne saurait être une propriété de l'être-en-soi. Par nature, il est un *réfléchi*, comme l'indique assez la syntaxe et, en particulier, la rigueur logique de la syntaxe latine et les distinctions strictes que la grammaire établit entre l'usage du *'ejus'* et celui du *'sui.'* Le *soi* renvoie, mais il renvoie précisément au *sujet*. Il indique un rapport du sujet avec lui-même et ce rapport est précisément une dualité, mais une dualité particulière puisqu'elle exige des symboles verbaux particuliers" (p. 118).

55. SUD, p. 44.

56. *Nicene and Post-Nicene Fathers*, ed. Philip Schaff, Vol. III, pp. 127–29.

57. SUD, p. 128.

58. SUD, p. 44. (Karl Jaspers makes the same point when he writes: "Wille ist *als Beziehung auf sich selbst*. Er ist ein Selbstbewusstsein, in dem ich mich nicht betrachtend sehe, sondern in dem ich mich aktiv zu mir verhalte" [*Philosophie*, Vol. II, p. 425].)

59. CUP, p. 311.

60. ". . . there arises the category: 'the individual,' the category which is so wedded to my name that I wish that on my grave might be put 'the individual' . . . (*Journals*, entry 657).

61. *CUP*, p. 309.

62. *Ibid.*, pp. 286–87.

63. *Ibid.*, p. 315.

64. *EO*, Vol. II, p. 214. Cf. *The Concept of Dread* (elsewhere cited as *CA*): " 'Self' signifies precisely the contradiction of positing the general as the particular (*Enkelte*)" (trans. Walter Lowrie [Princeton, N. J.: Princeton University Press, 1946], p. 70). For a helpful discussion of Kierkegaard on the problem of individuality, the reader is referred to Karl Löwith's careful treatment of the subject in his book *Von Hegel zu Nietzsche*: "Das zum Selbst gewordene Ich ist kein abstrakt vereinzeltes, sondern es drückt in seinem ganzen Leben konkret das allgemein-Menschliche aus. . . . Der wahrhaft existierende Mensch ist ein 'durchaus individueller Mensch ohne seinesgleichen und zugliech der allgemeine Mensch' " ([Stuttgart: W. Kohlhammer Verlag, 1941], p. 343).

65. *SZ*, p. 133.

66. Tillich, *Systematic Theology* (Chicago: University of Chicago Press, 1951), Vol. I, p. 62.

67. "Das 'Wesen' des Daseins liegt in seiner Existenz. . . . Das Sein, *darum* es diesem Seienden in seinem Sein geht, ist je meines" (*SZ*, p. 62).

68. *Ibid.*, p. 42.

69. *Humanismus*, p. 16.

70. Tillich, "Existential Philosophy," *Journal of the History of Ideas*, V (1944), p. 47.

71. Adolph Sternberger, *Der Verstandene Tod* (Leipzig: Verlag von Hirzel, 1934), p. 19. Max Müller has submitted the helpful distinction between "*ausstand*," or that which stands out from itself and is open to itself, and "*selbst-stand*," or that which stands-in-itself—the latter being the traditional meaning of substance. See *Existenz-philosophie im Geistigen Leben der Gegenwart* (Heidelberg: Kerle Verlag, 1949), p. 48.

72. *Humanismus*, p. 13.

73. *EO*, Vol. II, p. 180.

74. *SUD*, p. 45.

75. *SUD*, p. 44.

76. *CUP*, p. 85.

77. *SUD*, p. 53.

78. *Repetition*, trans. Walter Lowrie (Princeton, N. J.: Princeton University Press, 1946), p. 114.

79. *SUD*, p. 54. Cf. p. 57. The notion of possibility is one of Kierkegaard's most important notions, but unfortunately he has not wholly succeeded in freeing it from a certain ambiguity which emerges

from time to time in his writings. The reason for this is that he is using the same term in two different contexts of meaning. In the *Postscript* he sometimes speaks of possibility in the sense of logical or intellectual possibility, i.e., possibility in terms of pure potentiality in
abstraction from existence. In some of his other writings, particularly
The Sickness Unto Death and *The Concept of Anxiety*, possibility is
understood as a positive determination of existential reality—when he
says, for example, that the self is a synthesis of possibility and necessity.

80. *SUD*, p. 55.
81. *Ibid.*, p. 62.
82. "Das pure 'dass es ist' zeigt sich, das Woher and Wohin blei-
ben im Dunkel" (*SZ*, p. 134).
83. *SZ*, p. 137.
84. *L'Être et le Néant*, p. 588.
85. *Ibid.*, p. 605.
86. *SZ*, p. 143.
87. *Ibid.*, p. 143.
88. "Das Möglichsein, das je das Dasein existenzial ist, unterschei-
det sich ebensosehr von der leeren, logischen Moglichkeit wie von der
Kontingenz eines Vorhandenen, sofern mit diesem das und jenes 'pas-
sieren' kann. Als modale Kategorie der Vorhandenheit bedeutet Möglichkeit das *noch nicht* Wirkliche und das *nicht jemals* Notwendige.
Sie charackterisiert das *nur* Mögliche. Sie is ontologisch niedriger als
Wirklichkeit und Notwendigkeit" (*ibid.*, 143).
89. *SZ*, p. 346.
90. *Ibid.*, p. 181.
91. *Ibid.*, p. 198.

NOTES/CHAPTER III

1. *The Journals of Søren Kierkegaard*, ed. Alexander Dru (New
York: Oxford University Press, 1938), entries 841, 444, 705. Cited
hereafter as *Journals*.
2. Professor Tillich has called my attention to the fact that the
English rendering of *aengst* as "dread" in Walter Lowrie's translation
of *The Concept of Dread* (Princeton, N. J.: Princeton University Press,
1944) does not quite catch the meaning of the original. He has suggested the use of the term "anxiety" as being more *wortgetreu*. Therefore I have consistently used "anxiety" where Lowrie has translated
"dread," and the work is cited hereafter as *CA*.
3. Martin Heidegger, *Sein und Zeit* (Tübingen: Max Niemeyer
Verlag, 1953), p. 188. Cited hereafter as *SZ*.

4. CA, p. 38.

5. Heidegger, *Was ist Metaphysik?* (Frankfurt: Vittorio Klostermann, 1929), pp. 31–32. Cited hereafter as WM.

6. CA, p. 86.

7. SZ, p. 187. Cf. WM: "In der Halle des Blickes, den die frische Erinnerung trägt, müssen wir sagen: wovor und worum wir ängsteten, war 'eigentlich'—nichts. In der Tat: das Nichts selbst—als solches—war da" (pp. 32–33). Cf. also: "Die Angst ist dejenige Grundbefindlichkeit, die vor das Nichts stellt" (in Heidegger's *Kant und das Problem der Metaphysik* [Frankfurt: Vittorio Klostermann, 1929], p. 214; cited hereafter as KPM).

8. WM, p. 141.

9. "Dieses 'Furchtsamkeit' darf nicht im ontischen Sinne einer Faktischen, 'vereinzelten' Veranlagung verstanden werden, sondern als existenziale Möglichkeit der wesenhaften Befindlichkeit des Daseins überhaupt, die freilich nicht die einzige ist" (*ibid.*, p. 142).

10. *Journals*, entry 967.

11. *The Courage to Be* (New Haven: Yale University Press, 1952), p. 35.

12. WM, p. 28. Basically the same view is expressed by Paul Tillich when he writes: "It is of little significance that some logicians deny that non-being has conceptual character and try to remove it from the philosophical scene except in the form of negative judgments. For the question is: What does the fact of negative judgments tell us about the character of being? What is the ontological condition of negative judgments? How is the realm constituted in which negative judgments are possible?" (*The Courage to Be*, p. 34).

13. WM, p. 33.

14. KPM, p. 215.

15. SZ, p. 242.

16. WM, pp. 33, 38; KPM, pp. 71, 214.

17. WM, p. 39; cf. KPM, p. 204.

18. See Tillich, *Systematic Theology* (Chicago: University of Chicago Press, 1951), Vol. I, pp. 187–89, 253; and Heidegger, KPM, p. 71.

19. KPM, pp. 69–74.

20. CA, p. 40.

21. *Ibid.*, p. 50.

22. CA, p. 38. Karl Jaspers formulates a concept of anxiety identical with that of Kierkegaard: "Angst ist das Schwindligwerden und Schaudern der Freiheit, die vor der Wahl steht" (*Philosophie* [Heidelberg: Springer-Verlag, 1948], Vol. II, p. 522).

23. CA, p. 38.

24. *Ibid.*, p. 55.

25. *Ibid.*, p. 40.

26. "Adam is the first man; he is at once himself and the race.

. . . He is not essentially different from the race, for in that case there is no race; he is not the race, for in that case there is no race: he is himself and the race. Therefore what explains Adam explains the race, and vice versa" (*ibid.*, pp. 26–27). In this passage we find another exemplification of the cardinal principle of Kierkegaard's existentialism that the individual is the bearer of the universal.

27. CA, pp. 37, 44.

28. *Ibid.*, p. 41.

29. *Ibid.*

30. *Ibid.*, p. 32.

31. *Ibid.*, p. 83.

32. *Ibid.*, p. 100.

33. *Ibid.*, p. 52.

34. On the grounds of Kierkegaard's reflections relative to an objective anxiety which pervades the whole of creation, it would seem necessary to question Jean Wahl's interpretation when he argues that for Kierkegaard anxiety is only psychological and in no way cosmic. This, Wahl believes, constitutes the basic difference between Kierkegaard and Heidegger in their understanding of anxiety: "On voit qu'il y a une grande différence entre l'usage que Kierkegaard fait de l'idée d'angoisse et celui qu'en fera Heidegger. Pour Kierkegaard, il s'agit d'une angoisse psychologique et d'un rien qui est dans l'esprit. Pour Heidegger, l'angoisse est liée à un fait cosmique, au néant absolu sur lequel se détache l'existence." *Etudes Kierkegaardiennes* (Paris: Fernand Aubier, n.d.), p. 221.

35. CA, p. 99.

36. *Ibid.*, p. 82.

37. *Christian Discourses*, trans. Walter Lowrie (New York: Oxford University Press, 1939), p. 80.

38. CA, p. 82.

39. SZ, p. 186.

40. WM, p. 32.

41. SZ, p. 188.

42. "Das aufgehen im Man und bei der besorgten 'Welt' offenbart so etwas wie eine Flucht des Daseins vor ihm selbst als eigentlichem Selbst-sein-können" (*ibid.*, 184).

43. SZ, p. 188.

44. Kierkegaard, *Either/Or* (New York: Anchor Books, 1959), Vol. I, p. 29. Cited hereafter as *EO*.

45. *Ibid.*, p. 235.

46. WM, p. 30.

47. *Ibid.*, p. 31.

48. *Nausea*, trans. Lloyd Alexander (Norfolk, Conn.: New Directions, 1949), p. 210.

49. WM, p. 30. This theme of emptiness and indifference is vividly expressed in D. H. Lawrence's novel *Women in Love*. The

central character, Rupert Birkin, in a revealing soliloqy, expresses a profound indifference to life and the world: "Why strive for a coherent, satisfied life? Why not drift on in a series of accidents—like a picaresque novel? Why not? Why bother about human relationships? Why take them seriously—male or female? Why form a serious connection at all? Why not be casual, drifting along, taking all for what it was worth?" ([The Albatross: Modern Continental Library, 1949] p. 328).

50. *EO*, Vol. I, p. 239.

51. *Pensées*, ed Léon Brunschvicg (Paris: Libraire Hachette, 1904), entry 139.

52. Arthur Schopenhauer, *The World as Will and Idea*, trans. R. B. Haldane and J. Kemp (London: Kegan Paul, n.d.), p. 404.

53. *Ibid.*

54. *EO*, Vol. II, p. 159.

55. *Journals*, entries 359, 600, 754, 938; *SLW*, pp. 249, 342.

56. *The Courage To Be*, p. 65.

57. *Ibid.*, p. 66.

58. *CA*, p. 104.

59. *EO*, Vol. II, p. 157.

60. *Ibid.*, p. 158.

61. *Works of Love*, Trans. David Swenson and Lillian Swenson (Princeton, N. J.: Princeton University Press, 1946), p. 134.

62. *SUD*, p. 44.

63. *Ibid.*, p. 45. Kierkegaard's use of the Greek words ἄπειρον and πέρας in his footnote reference to Plato's *Philebus* (*ibid.*, p. 53n) points up an affinity of Kierkegaard's implicit ontology of the self to Plato's metaphysics as outlined in this dialogue. As the universe, according to the *Philebus*, is a mixture (μεικτόν) of the infinite (ἄπειρον) and the finite (πέρας) in which the indeterminate is determined, the unlimited limited, the formless informed, and the indefinite defined, so the self in Kierkegaard's analysis, as a polarity of infinitude and finitude expresses this synthesis of the indeterminate and determinate, indefinite and definite, unlimited and limited, and formless and formed.

64. *SUD*, p. 66.

65. *Philosophie*, Vol. II, p. 330.

66. *SUD*, p. 35.

67. *Ibid.*, p. 84.

68. *Ibid.*, p. 88.

69. *Ibid.*, p. 103.

70. *Ibid.*, p. 109.

71. *Ibid.*, p. 111.

72. *Ibid.*, p. 110.

73. *Ibid.*, p. 110.

74. *Ibid.*, pp. 113–14.

75. *The Rebel*, trans. Anthony Bower (New York: Vintage Books, 1956), p. 23.

76. *SUD*, p. 118.
77. *Ibid.*, p. 119.
78. Jaspers, *Philosophie*, Vol. II, pp. 552–64.
79. *EO*, Vol. II, p. 206n.

NOTES / CHAPTER IV

1. Berdyaev, *The Destiny of Man*, trans. Natalie Duddington (London: Geoffrey Bles, 1957), p. 335.
2. Søren Kierkegaard, *The Concept of Dread*, trans. Walter Lowrie (Princeton, N. J.: Princeton University Press, 1944), p. 83n. For reasons given in chap. iii, n. 2, this work is cited hereafter as *CA*.
3. Karl Jaspers, *Philosophie* (Heidelberg: Springer-Verlag, 1948), Vol. II, p. 483.
4. Martin Heidegger, *Sein und Zeit* (Tübingen: Max Niemeyer Verlag, 1953), p. 247. Cited hereafter as *SZ*.
5. *SZ*, p. 245.
6. "Es gibt nicht eine beharrende, als richtig auszusagende Stellung zum Tode. Vielmehr wandelt sich meine Haltung zum Tode in Sprüngen neuen Erwerbens durch das Leben, so dass ich sagen kann: *der Tod wandelt sich mit mir.* . . . Der Tod ist nur als ein Faktum eine immer gleiche Tatsache, in der Grenzsituation hört er nicht auf zu sein, aber er ist in seiner Gestalt wandelbar, ist so, wie ich jeweils als Existenz bin. Er is nicht endgültig, was er ist, sondern aufgenommen in die Geschichtlichkeit meiner sicher scheinenden Existenz" (*Philosophie*, Vol. II, p. 491).
7. Berdyaev, *op. cit.*, p. 319.
8. *Ibid.*, p. 320.
9. Jean-Paul Sartre, *L'Être et le Néant* (Paris: Gallimard, 1943), p. 621.
10. *Ibid.*, p. 628.
11. Kierkegaard, *Concluding Unscientific Postscript*, trans. David Swenson and Walter Lowrie (Princeton, N. J.: Princeton University Press, 1944), p. 151. Cited hereafter as *CUP*.
12. *Ibid.*, p. 152.
13. *Philosophie*, Vol. II, p. 491.
14. *CA*, p. 83n.
15. Kierkegaard, *Thoughts on Crucial Situations in Human Life*, trans. David Swenson (Minneapolis: Augsburg Publishing House, 1941), p. 78. Cited hereafter as *CS*.
16. *CA*, p. 83n.
17. *CS*, pp. 78–79.
18. *CUP*, p. 148.

19. *Ibid.*, p. 149.

20. *Ibid.*, p. 149.

21. *Ibid.*, p. 148.

22. *SZ*, p. 251.

23. *Ibid.*, p. 253.

24. *Ibid.*, p. 254.

25. "Alle Menschen, soweit man weiss, 'sterben.' Der Tod ist fur jeden Menschen im höchsten Grade wahrscheinlich, aber doch nicht 'unbedingt' gewiss. Streng genommen darf dem Tod doch 'nur' *empirische* Gewissheit zugesprochen werden" (*ibid.*, p. 257).

26. *CUP*, p. 151.

27. *Sechs Essays* (Heidelberg: L. Schneider, 1948), p. 64.

28. *The Challenge of Existentialism* (Bloomington: Indiana University Press, 1955), p. 119.

29. *CS*, pp. 101, 106.

30. *CUP*, p. 150.

31. *Ibid.*

32. *Ibid.*

33. Wach's book was published in Tübingen (Verlag von J. C. B. Mohr) in 1934. See p. 7. Cf. also *CUP*, p. 152.

34. *Philosophie*, Vol. II, pp. 484–85.

35. Berdyaev, *op cit.*, p. 320.

36. *SUD*, p. 25.

37. *Ibid.*

38. *SZ*, p. 236. Cf. *SZ*, p. 242. (In Heidegger's analysis the terms, "standing-out" (*Ausstehen*); protention" (*Entwurf*); "possibility-of-being" (*Seinkönnen*); and "ek-sistence" (*Ek-sistenz*) circumscribe the same reality structure and are used interchangeably. To say that the essence of *Dasein* resides in his ek-sistence means that human reality is always protentional or standing-out into its possibility-of-being.)

39. *Ibid.*, p. 234.

40. *Ibid.*, p. 252.

41. *Ibid.*, p. 240.

42. "Was zuvor *Begriff* war (*existenzialer Begriff*), wird nun Tätigkeit,—denn Übernehmen und Vorlaufen sind Tätigkeiten" ([Leipzig: Verlag von S. Hirzel, 1934], p. 92).

43. Cf. Alphonse de Waelhens, *La Philosophie de Martin Heidegger* (Louvain: Éditions de l'Institut Supérieur de Philosophie, n.d.): "L'existant authentique regarde la mort comme un indice affectant chacune de ses actions et chaque modalité de son être. Il vit dans *l'incessante anticipation* de mort" (p. 148).

44. *SZ*, p. 263.

45. *Ibid.*, p. 264.

46. "Das Sein zum Tode ist wesenhaft Angst" (*ibid.*, p. 266).

47. "Dasein ist . . . seinem Tod überantwortet" (*ibid.*, p. 251).

48. *Ibid.*, p. 248.

49. *Ibid.*, p. 247.

50. A case in point in the misinterpretation of Heidegger is the opinion expressed by Régis Jolivet in his book *Le Problème de la Mort chez Heidegger et Sartre* (Paris: Editions de Fontenelle, 1950). Jolivet links both Heidegger and Sartre with the materialistic world-view of the ancient Greek naturalists Epicurus and Lucretius (pp. 11, 13). Jolivet argues that both thinkers present a postulatory nihilism, in which any notion of immortality is an absurd myth. "Ces analyses, toutefois, chez Heidegger et chez Sartre, ne paraissent s'inspirer que d'un postulat nihiliste, où l'idée même d'immortalité perd toute espèce de signification et ne répond plus qu'à une mythologie parfaitement absurde" (p. 12). As we have suggested earlier, this may well be the case in Sartre's analysis, but it hardly expresses the view of Heidegger.

NOTES/CHAPTER V

1. Jean-Paul Sartre, *L'Être et le Néant* (Paris: Gallimard, 1943), p. 131.

2. Alfred North Whitehead, *The Concept of Nature* (New York: Cambridge University Press, 1930), p. 70. For a discussion of the relationship between Whitehead and Heidegger on the character of time and other points of doctrine, see the author's article, "Whitehead and Heidegger: Process Philosophy and Existential Philosophy," in *Dialectica*, XIII, No. 1 (1959), 42–56.

3. *Supra*, chap. ii.

4. Martin Heidegger, *Sein und Zeit* (Tübingen: Max Niemeyer Verlag, 1953), p. 404. Cited hereafter as SZ.

5. *Ibid.*, p. 406.

6. *L'Être et le Néant*, p. 131.

7. Søren Kierkegaard, *Either/Or* (New York: Anchor Books, 1959), Vol. II, p. 116. Cited hereafter as EO.

8. *Ibid.*, p. 14.

9. Kierkegaard, *The Concept of Dread*, trans. Walter Lowrie (Princeton, N. J.: Princeton University Press, 1944), p. 76. For reasons given in chap. iii, n. 2, this work is cited hereafter as CA.

10. *Ibid.*, p. 77n.

11. *Ibid.*, p. 77.

12. SZ, pp. 411 ff.

13. *Ibid.*, pp. 421, 422, 424, 426.

14. *Ibid.*, p. 423.

15. *Ibid.*, p. 426.

16. *Ibid.*, p. 329.

17. *L'Être et le Néant*, p. 150.

18. SZ, p. 250.

19. Biemel, *Le Concept de Monde chez Heidegger* (Paris: J. Vrin, 1950), p. 131.

20. SZ, p. 328. Cf. Biemel, *op. cit.*, p. 125.

21. EO, Vol. I, p. 181.

22. *Ibid.*, p. 182.

23. Frank, *Philosophical Understanding and Religious Truth* (London: Oxford University Press, 1945), p. 66.

24. Whitehead, *Adventures of Ideas* (New York: Macmillan Co., 1933), p. 246.

25. *L'Être et le Néant*, p. 188.

26. SZ, p. 426.

27. CA, p. 80.

28. *Ibid.*

29. SZ, p. 329.

30. " 'Zukunft' meint hier nicht ein Jetzt, das, *noch nicht* Wirklich' geworden, einmal erst *sein wird*, sondern die Kunft, in der das Dasein in seinem eigensten Seinkönnen auf sich zukommt" (SZ, p. 325).

31. Wild, *The Challenge of Existentialism* (Bloomington: Indiana University Press, 1955), p. 108. (For a discussion of Kierkegaard and his influence on contemporary existentialist philosophy with regard to the problems of cognition, time, and ethics, see an article by John Wild in the *Anglican Theological Review:* "Kierkegaard and Contemporary Existentialist Philosophy," Vol. XXXVIII (1956).

32. CA, p. 82. Heidegger makes precisely the same point here expressed by Kierkegaard when he writes in *Sein und Zeit:* "Anxiety is in anxiety over the naked *Dasein* in his uncanny abandonment. It brings *Dasein* back to the pure 'thatness' of his unique, individual abandonment. This return to himself is not a retreat into forgetfulness, but also not merely recollection. . . . To the contrary, anxiety brings *Dasein* back to his abandonment as a possibility of repetition" (p. 343).

33. *Philosophical Fragments*, trans. David Swenson (Princeton, N. J.: Princeton University Press, 1936), p. 56. Cited hereafter as PF.

34. "And as Christ is the Absolute, it is easy to see that with respect to Him there is only one situation: that of contemporaneousness. The five, the seven, the fifteen, the eighteen hundred years are neither here nor there; they do not change him, neither do they in any wise reveal who He was" (*Training in Christianity*, trans. Walter Lowrie [Princeton, N. J.: Princeton University Press, 1944], p. 67; cited hereafter as TC). Cf. PF, p. 48, and *The Journals of Søren Kierkegaard*, ed. Alexander Dru (New York: Oxford University Press, 1938), entry 417.

35. *Gospel of Suffering*, trans. David Swenson and Lillian Swenson (Minneapolis: Augsburg Publishing House, 1948), p. 43. Max Scheler has developed a similar analysis of the phenomena of repent-

ance and forgiveness in connection with the possible transformation of the meaning of the past in his essay "Reue und Wiedergeburt" in *Vom Ewigen im Menschen* (Leipzig: Der Neue Geist Verlag, 1923), Vol. I.

36. *Repetition*, trans. Walter Lowrie (Princeton, N. J.: Princeton University Press, 1941), pp. 3, 34.

37. *Ibid.*, p. 34.

38. CA, p. 19.

39. *Repetition*, pp. 144, 5.

40. *Ibid.*, p. 132

41. Kierkegaard, *Fear and Trembling*, trans. Robert Payne (New York: Oxford University Press, 1939), p. 37. Cited hereafter as *FT*.

42. EO, Vol. II, p. 114.

43. CA, p. 80.

44. PF, p. 13. Cf. *PF*, pp. 18, 39–43; CUP, pp. 505–15.

45. For a thorough and seminal interpretation of the Christological significance of the term *kairos*, as it relates to an understanding of time and history, see Paul Tillich's *The Interpretation of History* (New York: Charles Scribner's Sons, 1936), Part II, chap. ii, and *The Protestant Era* (Chicago: University of Chicago Press, 1948), chap. iii.

46. EO, Vol. II, p. 116.

47. CA, p. 75n.

48. *Ibid.*

49. PF, pp. 29ff. For an illuminating discussion of the meaning of paradox in Christian theology, see Paul Tillich's *Systematic Theology* (Chicago: University of Chicago Press, 1957), Vol. II, pp. 90–92.

50. Karl Jaspers, *Philosophie* (Heidelberg: Springer-Verlag, 1948), Vol. I, p. 404. Also cf. pp. 434 and 638, as well as Jaspers' discussion of Kierkegaard on this point in *Psychologie der Weltanschauungen* (Berlin: Verlag von Julius Springer, 1919), p. 99.

51. SZ, p. 338.

52. *Ibid.* p. 339.

53. *Ibid.*, p. 424.

54. SUD, p. 44. Cf. *CUP*: "An existing individual is constantly in the process of becoming" (p. 79).

55. PF, p. 60.

56. CA, p. 12.

57. *Ibid.*, p. 19. Cf. *PF*: "The necessary is the only thing that cannot come into being, because the necessary is," p. 61.

58. PF, p. 61.

59. *Ibid.*, p. 62.

60. CUP, p. 272n.

61. *Ibid.*

62. See particularly Dilthey's work, *Die geistige Welt: Einleitung in die Philosophie des Lebens* (*Gesammelte Schriften*, Vol. V [Leipzig: Verlag von B. G. Teubner, 1924]). "Die Endlichkeit jeder geschicht-

lichen Erscheinung, sei sie eine Religion oder ein Ideal oder philosophisches System, sonach die Relativität jeder Art von menschlicher
Auffassung is das letzte Wort der historischen Weltanschauung, alles
in einem Prozess fliessend, nichts bleibend" (p. 9).

63. Löwith, *Heidegger: Denker in Dürftiger Zeit* (Heidelberg:
Fischer Verlag, 1953), p. 46.

64. SZ. p. 376.

65. *Ibid.*, p. 373.

66. *Ibid.*, p. 375.

67. *Ibid.*, p. 392.

68. R. G. Collingwood has developed a foundational study of
these related problems in his epoch-making book, *The Idea of History*
(Oxford: Clarendon Press, 1946).

69. SZ, pp. 378–79.

70. *Ibid.*, p. 386. Although Heidegger points to the significance of
community for the understanding of history in his concept of *Geschick*,
the communal aspect of historicity remains inauspiciously neglected in
his analysis. For a critical statement on Heidegger's neglect of community in his views on history, see the author's article, "Phenomenology, Ontology, and History in the Philosophy of Heidegger,"
Revue internationale de Philosophie, Fasc. 2, No. 4 (1958).

71. SZ, p. 385.

72. "Die Wiederholung des Möglichen ist weder ein Wieder-
bringen des 'Vergangenen,' noch ein Zurückbinden der 'Gegenwart'
an das 'Uberholte.' Die Wiederholung lässt sich, einem entschlossenen
Sichentwerfen entspringend, nicht vom 'Vergangenen' überreden, um
es als das vormals Wirkliche nur wiederkehren zu lassen. Die Wiederholung *erwidert* vielmehr die möglichkeit der dagewesenen Existenz"
(*Ibid.*, pp. 385–86).

A point of clarification may be in order regarding the relation between Heidegger's notion of repetition as the "recurrence of the possible" and Nietzsche's doctrine of "eternal recurrence." Although
formally similar, the two concepts are materially distinct. As Heidegger
has shown in his essay on Nietzsche, Nietzsche's doctrine of eternal
recurrence is still rooted in the cosmological categories of traditional
metaphysics (*Holzwege* [Frankfurt: Vittorio Klostermann, 1950], p.
219). Nietzsche's doctrine is a survival of the myth of the eternal return as expressed in Greek religion and the non-historical religions of
the East. The doctrine of the eternal return is a *cosmological* myth in
which history is devaluated. The concept of repetition, as formulated by
Kierkegaard and Heidegger, is an *historical* and *existentialist* concept
which gives history a primal significance. For a profound treatment of
the myth of the eternal return in the history of religions, the reader is
referred to Mircea Eliade's book, *Cosmos and History* (Harper &
Bros., 1959).

73. EO, Vol. II, p. 112.

74. *Ibid.*, p. 113.

75. *Stages on Life's Way*, trans. Walter Lowrie (Princeton, N. J.: Princeton University Press, 1940), pp. 182–444.

76. *SZ*, p. 381.

77. *EO*, Vol. I, p. 55.

78. *PF*, p. 62.

79. "Das Geschehen dieser Entschlossenheit aber, das vorlaufend sich überliefernde Wiederholen des Erbes von Möglichkeiten, interpretierten wir als eigentliche Geschichtlichkeit" (*SZ*, p. 390).

Rudolph Bultmann has advanced an interpretation of history which draws heavily from the insights of both Kierkegaard and Heidegger. His debt to Heidegger in particular becomes evident in his book *The Presence of Eternity* (New York: Harper & Bros., 1957), where he writes: "Historicity now gains the meaning of responsibility over against the future, which is at the same time the responsibility over against the heritage of the past in face of the future. Historicity is the nature of man, who can never possess his genuine life in any present moment but is always on the way and yet is not at the mercy of a course of history independent of himself. Every moment is the *now* of responsibility, of decision" (p. 143).

NOTES/CHAPTER VI

1. *The Journals of Søren Kierkegaard*, ed. Alexander Dru (New York: Oxford University Press, 1938), entry 560. Cited hereafter as *Journals*.

2. Martin Heidegger, *Sein und Zeit* (Tübingen: Max Niemeyer Verlag, 1953), p. 269. Cited hereafter as *SZ*.

3. *Journals*, entry 1155.

4. *Ibid.*

5. Kierkegaard, *Christian Discourses*, trans. Walter Lowrie (New York: Oxford University Press, 1939), p. 144.

6. *Journals*, entry 1041.

7. *Ibid.*

8. *Ibid.*, entry 569.

9. Kierkegaard's attempt to proceed beyond the alternatives of heteronomy and autonomy anticipates a concept which was used by Troeltsch but which was first made central to the philosophy of religion by Paul Tillich. A theonomous view is one which affirms the presence of an unconditional and transcendent directive which is at the same time the fulfillment of man's own inner nature, e.g., freedom. In one of his essays Tillich has defined theonomy by differentiating it from

autonomy and heteronomy: "Autonomy asserts that man as the bearer of universal reason is the source and measure of culture and religion—that he is his own law. Heteronomy asserts that man, being unable to act according to universal reason, must be subjected to a law, strange and superior to him. Theonomy asserts that the superior law is, at the same time the innermost law of man himself, rooted in the divine ground which is man's own ground: the law of life transcends man, although it is, at the same time, his own" ("Religion and Secular Culture," *The Protestant Era* [Chicago: University of Chicago Press, 1948], pp. 56–57).

10. *SZ*, p. 269.

11. *Ibid.*, p. 278. Karl Jaspers advances an interpretation of conscience basically similar to that of Kierkegaard and Heidegger. Cf. his *Philosophie* (Heidelberg: Springer-Verlag, 1948): "Im Gewissen spricht eine *Stimme* zu mir, die *ich selbst* bin . . . Niemand ruft mich an; ich selbst spreche zu mir. Ich kann mir weglaufen und kann zu mir halten. Aber dies Selbst, das ich eigentlich bin, weil ich es sein könnte, ist nicht schon da, sondern spricht aus dem Ursprung her, mich in der Bewegung zu fuhren; es schweigt, wenn ich in der rechten Bewegung bin, oder wenn ich mich ganz verloren habe" (Vol. II, p. 524).

12. Explaining the point of view of his work as an author, Kierkegaard informs his readers that his "is a literary work in which the whole thought is the task of becoming a Christian." The *Concluding Unscientific Postscript*, he tells us, constitutes the turning point. "It presents the 'Problem,' that of becoming a Christian" (*The Point of View*, trans. Walter Lowrie [New York: Oxford University Press, 1939], pp. 41, 42).

13. *SZ*, p. 294.

14. *SZ*, p. 277.

15. *Ibid.*, p. 294.

16. *Ibid.*, p. 295.

17. Rudolf Bultmann obviously overlooks this point when he criticizes Heidegger's philosophy for developing a concept of salvation based on a self-realization which rests on human powers alone. Heidegger and Kamlah, Bultmann argues, "are convinced that all we need is to be told about the 'nature' of man in order to realize it" (*Kerygma and Myth*, ed. H. W. Bartsch and trans. R. H. Fuller [London: SPCK, 1954], p. 27). Although Heidegger may *personally* take such a position and express it by writing a "theology" which would advance an atheistic and nihilistic point of view, his *ontological analysis* of existence remains intentionally neutral to any religious or anti-religious interpretation.

18. *Concluding Unscientific Postscript*, trans. David Swenson (Princeton, N. J.: Princeton University Press, 1941), p. 470. Cited hereafter as *CUP*.

19. SZ, p. 288.

20. *Philosophie*, Vol. II, p. 463.

21. Kierkegaard, *The Concept of Dread*, trans. Walter Lowrie (Princeton, N. J.: Princeton University Press, 1944), p. 97. For reasons given in chap. iii, n. 2, this work is cited hereafter as CA.

22. Kierkegaard, *Either/Or* (New York: Anchor Books, 1959), Vol. I, pp. 113–33. Cited hereafter as EO.

23. *Ibid.*, p. 117.

24. *Ibid.* "When, therefore, Antigone in defiance of the king's prohibition resolves to bury her brother, we do not see in this so much a free action on her part as a predestined necessity, which visits the father's crime upon the children" (*ibid.*, p. 127). Antigone becomes guilty without the possibility of knowledge or action. Guilt is objectively conditioned. It is the result of the operation of fate.

25. *Ibid.*, p. 117.

26. *Ibid.*, p. 129.

27. Kierkegaard, *The Gospel of Suffering*, trans. David Swenson and Lillian Swenson (Minneapolis: Augsburg Publishing House, 1948), p. 92.

28. CA., p. 93.

29. *Ibid.*, p. 96.

30. *Philosophie*, pp. 506–7.

31. SZ, p. 283.

32. *Ibid.*, p. 285.

33. CA. p. 88.

34. *Ibid.*, p. 70.

35. *CUP*, p. 497.

36. *Ibid.*, p. 474.

37. *Ibid.*, p. 517.

38. *Ibid.*

39. *Ibid.*

40. Kierkegaard, *The Sickness Unto Death*, trans. Walter Lowrie (Princeton, N. J.: Princeton University Press, 1941), p. 142. Cited hereafter as *SUD*. Cf. p. 145: "What determinant is it then that Socrates lacks in determining what sin is? It is will, defiant will. The Greek intellectualism was too happy, too naive, too aesthetic, too ironical, too witty . . . to be able to get it sinfully into its head that a person knowingly could fail to do the good, or knowingly, with knowledge of what was right, do what was wrong. The Greek spirit proposes an intellectual categorical imperative."

41. CA, p. 56.

42. *CUP*, p. 481.

43. *Ibid.*, p. 473.

44. CA, p. 144.

45. On this point the idiosyncrasy of the German language makes any adequate translation impossible. In German one of the meanings

of guilt is "indebtedness." Hence it is both grammatically and semantically proper to say, *Ich bin ihm schuldig*, meaning that I am indebted to him. In English, however, it makes no sense to say, "I am guilty to him," thus seeking to express the notion of indebtedness.

46. "Schuldigsein hat dann die weitere Bedeutung vom 'schuld sein an,' das heisst Ursache—, Urheber-sein von etwas oder auch 'Veranlassung-sein,' für etwas" (SZ, p. 282).

47. *Philosophie*, Vol. II, pp. 507–8.

48. Ibid., p. 508.

49. Wild, *The Challenge of Existentialism* (Bloomington: Indiana University Press, 1955), p. 123.

50. SZ, p. 288.

NOTES/CHAPTER VII

1. Søren Kierkegaard, *Either/Or* (New York: Anchor Books, 1959), Vol. II, p. 146. Cited hereafter as *EO*.

2. Kierkegaard, *Concluding Unscientific Postscript*, trans. David Swenson (Princeton, N. J.: Princeton University Press, 1941), p. 470. Cited hereafter as *CUP*.

3. *The Journals of Søren Kierkegaard*, ed. Alexander Dru (New York: Oxford University Press, 1938), entry 1051. Cited hereafter as *Journals*.

4. *EO*, Vol. II, p. 179.

5. Ibid., p. 149.

6. Karl Jaspers, *Philosophie* (Heidelberg: Springer-Verlag, 1948), Vol. II, p. 446.

7. Jaspers, *Way to Wisdom*, trans. Ralph Manheim (New Haven: Yale University Press, 1951), p. 59.

8. *Philosophie*, Vol. II, p. 451.

9. Reinhardt, *The Existentialist Revolt* (Milwaukee: Bruce Publishing Company, 1952), p. 182.

10. *Philosophie*, Vol. II, p. 450. Cf. "Dann aber mache ich die Erfahrung, dass diese zeitlich bestimmte Wahl nicht *nur* das unvermeidliche Negative und Unfreie ist, das ohne Vollendung der Idee notgedrungen vollzogen werden muss, sondern in dieser *Wahl* bin ich mir erst der Freiheit bewusst, welche *ursprüngliche Freiheit* ist, weil ich erst in ihr mich eigentlich als mich selbst weiss" (p. 449).

11. For Marcel's criticism of Sartre's view of freedom see his book *The Philosophy of Existence* (London: The Harvill Press, 1948), chap. ii.

12. Jean-Paul Sartre, *L'Être et le Néant* (Paris: Gallimard, 1943), p. 61.

13. *Philosophie*, Vol. II, p. 441.

14. Paul Tillich, *Systematic Theology* (Chicago: University of Chicago Press, 1951), Vol. I, p. 183.

15. *L'Être et le Néant*, p. 520.

16. *Supra*, chap. v.

17. *Stages on Life's Way*, trans. Walter Lowrie (Princeton, N. J.: Princeton University Press, 1940), p. 430. Translator Walter Lowrie in a note in *Stages on Life's Way* suggests that "S. K.'s thought is more aptly rendered by 'existence-spheres' than by 'stages,' which commentators use far too commonly, for no better reason than that it is conspicuous as the title of this book. But even in this book S. K. was thinking of spheres which coexist and in part overlap, rather than of stages which in the sequence of time one completely surmounts" (pp. 335–36).

18. *EO*, Vol. II, p. 150.

19. *CUP*, p. 262.

20. Kierkegaard, *The Sickness Unto Death*, trans. Walter Lowrie (Princeton, N. J.: Princeton University Press, 1941), p. 54. Cited hereafter as *SUD*.

21. *EO*, Vol. II, p. 155.

22. *Ibid.*, p. 141.

23. *Ibid.*, p. 189.

24. *Supra*, chap. iii.

25. *EO*, Vol. II, p. 161.

26. *Ibid.*, p. 145.

27. Kierkegaard, *The Present Age*, trans. Alexander Dru and Walter Lowrie (New York: Oxford University Press, 1940), p. 28; *The Point of View*, trans. Walter Lowrie (New York: Oxford University Press, 1939), p. 61.

28. *Philosophie*, Vol. II, p. 453.

29. *The Point of View*, p. 116.

30. *Ibid.*, p. 120.

31. *EO*, Vol. II, p. 139.

32. *Supra*, chap. ii.

33. Martin Heidegger, *Sein und Zeit* (Tübingen: Max Niemeyer Verlag, 1953), p. 175. Cited hereafter as *SZ*.

34. *SZ*, p. 178.

35. *Ibid.*, p. 304.

36. The description of unauthenticity in connection with the objectification of human reality, although differently elaborated, is common to all the existentialist thinkers. Sartre develops the theme in his discussion of "bad faith" (*mauvaise foi*). "Bad faith" is the attitude by which man seeks to escape from himself as *pour-soi* (for-

itself) by existing in the mode of the *en-soi* (in-itself). He identifies himself with the solidity and plentitude of the in-itself and thus forfeits the nothingness and freedom which constitutes him as consciousness or for-itself. In this way man can escape from the urgency of choice. A thing or an object need not decide. One of Sartre's illustrations is the attitude taken by a woman who must deal with advances made by a persistent lover. She knows that she will need to make a decision, but she keeps postponing it. Finally, she deals with the situation by transforming herself as consciousness into the mode of objective being; "the hand rests inert between the warm hands of her companion—neither consenting nor resisting—a thing" (*L'Être et le Néant*, p. 95). This woman, says Sartre, exists in "bad faith." She has relinquished her freedom by identifying herself with the mode of "thinghood" (or *Vorhandenheit*, as Heidegger would say), and thus she abdicates her responsibility for decision.

37. In his book on Plato, Heidegger has presented, in a most illuminating and original manner, an existentialist interpretation of Plato's Allegory of the Cave. The people chained in the cave are confined in the prison of everydayness. Their movements are solely within the conventions of an average, everyday, mediocre circle of activities. They live unauthentic lives in which they have not yet found themselves. Only by proceeding from the confinement and darkness of the cave to the reality illumined by the sun do they arrive at an authentic understanding and existence. *Platons Lehre von der Wahrheit* (Bern: Francke Verlag, 1947), pp. 19–34.

38. SZ, p. 180.

39. In his *Lectures on Philosophy of Religion*, Hegel writes: "In philosophy religion gets its justification from thinking consciousness. . . . Thought is the absolute judge before which the content must verify and attest its claims" (trans. Spiers and Sanderson [London: Kegan Paul, 1895], Vol. III. p. 148).

40. SZ, p. 10 (Alphonse de Waelhens fails to take note of Heidegger's explicit statement on the autonomy of theology and the self-authenticating character of faith when he criticizes Heidegger for seeking to resolve the problem of original sin philosophically. "Heidegger ne sait pas encore s'il y a un problème de la corruption originelle, mais il sait déjà que si un tel problème se pose, il sera résolu par des méthodes philosophiques" [*La Philosophie de Martin Heidegger* (Louvain: Éditions de l'Institut Supérieur de Philosophie, n.d.), p. 31].)

41. *Wom Wesen des Grundes* (4th ed.; Frankfurt: Vittorio Klostermann, 1955), p. 39. Cited hereafter as WG.

42. EO, Vol. II, p. 141.

43. *Ibid.*, p. 150.

44. *Ibid.*, p. 159.

45. *Ibid.*, p. 193.

46. *Ibid.*, p. 149.

47. Kierkegaard, *Repetition*, trans. Walter Lowrie (New York: Oxford University Press, 1941), p. 144.

48. *CUP*, p. 262.

49. *EO*, Vol. II, pp. 209–10.

50. *Ibid.*, p. 149.

51. *Ibid.*

52. *Ibid.*, p. 143.

53. *SUD*, p. 43.

54. *Purity of Heart*, trans. Douglas Steere (New York: Harper and Bros., 1938), *passim*.

55. James Collins, *The Mind of Kierkegaard* (Chicago: Henry Regnery Co. 1953), p. 75.

56. *CUP*, p. 144.

57. *Supra*, chap. VI.

58. For a more thorough examination of Kierkegaard's distinction between the ethical as a universal moral requirement and the ethical as a mode of existence, see the author's article, "Note on Kierkegaard's Teleological Suspension of the Ethical," *Ethics*, LXX, No. 1 (October, 1959).

59. *EO*, Vol. II, p. 123.

60. *Ibid.*, p. 192.

61. *Ibid.*, p. 150.

62. *CUP*, p. 448.

63. See *Begriff der Ironie*, Übersetzt von Wilhelm Rütemeyer (München: Kaiser Verlag, 1929). Unfortunately, this important early work of Kierkegaard has not yet been made available in English.

64. *CUP*, p. 491n.

65. *Ibid.*, p. 450.

66. *Ibid.*, p. 451.

67. *L'Être et le Néant*, p. 614.

68. "Die anfangs nur ontologisch-methodisch erörterte Frage der Daseinsganzheit hatte ihr Recht, aber nur weil dessen Grund auf eine ontische Möglichkeit des Daseins zurückgeht" (*SZ*, p. 309).

69. *Ibid.*, p. 322.

70. *Way to Wisdom*, p. 59.

71. *SZ*, p. 320.

72. *Ibid.*, p. 303.

73. *Ibid.*, p. 322.

74. *Ibid.*

75. "Die eigentliche Existenz is nichts, was über der verfallenden alltäglichkeit schwebt, sondern existenzial nur ein modifiziertes Ergreifen dieser" (*ibid.*, p. 179).

76. *Ibid.*, p. 310.

77. *Ibid.*, p. 305.

78. *EO*, Vol. II, pp. 219–20.

79. Sartre, *Existentialism*, trans. Bernard Frechtman (New York: Philosophical Library, 1947), p. 21.

80. *Supra*, chap. ii.

81. Martin Buber, the Jewish existentialist thinker, has developed the same theme in his "I-Thou" philosophy. See his book *I and Thou* (2d ed.; New York: Charles Scribner's Sons, 1958).

82. "On My Philosophy," trans. Felix Kaufmann, as quoted in Walter Kaufmann, *Existentialism from Dostoevsky to Sartre* (New York: Meridian Books, 1956), p. 147.

83. *Philosophie*, Vol. II, p. 339.

84. *Ibid.*, p. 340.

85. *Man in the Modern Age*, trans. Eden and Cedar Paul (London: Routledge & Sons, 1933) p. 40.

86. *Supra*, chap. ii.

87. SZ, p. 298.

88. *Ibid.*, p. 297.

89. *Ibid.*, p. 298.

90. *Ibid.*

91. *Ibid.*

Bibliography

Books *

ALLEMAN, BEDA. *Hölderlin und Heidegger.* Zurich: Atlantis Verlag, 1954.

ALLEN, E. L. *The Self and Its Hazards: A Guide to the Thought of Karl Jaspers.* New York: Philosophical Library, 1951.

————. *Existentialism from Within.* New York: Macmillan Co., 1953.

ARENDT, HANNAH. *Sechs Essays.* Heidelberg: L. Schneider, 1948.

BARRET, W. *Irrational Man: A Study in Existential Philosophy.* New York: Doubleday Anchor Books, 1958.

BENSE, MAX. *Hegel und Kierkegaard.* Köln und Krefeld: Staufen Verlag, 1948.

BERDYAEV, NICOLAS. *Freedom and the Spirit.* Trans. Oliver Clarke. New York: Charles Scribner's Sons, 1935.

————. *Slavery and Freedom.* Trans. R. M. French. New York: Charles Scribner's Sons, 1944.

————. *The Destiny of Man.* Trans. Natalie Duddington. 3d ed. London: Geoffrey Bles, 1948.

BIEMEL, WALTER. *Le Concept de Monde chez Heidegger.* Paris: J. Vrin, 1950.

BLACKHAM, H. J. *Six Existentialist Thinkers.* London: Routledge & Kegan Paul, 1952.

BOCHENSKI, I. M. *Europäische Philosophie der Gegenwart.* München: L. Lehnen Verlag GMBH, 1951.

BOHLIN, TORSTEN. *Kierkegaard's dogmatische Anschauung.* Gütersloch: Bertelsmann Verlag, 1927.

BOLLNOW, OTTO. *Existenzphilosophie.* Stuttgart: W. Kohlhammer Verlag, 1949.

BRAND, GERD. *Welt, Ich und Zeit: Nach unveröffentlichen Manuskripten Edmund Husserls.* Den Haag: Martinus Nijhoff, 1955.

BRECHT, FRANS J. *Einführung in die Philosophie der Existenz.* Heidelberg: Heidelberg Skripten, 1948.

* Date of original publication listed in parentheses following title.

BROCK, WERNER. *Existence and Being*. London: Vision Press, 1949.

BULTMANN, RUDOLPH. *Kerygma and Myth*. Ed. Hans Bartsch and trans. Reginald Fuller. London: SPCK, 1954.

———. *Essays: Philosophical and Theological*. Trans. James C. Greig. New York: Macmillan Co., 1955.

———. *The Presence of Eternity*. New York: Harper & Bros., 1957.

CHESTOV, LEON. *Kierkegaard et la Philosophie Existentielle*. Paris: J. Vrin, n.d.

COLLINS, JAMES. *The Existentialists*. Chicago: Henry Regnery Co., 1952.

———. *The Mind of Kierkegaard*. Chicago: Henry Regnery Co., 1953.

CROXALL, T. H. *Kierkegaard Commentary*. London: James Nisbet & Co. Ltd., 1956.

———. *Kierkegaard: Johannes Climacus*. London: Adam & Charles Black, 1958.

DELPH, ALFRED. *Tragische Existenz*. Freiburg im Breisgau: Herder & Co. GMBH, 1935.

DEMPF, ALOIS. *Kierkegaard's Folgen*. Leipzig: J. Hegner, 1935.

DE WAELHENS, ALPHONSE. *La Philosophie de Martin Heidegger*. Louvain: Éditions de l'Institut Supérieur de Philosophie, n.d.

———. *Phénoménologie et Vérité*. Paris: Presses universitaires de France, 1953.

DIEM, HERMANN. *Philosophie und Christentum bei Soren Kierkegaard*. München: C. Kaiser Verlag, 1929.

DUFRENNE, M. and P. RICOEUR. *Karl Jaspers et la Philosophie de l'Existence*. Paris: Editions du Seuil, 1947.

FARBER, M. *The Foundation of Phenomenology: Edmund Husserl and the Quest for a Rigorous Science of Philosophy*. Cambridge, Mass.: Harvard University Press, 1943.

FEIFEL, HERMAN (ed.). *The Meaning of Death*. New York: McGraw-Hill Book Co., 1959.

FISCHER, ALOIS. *Die Existenzphilosophie Martin Heideggers*. Leipzig: Felix Meiner Verlag, 1935.

FISCHER, FRIEDRICH C. *Die Nullpunkt-Existenz*. München: C. H. Beck'sche Verlagsbuchhandlung, 1933.

FOLWART, HELMUT. *Kant, Husserl, Heidegger: Kritizismus, Phänomenologie, Existenzialontologie*. Breslau: H. Eschenhagen, 1936.

FRANK, ERICH. *Philosophical Understanding and Religious Truth*. New York: Oxford University Press, 1945.

FÜRSTENAU, PETER. *Heidegger, Das Gefuge seines Denkens*. Frankfurt: Vittorio Klostermann, 1958.

GEISMAR, EDUARD. *Sören Kierkegaard*. Gutersloh: C. Bertelsmann Verlag, 1925.

GILSON, E., et al. *Existentialisme Chrétien: Gabriel Marcel*. Paris: Librairie Plon, 1947.

GRENE, MARJORIE. *Dreadful Freedom*. Chicago: University of Chicago Press, 1948.

————. *Martin Heidegger*. New York: Hillary House, Inc., 1957.

GRIMSLEY, RONALD. *Existentialist Thought*. Cardiff: University of Wales Press, 1955.

HAECKER, THEODOR. *Sören Kierkegaard und die Philosophie der Innerlichkeit*. München: J. F. Schreiber, 1913.

————. *Opuscula*. München: Hegner Verlag, 1949.

HEGEL, G. W. F. *Lectures on the Philosophy of Religion*. Trans. Spiers. 3 vols. London: Kegan Paul, 1895.

————. *Phenomenology of Mind*. Trans. J. B. Baille. Rev. 2d ed. London: George Allen & Unwin Ltd., 1949.

————. *Science of Logic*. Trans. Johnston and Struthers. 2 vols. New York: Macmillan Co., 1951.

HEIDEGGER, MARTIN. *Die Kategorien- und Bedeutungslehre des Duns Scotus*. Tübingen: J. C. B. Mohr, 1916.

————. *Die Selbstbehauptung der Deutschen Universität*. Breslau: W. G. Korn, 1933.

————. *Platons Lehre von der Wahrheit*. Bern: Francke Verlag, 1947.

————. *Über den Humanismus*. Frankfurt: Vittorio Klostermann, 1947.

————. *Holzwege*. Frankfurt: Vittorio Klostermann, 1950.

————. *Erläuterungen zu Hölderlins Dichtung*. Frankfurt: Vittorio Klostermann, 1951.

————. *Kant und das Problem der Metaphysik* 2d ed. Frankfurt: Vittorio Klostermann, 1951.

————. *Einführung in die Metaphysik*. Tübingen: Max Niemeyer Verlag, 1953.

————. *Sein und Zeit*. 7th ed. Tübingen: Max Niemeyer Verlag, 1953.

————. *Aus der Erfahrung des Denkens*. Tübingen: Günther Neske Pfullingen, 1954.

————. *Vom Wesen der Wahrheit*. Frankfurt: Vittorio Klostermann, 1954.

————. *Vorträge und Aufsätze*. Tübingen: Günther Neske Pfullingen, 1954.

————. *Was Heisst Denken?* Tübingen: Max Niemeyer Verlag, 1954.

————. *Wom Wesen des Grundes*. 4th ed. Frankfurt: Vittorio Klostermann, 1955.

————. *Was ist Metaphysik?* 7th ed. Frankfurt: Vittorio Klostermann, 1955.

————. *Der Feldweg*. Frankfurt: Vittorio Klostermann, 1956.

————. *Zur Seinsfrage*. Frankfurt: Vittorio Klostermann, 1956.

————. *Was ist Das—die Philosophie?* Tübingen: Günther Neske Pfullingen, 1956.

————. *Identität und Differenz*. Tübingen: Günther Neske Pfullingen, 1957.

————. *Hebel: Der Hausfreund*. Tübingen: Günther Neske Pfullingen, 1957.

————. *Satz vom Grund* 2d ed. Tübingen: Günther Neske Pfullingen, 1958.

Heinemann, F. H. *Existentialism and the Modern Predicament*. New York: Harper & Bros., 1954.

Hirsch, Emmanuel. *Kierkegaard-Studien*. 2 vols. Gütersloh: C. Bertelsmann Verlag, 1933.

Hoberg, Clemens August. *Das Dasein des Menschen: Die Grundfrage der Heideggerischen Philosophie*. Zeulenroda: Bernhard Sporn Verlag, 1937.

Husserl, Edmund. *Ideen: zu einer reinen Phänomenologie und phänomenologischen Philosophie (Husserliana*, Vol. III). Den Haag: Martinus Nijhoff, 1950.

————. *Logische Untersuchungen*. 2d ed. 2 vols. Halle: M. Niemeyer Verlag, 1913–21.

Janssen, Otto. *Dasein und Wirklichkeit*. München: Ernst Reinhardt Verlag, 1938.

Jaspers, Karl. *Allgemeine Psychopathologie*. 2d ed. Berlin: Springer-Verlag, 1919.

————. *Psychologie der Weltanschauungen*. 3rd ed. Berlin: Springer-Verlag, 1925.

————. *Man in the Modern Age* (1931). Trans. Eden and Cedar Paul. London: Routledge & Sons, 1933.

————. *Reason and Existenz* (1935). Trans. William Earle. London: Routledge & Kegan Paul, 1956.

————. *Nietzsche: Einführung in das Verständnis seines Philosophierens*. Berlin: Walter de Gruyter & Co., 1936.

————. *Existenzphilosophie*. Berlin: Walter de Gruyter & Co., 1938.

————. *Die Schuldfrage*. Heidelberg: Verlag Lambert Schneider, 1946.

————. *Philosophie*. 2nd ed. Heidelberg: Springer-Verlag, 1948.

————. *The Perennial Scope of Philosophy* (1948). Trans. Ralph Manheim. London: Routledge & Kegan Paul, 1950.

————. *The Origin and Goal of History* (1949). Trans. Michael Bullock. New Haven: Yale University Press, 1953.

————. *Way to Wisdom* (1950). Trans. Ralph Manheim. New Haven: Yale University Press, 1951.

Harper, Ralph. *Existentialism: A Theory of Man*. Cambridge, Mass.: Harvard University Press, 1948.

Hessen, J. *Existenz-Philosophie*. Basel: Morus-Verlag, 1948.

Jolivet, Régis. *Les Doctrines Existentialistes*. Paris: Editions de Fontenelle, 1948.

————. *Le Problème de la Mort chez Heidegger et Sartre*. Paris: Editions de Fontenelle, 1950.

————. *Introduction to Kierkegaard*. Trans. W. H. Barber. New York: E. P. Dutton & Co., 1951.

Kahl-Furtlmann, G. *Das Problem des Nicht*. Berlin: Junker und Dünnhaupt Verlag, 1934.

Kaufmann, Walter. *Existentialism from Dostoevsky to Sartre*. New York: Meridian Books, 1956.

KIERKEGAARD, SØREN. *Der Begriff der Ironie* (1841). Übersetzt von Wilhelm Rütemeyer. München: Kaiser Verlag, 1929.

————. *Either/Or: A Fragment of Life* (1843). Trans. David Swenson and Lillian Swenson. 2 vols. Princeton, N. J.: Princeton University Press, 1949.

————. *Fear and Trembling: A Dialectical Lyric* (1843). Trans. Robert Payne. New York: Oxford University Press, 1939.

————. *Repetition: An Essay in Experimental Psychology* (1843). Trans. Walter Lowrie. New York: Oxford University Press, 1941.

————. *Edifying Discourses* (1843–46). Trans. David Swenson and Lillian Swenson. 4 vols. Minneapolis: Augsburg Publishing House, 1943–46.

————. *The Concept of Dread* (1844). Trans. Walter Lowrie. Princeton, N. J.: Princeton University Press, 1944.

————. *Philosophical Fragments or a Fragment of Philosophy* (1844). Trans. David Swenson. Princeton, N. J.: Princeton University Press, 1936.

————. *Stages on Life's Way* (1845). Trans. Walter Lowrie. Princeton, N. J.: Princeton University Press, 1940.

————. *Thoughts on Crucial Situations in Human Life* (1845). Trans. David Swenson. Minneapolis: Augsburg Publishing House, 1941.

————. *Concluding Unscientific Postscript* (1846). Trans. David Swenson. Princeton, N. J.: Princeton University Press, 1941.

————. *The Present Age* (1846). Trans. Alexander Dru and Walter Lowrie. New York: Oxford University Press, 1940.

————. *The Gospel of Suffering* (1847). Trans. David Swenson and Lillian Swenson. Minneapolis: Augsburg Publishing House, 1948.

————. *Purity of Heart* (1847). Trans. Douglas V. Steere. New York: Harper & Bros., 1938.

————. *Works of Love* (1847) Trans. David Swenson and Lillian Swenson. Princeton, N. J.: Princeton University Press, 1946.

————. *Christian Discourses* (1848). Trans. Walter Lowrie. New York: Oxford University Press, 1939.

————. *The Sickness Unto Death* (1849). Trans. Walter Lowrie. Princeton, N. J.: Princeton University Press, 1941.

————. *Training in Christianity* (1850). Trans. Walter Lowrie. Princeton, N. J.: Princeton University Press, 1944.

————. *For Self-Examination and Judge for Yourselves!* (1851). Trans. Walter Lowrie. New York: Oxford University Press, 1941.

————. *Attack Upon Christendom* (1854–55). Trans. Walter Lowrie. Princeton, N. J.: Princeton University Press, 1944.

————. *The Point of View* (1859). Trans. Walter Lowrie. New York: Oxford University Press, 1939.

————. *The Journals of Soren Kierkegaard* (18??). Trans. Alexander Dru. New York: Oxford University Press, 1938.

KRAFT, JULIUS. *Von Husserl zu Heidegger: Kritik der phänomenologischen Philosophie.* Leipzig: Hans Buske, 1932.

KUHN, HELMUT. *Encounter with Nothingness*. London: Methuen & Co., 1951.

LANGAN, THOMAS. *The Meaning of Heidegger*. New York: Columbia University Press, 1959.

LEHMANN, GERHARD. *Die Ontologie der Gegenwart in ihren Grundgestalten*. Halle: M. Niemeyer Verlag, 1935.

LEHMANN, KARL. *Der Tod bei Heidegger und Jaspers*. Heidelberg: Evangelischer Verlag, 1938.

LÖWITH, KARL. *Das Individuum in der Rolle des Mitmenschen*. München: Drei Masken Verlag, 1928.

———. *Kierkegaard und Nietzsche*. Frankfurt: Vittorio Klostermann, 1933.

———. *Heidegger: Denker in Dürftiger Zeit*. Heidelberg: Fischer Verlag, 1953.

———. *Von Hegel zu Nietzsche*. 3d ed. Stuttgart: W. Kohlhammer Verlag, 1953.

———. "Natur und Humanität des Menschen." *Wesen und Wirklichkeit des Menschen: Festscrift fur Helmuth Plessner*. Göttingen: Klaus Ziegler Verlag, 1957.

MACQUARRIE, JOHN. *An Existentialist Theology*. London: SCM Press, 1955.

MARCEL, GABRIEL. *Metaphysical Journal* (1927). Trans. Bernard Wall. Chicago: Henry Regnery Co., 1951.

———. *Being and Having* (1935). Trans. Katherine Farrer. Westminster: Dacre Press, 1949.

———. *Homo Viator: Introduction to a Metaphysic of Hope* (1944). Trans. Emma Craufurd. Chicago: Henry Regnery Co., 1951.

———. *The Philosophy of Existence* (1946). Trans. Manya Harari. London: Harvill Press, 1948.

———. *The Mystery of Being* (1951). Vol. I: *Reflection and Mystery*. Trans. G. Fraser. Vol. II: *Faith and Reality*. Trans. R. Hague. Chicago: Henry Regnery Co., 1951.

MAY, ROLLO, et al. *Existence: A New Dimension in Psychiatry and Psychology*. New York: Basic Books, Inc., 1958.

MEERPOHL, BERNHARD. *Die Verzweiflung als metaphysisches Phänomen in der Philosophie Sören Kierkegaards*. Würzburg: C. J. Becker Verlag, 1934.

MERLEAU-PONTY, M. *Phénoménologie de la Perception*. Paris: Librairie Gallimard, 1945.

———. *La Structure du Comportement*. Paris: Presses universitaires du France, 1953.

MESNARD, P. *Le Vrai Visage de Kierkegaard*. Paris: Gabriel Beauchesne et ses Fils, 1948.

METZGER, ARNOLD. *Phänomenologie und Metaphysik*. Halle: M. Niemeyer Verlag, 1933.

MICHALSON, CARL (ed.). *Christianity and the Existentialists*. New York: Charles Scribner's Sons, 1956.

Möller, Joseph. *Existenzialphilosophie und katholische Theologie.* Baden-Baden: Verlag für Kunst und Wissenschaft, 1952.

Müller, Helmut Ernest *Der Zeitbegriff Deutingers und Heideggers.* Würzburg: Richard Mayr, 1934.

Müller, Max. *Existenzphilosophie im Geistigen Leben der Gegenwart.* Heidelberg: Kerle Verlag, 1949.

Natanson, M. *A Critique of Jean-Paul Sartre's Ontology.* Lincoln: University of Nebraska Press, 1951.

Pascal, Blaise. *Pensées.* Ed. Leon Brunschvicg. Paris: Librairie Hachette, 1904.

Pfeiffer, Johannes. *Existenzphilosophie: Eine Einführung in Heidegger und Jaspers.* 3d ed. Hamburg: Richard Meiner Verlag, 1952.

Ricoeur, P. *Gabriel Marcel et Karl Jaspers: Philosophie du Mystère et Philosophie du Paradoxe.* Paris: Editions du Temps présent, 1947.

Ruttenbeck, W. *Sören Kierkegaard: Der Christliche Denker und sein Werk.* Berlin: Trowitzsch, 1929.

Sack, Max. *Die Verzweiflung: Eine Untersuchung ihres Wesens und ihrer Entstehung.* Källmunz: Michael Kassleben, n.d.

Sartre, Jean-Paul. *The Transcendence of the Ego* (1936–37). Trans. Forrest Williams and Robert Kirkpatrick. New York: Noonday Press, 1947.

———. *Existentialism* (1946). Trans. Bernard Frechtman. New York: Philosophical Library, 1947.

———. *L'Être et le Néant.* 18th ed. Paris: Librairie Gallimard, 1949.

———. *Nausea.* Trans. Lloyd Alexander. Norfolk, Connecticut: New Directions, 1949.

———. *Théatre.* Paris: Librairie Gallimard, 1947.

Schott, Erdmann. *Die Endlichkeit des Daseins Nach Martin Heidegger.* Berlin: Walter de Gruyter Verlag, 1930.

Schulz, Walter. "Existenz und System bei Soren Kierkegaard." *Wesen und Wirklichkeit des Menschen: Festschrift für Helmuth Plessner.* Gottingen: Klaus Ziegler Verlag, 1957.

Seifert, Hans. *Die Konkretion des Daseins bei Sören Kierkegaard.* Erlangen: Reinhold & Limmert, 1929.

Sternberger, Adolf. *Der verstandene Tod.* Leipzig: Verlag von S. Hirzel, 1934.

Tillich, Paul. *The Courage to Be.* New Haven: Yale University Press, 1952.

———. *The Interpretation of History.* New York: Charles Scribner's Sons, 1936.

———. *The Protestant Era.* Trans. James Luther Adams. Chicago: University of Chicago Press, 1948.

———. *Systematic Theology.* 2 vols. Chicago: University of Chicago Press, 1951, 1957.

Troisfontaines, R. *Existentialism and Christian Thought.* Trans. M. Jarret-Kerr. London: A & C Black, 1950.

USSHER, A. *Journey Through Dread*. New York: Devin-Adair, 1955.

VOGT, ANNEMARIE. *Das Problem des Selbstseins bei Heidegger und Kierkegaard*. Emsdetten: Heinrich & Lechte, 1936.

WACH, JOACHIM. *Das Problem des Todes in der Philosophie unserer Zeit*. Tübingen: J. C. B. Mohr Verlag, 1934.

WAHL, JEAN. *Etudes Kierkegaardiennes*. Paris: Fernand Aubier, n.d.

——. *Vers le Concret: Etudes d'Histoire de la Philosophie Contemporaine*. Paris: Joseph Vrin, 1932.

——. *A Short History of Existentialism*. Trans. Forrest Williams and Stanley Maron. New York: Philosophical Library, 1949.

WILD, JOHN. *The Challenge of Existentialism*. Bloomington: Indiana University Press, 1955.

——. *Human Freedom and Social Order*. Durham: Duke University Press, 1959.

WYSCHOGROD, MICHAEL. *Kierkegaard and Heidegger*. London: Routledge & Kegan Paul, 1954.

Articles

BARTH, H. "Heidegger und Kant," *Theologische Blätter*, XL (1930).

——. "Kierkegaard als Denker," *Zwischen den Zeiten* (1926).

——. "Philosophie, Theologie, und Existenzproblem," *Zwischen den Zieten* (1932).

BECK, M. "Ontologie der Gegenwart," *Philosophische Hefte*, VIII (1928).

BOHLIN, TORSTEN. "Luther, Kierkegaard und die dialektische Theologie," *Zeitschrift fur Theologie und Kirche* (1926).

BRUNNER, EMIL. "Das Grundproblem der Philosophie bei Kant und Kierkegaard," *Zwischen den Zeiten* (1924).

——. "Theologie und Ontologie—oder die Theologie am Scheidewege," *Zeitschrift fur Theologie und Kirche* (1930).

BULTMANN, R. "Die Geschichtlichkeit des Daseins und der Glaube," *Zeitschrift für Theologie und Kirche* (1930).

CASSIRER, E. "Kant und das Problem der Metaphysik," *Kant-Studien*, XXXVI (1931).

CERF, WALTER. "An Approach to Heidegger's Ontology," *Philosophy and Phenomenological Research*, I (1940).

CLIVE, GEOFFREY. " 'The Teleological Suspension of the Ethical' in Nineteenth-Century Literature," *Journal of Religion*, XXXIV (1954).

EARLE, WILLIAM. "Wahl on Heidegger on Being," *Philosophical Review*, LXVIII (1958).

ERNST, W. "M. Heidegger und dialektische Theologie," *Zeitschrift für systematische Theologie*, IX (1932).

FARBER, MARVIN. "Heidegger on the Essence of Truth," *Philosophy and Phenomenological Research*, XVIII (1958).

FREUND, ERNEST. "Man's Fall in Martin Heidegger's Philosophy," *Journal of Religion*, XXIV (1944).

GEISMAR, EDUARD. "Das ethische Stadium bei Soren Kierkegaard," *Zeitschrift für systematische Theologie*, I (1923).

———. "La Personnalité de Kierkegaard," *Revue de Métaphysique* (1933).

GRAY, J. GLENN. "Heidegger's 'Being,' " *Journal of Philosophy*, XLIX (1952).

GRAY, J. GLENN. "Heidegger's Course: From Human Existence to Nature," *Journal of Philosophy*, LIV (1957).

———. "Heidegger Evaluates Nietzsche," *Journal of the History of Ideas*, XIV (1953).

GRUNDMANN, W. "Heideggers Sein und Zeit und die Christliche Verkündigung," *Die Furche*, XVII.

HARTT, JULIAN. "God, Transcendence and Freedom in the Philosophy of Jaspers," *Review of Metaphysics*, IV (1950).

HEIM, KARL. "Ontologie und Theologie," *Zeitschrift für Theologie und Kirche* (1930).

HINNERS, RICHARD. "Freedom and Finiteness in Heidegger," *The New Scholasticism* (1959).

ITTEL, GERHARD. "Der Einfluss der Philosophie M. Heideggers auf die Theologie R. Bultmanns," *Kerygma und Dogma*, II (1956).

KAUFMANN, F. W. "The Value of Heidegger's Analysis of Existence for Literary Criticism," *Modern Language Notes*, XLVIII (1933).

KRAFT, JULIUS. "The Philosophy of Existence, *Philosophy and Phenomenological Research*, I (1941).

KRONER, RICHARD. "Heidegger's Private Religion," *Union Seminary Quarterly Review*, XI (1956).

LEVINAS, E. "M. Heidegger et l'Ontologie," *Revue Philosophique* (1932).

LEVY, H. "Heideggers Kant-interpretation," *Logos*, XXI (1932).

LEWKOWITZ, ALBERT. "Vom Sinn des Seins, zur Existenzphilosophie Heideggers," *Montasschrift für Geschichte und Wissenschaft des Judentums* (1936).

LÖWITH, KARL. "Grundzüge der Entwicklung der Phänomenologie zur Philosophie und ihr Verhaltnis zur protestantischen Theologie," *Theologische Rundschau* (1930).

———. "Phänomenologische Ontologie und protestantische Theologie," *Zeitschrift für Theologie und Kirche* (1930).

———. "Heidegger: Problem and Background of Existentialism," *Social Research* (XV).

———. "L'Achèvement de la Philosophie," *Recherches Philosophiques* (1934).

McINERNY, RALPH. "Ethics and Persuasion: Kierkegaard's Existential Dialectic," *The Modern Schoolman*, XXXIII (1956).

MARX, WERNER. "Heidegger's New Concept of Philosophy: The Second Phase of Existentialism," *Social Research*, XXII (1953).

MERLAN, PHILIP. "Time Consciousness in Husserl and Heidegger," *Philosophy and Phenomenological Research*, VIII (1947).

MESNARD, PIERRE. "Philosophie de Kierkegaard," *Revue d'Histoire et de Philosophie Religieuses* (1955).

MESSER, A. "Über das Nichts: Eine Auseinandersetzung mit Heidegger," *Philosophie und Leben* (1931).

MINKOWSKI, E. "Le Problème du Temps Vécu," *Recherches Philosophiques* (1935–36).

MISCH, G. "Lebensphilosophie und Phänomenologie," *Philosophischer Anzeiger* (1929–30).

NINK, E. "Grundbegriffe der Philosophie Martin Heideggers, *Philosophisches Jahrbuch*, XI (1932).

PICARD, YVONNE. "Le Temps chez Husserl et chez Heidegger," *Deucalion, Cahiers de Philosophie*, No. 1 (1946).

REISNER, E. "Existenzialphilosophie und existenzielle Philosophie," *Zwischen den Zeiten* (1933).

RICHEY, CLARENCE W. "On the Intentional Ambiguity of Heidegger's Metaphysics," *Journal of Philosophy*, LVIII (1958).

SCHRADER, GEORGE. "Heidegger's Ontology of Human Existence," *Review of Metaphysics*, X (1956).

SCHRAG, CALVIN O. "Phenomenology, Ontology, and History in the Philosophy of Heidegger," *Revue Internationale de Philosophie*, No. 44 (1958).

———. "Whitehead and Heidegger: Process Philosophy and Existential Philosophy," *Dialectica*, XIII (1959).

———. "Existence and History," *Review of Metaphysics*, XIII (1959).

———. "Kierkegaard's Existential Reflections on Time," *Personalist*, XLII, No. 2 (1961).

———. "Note on Kierkegaard's Teleological Suspension of the Ethical," *Ethics*, LXX (1959).

SCHULZ, WALTER. "Uber den philosophiegeschichtlichen Ort Martin Heideggers," *Philosophische Rundschau* (1953/54).

SIMMEL, G. "Zur Metaphyzik des Todes," *Logos* (1910).

STERN (ANDERS), GUENTHER. "On the Pseudo-concreteness of Heidegger's Philosophy," *Philosophy and Phenomenological Research*, VIII (1948).

STRASSER, STEPHEN. "The Concept of Dread in the Philosophy of Heidegger," *Modern Schoolman*, XXXV (1957).

TAUBES, SUSAN. "The Gnostic Foundations of Heidegger's Nihilism," *Journal of Religion*, XXXIV (1954).

TIEBOUT, H. M. "Freud and Existentialism," *Journal of Nervous and Mental Disease*, CXXVI (1958).

———. "Tillich, Existentialism, and Psychoanalysis," *The Journal of Philosophy*, LVI (1959).

TILLICH, PAUL. "Existential Philosphy," *Journal of the History of Ideas*, V (1944).

————. "The Nature and the Significance of Existentialist Thought," *The Journal of Philosophy*, LIII (1956).

TINT, H. "Heidegger and the Irrational," *Proceedings of the Aristotelian Society*, LVII (1957).

TRAUB, F. "Existenzielles Denken," *Zeitschrift für Theologie und Kirche* (1931).

TRIVERS, HOWARD. "Heidegger's Misinterpretation of Hegel's Views on Spirit and Time," *Philosophy and Phenomenological Research*, III (1943).

TURNBULL, ROBERT G. "Heidegger on the Nature of Truth," *Journal of Philosophy*, LVIII (1957).

UNGER, ERIC. "Existentialism, I & II," *Nineteenth Century and After*, CXLII (1947), CXLIII (1948).

WAHL, J. "Heidegger et Kierkegaard," *Recherches Philosophiques*, II (1932–33).

WEISS, HELEN. "The Greek Conceptions of Time and Being in the Light of Heidegger's Philosophy," *Philosophy and Phenomenological Research*, II (1941).

WERKMEISTER, W. "An Introduction to Heidegger's 'Existential Philosophy,'" *Philosophy and Phenomenological Research*, II (1941).

WILD, JOHN. "Kierkegaard and Classic Philosophy," *The Philosophical Review* (1940).

————. "The New Empiricism and Human Time," *Review of Metaphysics*, VII (1954).

————. "Kierkegaard and Contemporary Existentialist Philosophy," *Anglican Theological Review* (1956).

Index

A NOTE ON MANUFACTURE

THE TEXT of this book is set in Linotype ELECTRA, a face designed by the late William A. Dwiggins (1880–1956). Light in color, large on the body, and somewhat condensed, *Electra* is easily read in the smaller point sizes and permits the setting of more matter per page than comparable faces.

Not the least of his contributions to the art of the book were Dwiggins' binding designs which combined abstract brush-drawn or stencilled motifs and his highly original calligraphy. As with all machine-manufactured books, these designs were stamped on the case by heated dies of brass struck on ribbons of metallic or pigment foil. The resulting impression tends to be heavier in weight than the letter as drawn, a fact which must be taken into account by the designer. If the title and author's name are to be read while the book is standing upright they must be large enough and yet condensed so as to allow fitting on the relatively narrow shelfback. Counters (for instance, the area enclosed within the bowl of the letter "P") must be kept open to prevent filling with foil. A study of some of the original art work prepared for the die-maker by W. A. Dwiggins strongly suggests the possible genesis of *Electra* and gives hint to the logic underlying its construction.

This book was composed, printed, and bound by KINGSPORT PRESS, INC., *Kingsport, Tennessee.* MEAD PAPERS, INC., DAYTON, OHIO, *manufactured the paper. The typography and binding designs are by Guy Fleming.*